GENERALS

by the same author

WAR IN AFGHANISTAN
SOVIET LAND POWER
UK EYES ALPHA
BIG BOYS' RULES
THE MAN WHO BROKE NAPOLEON'S CODES
RIFLES

Generals

Ten British Commanders
who Shaped the World

MARK URBAN

faber and faber

First published in 2005
by Faber and Faber Limited
3 Queen Square London WC1N 3AU

Photoset by RefineCatch Ltd, Bungay, Suffolk
Printed in England by Mackays of Chatham plc, Chatham, Kent

A CIP record for this book is available from the British Library

ISBN 0-571-22485-7

2 4 6 8 10 9 7 5 3 1

Contents

Illustrations

[vi]

PICTURES IN TEXT

page 1 The 'Captaine Generall of all his Majesties Land forces' depicted in later life (and indeed more than a century after his death). He had already emerged by the early 1800s as a hero for Tories and a figure of suspicion to Whigs. *Etching by an unnamed artist published by Harding, 1800.*

page 29 This early 19th Century depiction of Marlborough shows him in Napoleonic period uniform. A French engraving, it serves to illustrate how far the general had entered the psyche of that nation as the personification of the British bogeyman. *Unattributed woodcut on an early 19th century French song sheet in Bibliotheque Nationale, Paris.*

page 63 William Howe somehow managed to live through the golden age of British caricature without being lampooned. Instead we have only such engravings by which to judge him. We know, in any case, that by the time he assumed command in America he had lost many teeth and that age had also had its impact on his mental faculties. *Unattributed engraving.*

page 93 The Duke of York caricatured shortly after his marriage to Princesse Friedericke of Prussia. This is one of the kindest depictions of him from an age where satirists were often merciless. Even so, his double chin and ample girth are drawn in deliberate contrast to his bride's delicate physique. Seen this way, as the stout Englishman, Frederick seems to personify John Bull. *Etching by James Gillray, London, 14 December 1791.*

page 121 This arresting image by William Heath was one of the most famous of the 'Wellington Boot'. Caricaturists hardly bothered with Wellington before Waterloo and the few pre–1815 cartoons that exist bear little resemblance to him. It was once the Duke set himself on a political career (and indeed became a familiar figure on London's streets) that he evolved into an irresistible target for lampoon. Heath was the most skilful of Wellington's mockers and many of his drawings reflected the British unease with the victorious general who had turned to politics.

page 151 Gordon is depicted by Punch, holed up in Khartoum and wondering whether he has spotted, "the quick gleam of English steel, or but a desert dream". This image dates from the spring of 1884 when public pressure on Gladstone to send a rescue mission had reached its peak. The earlier satirical styles of Gillray or Heath had by this time been replaced by one of irony-free Imperial propaganda. *Punch, April 12, 1884.*

page 183 Introvert and diffident, Kitchener's image was defined by others. Newspapermen in Sudan wrote him up as a brutal unfeeling 'easterner'; others later suggested he had the machine-like efficiency needed to beat the Germans. This postcard dates from 1914, redefining K of K (Earl Kitchener of Khartoum) once again as the paragon of British patriotism.

page 213 Sacre's 1918 caricature of Allenby displays his public persona. It calls to mind novelist C.S. Forester's line about, "a huge man with a face the colour of mahogany". The General dominated those around him with brutal cross-examinations, uncompromising orders and a refusal to tolerate failure. By contrast, the private Allenby was a loving husband and father, immensley well read and acutely sensitive to the historical ramifications of campaigning in Palestine.

page 241 The British fascist magazine 'Action' depicted Fuller as a scarily bright ideologue. To modern eyes the shape given to his head and ears suggest an almost alien lack of emotion. Fuller joined the fascist bandwagon in the late 1930s when many other Britons were leaving it. His identification with such ideas and admiration for Hitler have made it hard ever since to assess his military ideas dispassionately. *Action, Issue No. 59.*

page 267 Monty never missed an opportunity to publicise himself and he used this image for his 1943 Christmas card. It frames his features with symbols emphasising his identity as a soldier, notably his Royal Tank Regiment beret, marks of rank and medal ribbons. In this sense self-image coincides with legacy, for it is as a consummate professional that he is best remembered.

Illustrations in the plate sections are reproduced by kind permission of the following: National Army Museum, London (1, 4, 6, 10, 15); Imperial Defence College, Camberley / Bridgeman Art Library (2); Mary Evans Picture Library (3); Private Collection, © Bonhams, London / Bridgeman Art Library (5); New York Historical Society / Bridgeman Art Library (7); Museum of Fine Arts, Boston / Gift of Howland S. Warren / Bridgeman Art Library (8); Private Collection, © Christie's Images / Bridgeman Art Library (9); Victoria and Albert Museum, London (11); Apsley House, The Wellington Museum, London / Bridgeman Art Library (12); AKG Images (13, 14, 21, 23); Imperial War Museum (16, 18, 19, 20, 22); Walker Art Gallery (17); Corbis (24, 26, 27); Getty Images (25).

Illustrations in the text are reproduced by kind permission of the following: Mary Evans Picture Library (1, 2, 3, 5, 7, 8); AKG Images (4); Punch picture library (6); Getty Images (10).

Maps

Introduction

Not everyone in an army is created equal. Rather, the opinions of those at the top of the hierarchy, the generals, count most; and their actions have the greatest potential for good – or harm. This might seem glaringly obvious, but there has been such a tendency in recent writing about war to examine the deeds of the ordinary soldier that it is sometimes forgotten. Indeed one of the twentieth century's most respected war correspondents commented that the journalist's job was to tell the story of the little people rather than those in power. This is a false dichotomy: I am as interested as anyone in the deeds or suffering of the ordinary soldier (hence the subject of my last book, *Rifles*) but I also want to know who gave the orders and why.

It is my desire here to examine the impact on the wider world of some towering British military figures. Few people in modern Britain want to boast about these powerful men; indeed, in large parts of society the names have been forgotten, if they were ever known. The urge to write about these subjects does not come from some sense of post-imperial nostalgia, but from a feeling that enough time has passed to examine their lives in a detached way.

Of course, the role of British generals has evolved in tandem with the growth of democracy in this country. Compared to Marlborough, Montgomery was a great deal more constrained by politicians, public opinion and the attitudes of a huge army of citizen soldiers. Nevertheless, there can be no doubt that even in 1945, a military Commander-in-Chief held vastly more votes in the electoral college of a democratic army than his soldiers did. What Marlborough and Montgomery had in common was ultimate responsibility to a political master who could sack them. This is the essential context of this book and its subjects.

I cannot compare the deeds of a general in 1815 or 1915 with those of Henry V or even Cromwell – figures who combined military with supreme political or dynastic power. This book is about succeeding or failing militarily when authority was divided. It is about command in *modern* Britain, even if Parliamentary democracy in the late seventeenth or early eighteenth century was callow and poorly formed. We must never forget how many of this army's opponents – most famously Napoleon – unified military and civil authority, suffering less from the constraints imposed by lay decision-makers representing a free society.

The choice of subjects is entirely personal – and, of course, could be debated endlessly. It is also true that in seeking to pack ten of them into one modest volume, I can give no more than a flavour of their lives and why they were important. The chapters are based on episodes or vignettes that dramatise the contributions of each life, rather than an attempt at birth-to-death biography. The *whole* story has, in the case of some of these subjects, required multi-volume biographies. I have consulted many sources, but the primary ones tend to be published memoirs or collections of letters rather than the scratchy manuscripts in draughty country houses that were vital to my last two books. My aim, with the bibliography given for each chapter, is to allow the interested reader to follow up with further reading of their own.

As for the omissions . . . What about Clive of India? And, what, no Slim? What I was aiming to do was find ten men whose deeds have resonance, and provide some definite legacy, even today. That is not necessarily the same as choosing the best commanders on the battlefield.

Another problem with defining the criteria is that they have to evolve in tandem with the army and wider society. If, for example, you just want those who conquered or lost large parts of the world for Britain, then there are five or six strong candidates in the first half of the eighteenth century, but fewer as time went on and European powers divided the world. I wanted to spread my subjects across nearly three centuries, in order to show how the factors affecting commanders developed, and highlight the different preconditions for success, for example, in the twentieth century.

For me, the most problematic omission is India. One of the most important legacies of British military power is the world's largest democracy. My difficulty was that the creation of the Raj involved several leading generals over a long period of history. Clive's successes in the mid-eighteenth century had to be followed by those of Cornwallis, the campaigns against the Marathas, the Sikh Wars and even the suppression of the mutiny in 1857. Clive was undoubtedly vital but he secured only a toehold, and the French in the 1780s, for example, might still have prevailed. So I have not been able to award the laurels for India to any one man.

Lists of great people, while in some ways arbitrary and utterly subjective, do at least have the advantage of imposing some discipline on their compilers. I have had to mull over the choices and debate them with others so many times that in the end I feel able to defend my subjects passionately. Those chosen stand in their own right; comparison between some of them may seem very difficult if not impossible. But I think there are threads running through these lives, as I will show at the end.

Quite a few of the subjects are shown warts and all, since this is not an attempt to reinvent Victorian-style hero worship (*The Bumper Book of British Generals for Boys!*). Equally, it is not an exercise in ridicule (*Britain's Ten Worst Brass-Hat Blunderers*) designed to show up the whole military enterprise as a cavalcade of folly and stupidity. It is intended rather to examine the impact of some individuals who may have been brilliant, charming, dull or vile in various combinations. Inevitably, eschewing historical caricature, there are plenty of perplexing amalgams of qualities and faults in these figures, and ultimately there were a couple whom I couldn't decide whether I admired or loathed.

The task of editing the book and enhancing its coherence has fallen to Julian Loose and Henry Volans at Faber. I am grateful once again for the expert advice and professionalism of Jonathan Lloyd, Will Atkinson and Stephen Page.

My task of researching these subjects was made much easier by John Montgomery, Nick Menzies, Susan Ranson and John Litchfield. I have been indulged once more by my *Newsnight* editors – George Entwistle, Peter Barron and Mary Wilkinson.

The last but supreme decoration needs to be awarded to my wife Hilary and to our small Urbans, Isabelle, Madeleine and Sol, for their forbearance and support.

In memory of my father

George Monck

1608–1670

*The heaviest man in the world, but stout and
honest to his country.*
SAMUEL PEPYS

THE HAMMERING OF CARPENTERS could be distinctly heard above the cacophony of battle in the streets of Stirling. Lieutenant General George Monck went to inspect the work, eyeing the arcs of fire, conferring with his gunners, and chewing on a quid of tobacco so that he might ruminate well on the problem at hand.

It was 12 August 1651. Little more than a week had passed since Oliver Cromwell had begun his march back into England, delegating the command in Scotland to Monck. Cromwell had dealt a heavy blow to Parliament's enemies in battle at Dunbar, but most of the land was still in open revolt. An unholy alliance of Scottish Presbyterians and Royalists declared themselves loyal to Charles II, the exiled monarch, and Stirling Castle was one of their strongest outposts.

The general was a stout, barrel-chested man. He spoke with the accent of his native Devon. His straightforward manner and reputation for doing exactly what he said he would do appealed to many, making him an early archetype for the British soldier. A kinsman gave the following testament of Monck:

he was a plain downright Englishman, a rough soldier bred in camps, unskill'd and detesting the servile arts practised in courts . . . he was not a man of what is commonly understood by quick parts: but if he was slow in considering, he was sure in acting: Solidity of judgement, indefatigable industry and intrepid courage were the qualities best adapted for the work he was performing.

Monck's campaign might have been only a few days old, but he was determined to prosecute it with all due dispatch. He had been a professional soldier for twenty-five years and knew that fortresses had to be taken swiftly and without reverses, or his men's fighting spirit could collapse: 'the malice of a great army is broken, and the force of it spent in a great Siege'. For this reason, Monck eyed his wooden gun platforms with some satisfaction.

Inside Stirling's walls, the governor, William Cunningham, was confident. There were 300 determined men under his command, a castle of great strength, 27 cannon, hundreds of barrels of powder and victuals for months. They had other, more symbolic, reasons to hold out, too: the regalia and records of the ancient kings of Scotland had been lodged in the fortress and, as every Scot knew, English arms had been humiliated before at Stirling. But Cunningham did not understand what Monck had in store for him.

So it was that when Monck sent a messenger forward, that afternoon of 12 August, to request the garrison's surrender, he received a defiant reply from Cunningham. The governor told his attackers that he would hold out as long as he could.

That evening, four great guns and two mortars were brought onto their wooden platforms outside the castle. Parliament had hired the services of a Dutch master gunner, Joachim Hane, but Monck was an expert artillerist himself, having been given overall command of the Ordnance by Cromwell. Cunningham's men studied the scene from the battlements as the great metal destroyers were hoisted onto their firing platforms with cranes, block and tackle. All of the principal players – Cunningham, Monck and Hane – knew that the English guns, though powerful, would take many days to batter breaches in Stirling's thick walls. But those inside had no understanding of what the two great mortars could do. Although such weapons had been used in various continental sieges, there were few soldiers in Britain who had ever seen then in action.

Not long after daybreak on the 13th there was a terrific crump as the first mortar fired. Its shell took a quite different trajectory to the cannon balls of the four siege guns: the 1.75-pound metal sphere soared upwards at a steep angle, sailing high over the walls, before dropping and exploding. Hane noted the distances, performed his calculations and prepared a second shell.

As the great granado travelled up into the sky, the eagle-eyed might have spotted the burning fizz of its fuse. A skilful master gunner would trim its length with such fine judgement, matching the time of flight and burning speed of the igniter, that the powder inside would be detonated just above the targets' heads, showering them with lumps of the shell's iron casing. And that was precisely what happened. The second English shell plunged into the castle courtyard, exploding just a few feet above the ground, cutting down thirty men with its terrible blast.

Next day, after twenty-four mortar shells had been fired, Stirling's garrison mutinied. The soldiers, Highlanders for the most part, had not seen modern warfare before and they were terror-struck. Just two days after his defiant refusal of terms, Cunningham had to surrender. The English general had cracked one of Scotland's toughest fortresses without having to ask his army to storm it. One of his admirers wrote: 'Monk shewed what was the difference between a Professor in the Art of War, well studied in all its rules, and a Fanatick Soldier that fights by inspiration.'

The wars that racked the British Isles from 1642 had certainly unleashed a startling array of fanatics – religious fervour infused Protestant dissenting sects, Royalist volunteers or Irish Catholic bands with murderous self-righteousness. It did not though provide most of them with the slightest clue about how to fight successfully. Monck had begun the Civil War as a Royalist general, but he had been captured, and the Parliamentarians had managed to turn him to their side by offers of cash and rank.

Thomas Fairfax, the general who brought organisation to the Parliamentary cause by creating the New Model Army in 1645, called Monck 'a man worth the making'. The two officers, cast initially on opposite sides in the war, had learned their profession together, fighting in the Netherlands in the 1630s. It was there that Monck picked up many practical skills in such arcane matters as siege warfare. He was not only practiced in his profession but understood soldiers very well, earning the accolade in Ireland, scene of one of his early campaigns, of 'the most beloved by the soldiers of any officer in the army'.

One week after reducing Stirling, Monck's army was off again, marching on Dundee. He could not dawdle, aiming to crush his enemy before winter. Cromwell had confided a sizeable force to his lieutenant: four regiments of horse, one of dragoons and ten of infantry. The marching regiments of foot were the core of his army, but with each success Monck had to leave detachments, and men were cast about in order to prevent further insurrection. He knew from campaigns in Ireland the importance of retaining a powerful army under his own hand, without leaving too many soldiers on garrisons duty, and these considerations added urgency to his movements that August.

At this time, midway through the seventeenth century, the revolution in warfare brought about by gunpowder was still only half done. Each regiment that marched towards Dundee had to combine pikemen, often armoured with a helmet and breastplate, with other soldiers lugging great muskets. The firearms were inaccurate, difficult to load, and hardly usable at all in wet weather, when the slow-burning matches used to fire them might get drenched. For this reason, the pikemen, armed with 15–20-foot pikes, were there as a kind of insurance against mishaps, and to form a solid hedgehog in close combat against enemy horse or infantry.

Just as the pikemen fought in a way basically unchanged since the times of Alexander the Great, so too the horse were expected to charge into their enemies and run them through with cold metal. Only the dragoons, hybrid soldiers who rode between battles but often fought in them dismounted, using firearms, showed the advance of military science.

As to the human make-up of Monck's Scottish army, they were a diverse bunch, a product of their recruitment in several waves. Some were long-term survivors of the Parliamentary army, who had come into it nine years earlier, at the very start of the war, from the trained bands, militia forces of volunteers, often from quite educated or skilled backgrounds. Many in this category had joined in their teens, and seen battle many times. As the war progressed, though, volunteers dried up, leading the belligerent armies to use the press, or compel men to serve. This initially dragged in various unwilling farm labourers, servants and the like, but constables in the shires soon took advantage of the chance to empty their prisons. The men were therefore often serving unwillingly and could only hope that pay promised to them (but rarely delivered) would eventually give them some reward for their dangerous service.

When he summoned Robert Lumsdaine, governor of Dundee's fortress, on 26 August, Monck had many considerations on his mind. His siege train was moving very slowly, so he knew that he might not have at his disposal the same means that he had used at Stirling to bludgeon Dundee's defenders. Furthermore, the men were impatient for plunder and their morale might prove brittle if some precipitate attempt on the works was beaten back. So, concerned as he must have been, it can be imagined that Monck was nettled when Lumsdaine replied cheekily that he would offer the English army one last chance to surrender and take safe passage out of Scotland.

Monck brought cannon from some nearby ships, but they were simply not powerful enough to reduce Dundee's walls quickly. Time was slipping away; he needed a different approach.

His answer lay with a young boy who boasted that he could make his way in and out of the town at will. Monck employed him as a spy, and every day the urchin made a report to his new paymaster, often scampering over the works to the crack and whistle of musket balls fired at him by the defenders. Several more days elapsed, but when the siege guns finally arrived, Monck had what he needed to concert his plan. From his spy, he knew that the garrison were in the habit of getting blind drunk every night. He therefore resolved to attack in the morning, early enough to make the most of their collective hangover.

In the small hours of 1 September, the English army prepared its storming parties. Confusion reigned in such operations, so it was vital to be able to tell friend from foe. The usual procedure was to tie a strip of cloth around one arm. Monck's was a little different: he got the men to pull out their shirt tails, over their backsides. This system was all very well for the stormers as long as they kept going forward, but if a man turned to flee, there was no telling what might happen to him. As the Parliamentarians primed their pistols and burnished their swords, the password 'God With Us!' was whispered among them.

When the storm went in, Monck hit the town from two sides at once and resistance lasted little more than half an hour. Governor Lumsdaine received payback for the 'impertinent gallantry' with which he had received Parliament's summons and was put to the sword.

Dundee turned out to be packed with valuables, mostly the property of Lowland Royalists who had gone there for safety. For three days the English army sacked the place, stealing and boozing, before Monck could reimpose order.

In a campaign of just a few weeks Monck took several towns, captured enemy ringleaders and scattered resistance into the Highlands. He had successfully mopped up any organised remnants of the enemy army and, in doing so, made his reputation with Cromwell.

If Monck was a good general, his success in war did not match that of Cromwell. Yet it is Monck whose legacy was the greater for Britain and its army. This judgement might seem perverse, but while Cromwell had been the leading light in the execution of King Charles I, and the master of many battlefields, when he styled himself Lord Protector in December 1653 his journey reached a political dead end. Even Cromwell understood that in seeking to fill the void left by the beheaded Charles he could not crown himself king and be done with it. His problem was that he ran out of inspiration in his struggle to restore viable relations between Britain's landowners, army and himself, as ruler. So the atmosphere became increasingly fraught, with extreme religious ideas flourishing, near mutinous regiments refusing to disband themselves and continuous unrest in the provinces. This period was characterised by many of those who lived through it as a 'state of nature'.

Not long after assuming the title of Lord Protector, Cromwell drew up orders to send Monck – whose duties had taken him elsewhere for two years – back to Scotland. He packed up his trunks, leaving the post of 'General at Sea', an arrangement under which he had successfully commanded a naval squadron during a short-lived outbreak of Anglo–Dutch hostilities, and returning to Caledonia. In Monck's absence, the rebels had become increasingly daring, and the Parliamentry army was suffering from poor morale and discipline.

Terms set out in the parchment presented to the Royalist officer turned Cromwellian troubleshooter in April 1654 gave him enormous authority. Appointing Monck 'Commander in Chief of the Army and forces in Scotland', Cromwell gave him 'full power to rule, govern and command against rebels and enemies of the public peace'. The attainment of this aim even entitled the new pro-consul to take measures to protect the 'true religion', Protestantism, gave him the ability to raise revenue through imposing new customs duties, and do everything necessary to keep his army in order. In short, Monck was a plenipotentiary who would take care of business north of the Tweed for a master with too many other demands on his time. Indeed, the job created for Monck gave him a situation that was in many respects more powerful and less complicated than that of the Lord Protector himself in London.

The English general and his wife even managed a modest form of court life in Edinburgh, and some of the gentry, at least, were willing to be patronised at their table. Monck's wife, Ann, was eleven years his junior. They had met in 1644 while he was a Royalist prisoner in the

Tower, before he decided to switch his services to the Parliamentary cause. She is described, a little unkindly, in some accounts as a washerwoman who 'did' for the inmates. Small, shrewish and of volatile temper, one account calls her 'a lady of low origin, she having been formerly employed in one of the mercer's shops in the Exchange in London . . . her former station shows itself in her manners and dress'. Another states, 'Monk was more fearful of her than of an army. It is said she would even give him manual correction.'

Some suggest that Monck, through his long campaigning, knew little of the opposite sex, and that Ann was the only woman with whom he ever had, if the term is appropriate for an occasionally battered husband, a loving relationship. Reading between the lines, it is evident that some of Monck's military adventures provided welcome relief from Ann. Even so, he certainly loved her and was able to stand up for himself *in extremis*.

But if Monck did not always rule his own roost, he managed to run Scotland as a benign dictator: he used flying columns of dragoons and infantry to hunt down rebels; established a substantial network of informers; tried to put the nation's finances on a proper footing; kept his regiments in good military order; and checked some of the more radical preachers. However, the English Revolution made possible many new forms of religious worship, which gave the ruler of Scotland some insoluble problems. Cromwell believed strongly in this freedom, but Monck disliked many of the new groups, believing that the ideas flowing from various pulpits or meetings could allow extremists to foment social strife. He was concerned that firebrand preachers could subvert his soldiers and provoke conflict with Scottish Presbyterian ministers.

Monck could not completely suppress all these new sects – Baptists, Congregationalists, Quakers, Anabaptists and Fifth Monarchy Men – because the Protector decreed tolerance. Thus, the Presbyterians were annoyed that the nonconformists were allowed to operate at all, while the sectaries despised the general because he occasionally sought to restrain some of their wilder agitation.

Monck's security operations made any overt displays of loyalty to the Stuarts impossible across most of the country. They also made Scotland, for perhaps the only time that century, a more lawful place than England. One contemporary (by no means friendly to Monck) paid this tribute to his administration there: 'As he was feared by the nobility and hated by the clergy, so he was not unloved by the common people, who received more justice and less oppression from him than they had been accustomed to under their own lords.'

A little over one year after assuming his post, Monck decided that he had made sufficient progress in pacifying the country to begin reducing his garrison. This was an urgent necessity, since the cost of the army in Scotland was about double the revenue that the country itself could produce in various duties. But Britain's military rulers had reached a point where they could not afford to pay off the men. In Scotland, during the summer of 1655, Monck calculated his regiments' arrears at £80,000. They could not simply be sent packing, since they had campaigned for years in expectation of this money and would either mutiny or turn to crime if they did not receive it.

Monck applied the ingenuity that had served him so well at Stirling and Dundee to the disbandment problem. He encouraged soldiers to take jobs as mercenaries in Holland and France, or to emigrate to the colonies. He also cashiered some officers whom he believed had fallen under the spell of more radical sectaries. By these means, he managed a reduction of several regiments. Even so, the problem was only partially dealt with in Scotland, and even less so in England.

The ferment and ideological upheaval in 1650s Britain was such that it can easily be compared to France after 1789 or Iran after 1979. Fifth Monarchy Men and other millenarian sects were marching about, led by preachers who confidently asserted that Christ would make His second coming in England at any moment. Villagers fed up with being robbed by unpaid soldiers or set upon by thousands of 'fanatick' pilgrims formed armed groups, the Clubmen, who set upon any suspicious characters they met. Other factions, such as the Levellers and the Diggers, were advocating what we might now call a redistribution of wealth. The garrisons of what had once been a fine New Model Army could exert only a limited influence. In any case, many officers sympathised with the religious sectaries or Levellers, and the army was unhappy, owed huge amounts of money and refusing to disband itself. In short, it was holding the country to ransom.

During the five and a half years that Monck ruled Scotland, he tried to reconcile competing religious, military and budgetary demands. His solutions were subtly different from those in England. There was less religious tolerance in Scotland under the period of military rule, and certainly those members of the garrison who fell in with the Quakers or Fifth Monarchy Men often found themselves being dismissed from the army. Monck sought to maintain the military effectiveness of his regiments by curbing religious politics within their ranks, straining every sinew to pay them regularly and keeping them under command of trusted subordinates. All the while, he tried to protect himself against nasty political surprises by retaining a network of correspondents in London, his native Devon and the garrisons of Ireland and England – people of like mind, many of them professional soldiers.

At times, Monck tired of his burden and sought to resign, but Cromwell wouldn't let him. The Lord Protector had become such an admirer that he even preferred to overlook the ways in which Monck had subverted his Puritan experiment. Some of those black-suited ideologues who did not like what they heard from Edinburgh tried to convince Cromwell that Monck's heart remained true to the Stuarts and that the general was one of those who sought to restore Charles II to the throne.

Writing to Monck in August 1655, Cromwell referred to these rumours, going as far as to make a joke of them: 'There be some that tell me that there is a certain cunning fellow in Scotland called George Monck *who* is said to lie in wait there to introduce Charles Stuart; I pray you must use your diligence to apprehend him and send him up to me.'

Why did Cromwell leave him in Scotland, at the head of one of the few effective garrisons left in the army? The Lord Protector knew his general well enough to realise that the sense of military honour that bound Monck to serve, after having agreed to take up the Scottish position, would be sufficient to prevent him betraying the Commonwealth's trust. It was a sound judgement, and indeed was exactly the same one reached by a Royalist peer in considering whether Monck might be turned to the Stuart cause. The leading Stuart supporter put it thus: 'The only ties that have hitherto kept [Monck] from grumbling have been the vanity of constancy to his professions, and his affection to Cromwell's person.' In this last comment the Royalist had realised something that the Lord Protector apparently had not. Monck respected Cromwell as a general and as a strong hand, holding the country back from even worse confusion and Puritan zealotry.

When Cromwell died, in September 1658, the country reached a crossroads. For a few months, his son Richard was able to rule, but challenges to his authority began appearing almost immediately. The ties between Oliver Cromwell and his generals had been dissolved. They began vying for power and, increasingly, Richard became a marginal figure. As Monck's correspondents in London told him of each new twist and turn, he decided that he could not remain indifferent in the power struggle. He prepared to hurl himself out of Scotland, exploding with all the force of a political mortar bomb.

It was late in the evening of 8 December 1659 when Monck and his party arrived in Coldstream, a small village on the Scottish side of the Tweed. The ground was blanketed with snow, and stones in the stream that marked the English border were wreathed in ice. Several regiments of Monck's Scottish army had already billeted themselves on the locals, having marched there on the general's orders. At a time of night when the embers in Coldstream's hearths would normally have been dying, smoke billowed into the crisp night from its chimneys, bearing witness to the many rough soldiers who had been packed into each home or barn.

One of Monck's party recalled their arrival at 11 p.m.: 'The honest Red-coats did bid us heartily welcome, but the Knaves had eat up all the Meat, and drank all the Drink of the Town . . . the General lodged, falling to his good Cheer, which was his chewing tobacco (which he used to commend so much).' Monck and his people finally found beds for the night at a house just outside the village.

Monck's days in Coldstream were the most fateful of his life. For it was there, gripped in the depths of the Scottish winter, that he had to decide whether to cross the Tweed, march to London and seize power. Ann appeared on a couple of occasions, but Monck packed her off the following morning. He did not want her there as he approached his moment of decision.

Fifteen months had passed since Oliver Cromwell's death. His son Richard had inherited the title of Lord Protector but immediately it had become apparent that he did not have either the strength of character or the army following to wield supreme power. Certain warlords – veteran army commanders – soon decided to ignore Richard and took steps to dictate their terms to what remained of Parliament.

Cromwell's side in the Civil War had, of course, fought in the name of Parliament, but by 1659 that assembly was a shadow of its former self. Its remaining members were those who had survived the 1648 purge of 231 Royalists and the following year's abolition of the Lords.

Monck signalled by letter his opposition to the actions of the military opportunists who now attempted to coerce the MPs. The principal among these warlords, Major General John Lambert, had marched north with a small army, ready to confront Monck if he sought to follow his words in support of Parliament with deeds. Lambert was a gifted cavalry commander who had campaigned on the same side as Monck and Cromwell in Scotland seven years previously. But now he coveted the title of Lord Protector and had garnered some support among Puritan officers.

The choice thus confronting Monck as he reviewed his regiments in Coldstream was whether to risk a further civil war involving years more bloodletting. He wrote to Lambert: 'It is much upon my spiritt that this poore Commonwealth can never be happy if the army make itself a divided interest from the rest of the nation.' But Monck was not just opposed to rule by military diktat. His belief that England would have to revert to its traditional form of government included a more explosive agenda: that only the Restoration of King Charles II could end the chaos in his country. He stood ready to usher in a new order, but his road to Westminster was full of dangers, which meant he could not state his aims plainly. Army and society had been shattered by seventeen years of strife. There were all manner of disparate sects and interests that disagreed about most things but still denounced the Stuart monarchy loudly and might unite against anyone proposing Restoration.

We are fortunate that some of the greatest English writers – John Milton, Samuel Pepys and Thomas Hobbes – lived through this crisis and recorded their views about what Monck did next. 'If [Monck] had declared for the King or for a free Parliament,' noted Hobbes, explaining the general's subterfuge, 'all the armies in England would have joined against him.'

Monck's first priority during those days in Coldstream was therefore to assure himself of the loyalty of his own troops and that other garrisons in England and Ireland would acquiesce to his entering the political fray with his secret objectives. As he waited in the little border village, mud-spattered messengers on foaming horses arrived regularly, carrying dispatches from his correspondents across the country.

Monck had gone to the utmost care to cultivate these contacts during the preceding months, and to ensure that they went undiscovered by spies or gossips. Thomas Gumble, one of the general's chaplains, recorded, 'He had constantly Letters directed to Scotch Names at Edenbourgh, about Merchant affairs, and also other private business; and the whole Intelligence wrapt in certain words to be read in certain places . . . he had several Messengers that came as often as there was occasion, through by-ways, and not in the great Road.'

Others, too, arrived to see him: for example, a relative of Thomas Fairfax, the erstwhile commander of the Roundhead armies who, during Cromwell's later years, had shut himself away in Yorkshire. During the Civil War, Fairfax had been Monck's adversary and Lambert's friend, but over time he had come to conclude that England's best course back towards stability consisted of restoring the monarchy. Now he was ready to declare his support for Monck as soon as he crossed the Tweed, and to bring numerous influential northern gentlemen with him.

These secret preparations were so effective that Monck wrong-footed many of those who now sought power but who had written him off as a dull plodder. Hobbes wrote, 'they thought not of him; his gallantry had been shown on remote stages . . . [but] after General Monk [sic] had signified by letter his dislike of the proceedings of Lambert and his fellows, they were much surprised, and began to think him more considerable than they had done; but it was too late'.

By Christmas Day 1659, Monck's conspiracy was nearing fruition. He knew that many in London were desperate for deliverance from religious extremists relying on armed force, and that others in the army would either support him or at least stand aside and watch. But what about the loyalty of his own troops?

A little over two months before, on 19th October, the issue of allegiance had reached a tense crisis in Edinburgh. Monck had been forced to use loyal soldiers to face down those of his own and another regiment who had fallen under the spell of officers sympathetic to Lambert. Addressing the troops during this stand-off, with musketeers blowing on their smouldering matches, ready to give fire at any moment, Monck appealed direct to the rank and file, bellowing out in his Devon accent a promise that he would guarantee them their back pay. The men began cheering for their general; when shots rang out, mercifully they came in the form of a salute for Monck. With the threat of bloodshed averted, Monck had to dismiss the lieutenant colonel of his own regiment and six of its ten company commanders; all had shown themselves loyal to Lambert and the other army plotters in London.

With this crisis behind him, and the army readied in Coldstream, Monck's careful management of his soldiery during the previous four years paid dividends. Those in the ranks knew that 'honest George Monck' had seen to it that they were paid more often than the men of other garrisons and now they also had that promise of the remainder of their due. Occasional fighting against Highland rebels meant the regiments had retained their spirit. His popularity in this small force was such that when Monck rode among his men, he would often hear them shout that he should make himself Lord Protector in Richard Cromwell's stead.

On 1 January 1660, Monck's first brigade marched across the bridge at Coldstream. His destiny was sealed. Thomas Gumble, his chaplain, recorded breathlessly that setting out on New Year's Day was 'a good *omen* to begin a New World in *England*'.

The Scottish army marching south consisted of four regiments of horse and six of foot. They were divided into two brigades, the second of which, accompanied by Monck himself, crossed the Tweed on 2 January. The total strength of this force was fewer than 6,000 men, and they were soon known as the Coldstreamers. Gumble compared them to the Nobles of Israel, 'because they offered themselves willingly among the people, and jeoparded their lives unto death in the high places of the field'.

Ten days after their departure, when the Coldstreamers marched into York, the immediate prospect of bloodshed had receded somewhat. Yorkshire had risen in support of Monck, and Lambert's army melted away. Various worthies who presumed to speak for Parliament now began frantic negotiations with Monck, realising at last that he had become England's kingmaker. Associations around the country began sending petitions to York, where the general paused for five days while considering his next step.

Fairfax was one of the first to come and see Monck, and urged him to declare for Charles II. But he was disappointed when the Coldstreamers' leader gave him no clear answer. There were different proposals flying about that fell short of this dramatic step and were therefore worthy of consideration. Many of the arguments centred on whether some sort of national equilibrium could be restored if the MPs purged, or 'secluded', in 1648 – at least those who had survived – could be recalled to the Commons. Those opposed to this measure knew it would lead inexorably to the return of a Stuart king.

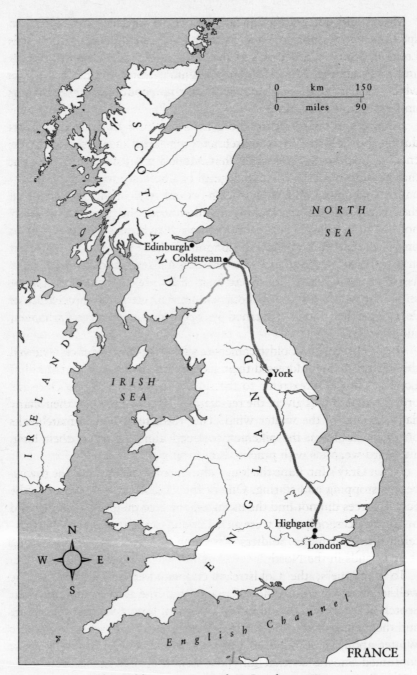

The Coldstreamers march to London, 1660

Monck did not gratify Fairfax, or the others who wanted him to spell out his position in York. Instead he resumed his march towards London. Some regarded this as indecision and funk. A contemporary and rival damned Monck as 'instrumental in bringing things to pass which he had neither wisdom to forsee nor courage to attempt nor understanding to continue'.

Admirers, though, regard the general's refusal to declare his aims during the Coldstreamers' march as a masterful tactic to prevent his enemies coalescing. It is clear that Monck wanted Restoration, but that he did not dare articulate it until he could see for himself the situation in London and know that he could rely on the support of all the main garrisons. In cloaking his intentions, the general was ready not just to be evasive but to resort to downright lies. Monck wrote to one of the old Roundheads in London: 'Believe me, Sir, for I speak it in the presence of God, it is the desire of my soul, and shall (the Lord assisting) be witnessed by the actions of my life, that these nations be so settled in a free state, without a king, a single person, or House of Peers, that they may be governed by their representatives in Parliament successively.'

On 3 February the Coldstreamers reached Highgate. Monck reviewed the regiments and addressed them as they gazed south from the hill at London's northern extreme to the smoky metropolis below. Once the order to march was given, the regiments filed down the hill, their many flags dancing in the winter wind. The musketeers lugged matchlocks on their shoulders, the pikemen tramped along, carrying their long, awkward weapons with practised ease.

Down Gray's Inn Lane the long columns of soldiers went, the townspeople stopping and staring. One of the Coldstreamers recorded, 'the Scotch forces did not find the usual welcome of the people, as they did in other places; only they were gazed upon, and that was all their entertainment. Which the Soldiers observing, wished themselves among their Friends in the North.'

To Londoners, the Coldstreamers looked quite different to the well-fed garrison troops they were used to. One account stated, 'Their Scotch horse were thin and out of case with long and hard Marching; and the men as rough and weather beaten, having marched in a severe Winter about three hundred Miles in length, and through deep and continued Snows; so that all their Way they had scarce seen their native Country.' They proceeded to Westminster, where Monck went in search of the Speaker of the Commons. Londoners gradually understood what the arrival of this new army meant.

Samuel Pepys noted in his diary on 6 February, 'I stood upon the steps and saw Monk go by, he making observances to the judges as he went along.' The next day, he saw some of Monck's men manhandling some Quakers, evidently having taken their commander's dislike of the religious sects to heart, and noted disapprovingly, 'indeed the soldiers did use them very roughly and were to blame'. A few days later, once a letter by Monck in favour of restoring the secluded Members of Parliament had become public, Pepys raced to the Guildhall in the City and found a very different scene:

the Hall was full of people expecting Monk and the Lord Mayor to come thither, and all very joyfull. Met Monk coming out of the chamber . . . but such a shout I never heard in all my life, crying out 'God Bless Your Excellence' . . . I saw many people give the soldiers drink and money, and all along the street cried, 'God Bless them!' and extraordinary good words.

Monck's position had at last become clear. The MPs purged in 1648 were those who had refused to go along with the trial and execution of Charles I. Bringing them back into the House would create a majority in favour of Restoration. People in the City, in particular, longed for it, and the explosion of joy witnessed by Pepys can be seen in that light. However, not everyone agreed to this step, and those who thought Monck's request a betrayal of everything gained in the Civil War met urgently at Westminster, and agreed to elect a completely new House of Commons.

It is a measure of how far Monck had thought ahead and prepared the ground through his secret correspondence and messengers that on 21 February, when his opponents were about to dissolve the House and declare a new election, one of his staff appeared at the Commons with seventy-three of the Members purged a dozen years before. Resuming their seats, and to the consternation of the Puritan zealots, these Members immediately changed the balance of the House. There could be no thought of casting out these returning gentlemen, because the other MPs knew that the force of Monck's army stood behind them. The Restoration of Charles II became inevitable.

Three months later, on 25 May, a large crowd of dignatories assembled on the quay at Dover. It was approaching 1 p.m. and the assembled party watched as a ship of the line approached. The warship had, until three days before, been called *Naseby*, after one of of Parliament's great victories. In view of its mission that day, it had been tactfully renamed the *Royal Charles*. The Mayor of Dover and his retinue fussed about, standing under the ornate canopy they had erected for the occasion. A large Bible, with golden clasps, sat on a lectern, awaiting presentation to His Majesty.

One guest, though, upstaged all the others. Monck had been summoned urgently to Dover after a letter arrived from Charles II saying that he would not land unless he was sure the general was there to meet him.

As the statuesque figure of the King – over six feet tall, with flowing locks and courtly robes – came ashore, cannon boomed out a salute from the castle. 'The General received him with becoming duty', recorded Gumble, who was standing just behind Monck, 'but his Majesty embraced him with an affection so absolute and vehement, as higher could not have been expressed by a Prince to a subject. He embraced and kissed him.' Pepys, who had been aboard the *Royal Charles*, sharing the King's breakfast of 'pease, pork and boiled beef', noted that after the embraces 'the shouting and joy expressed by all is beyond imagination'.

They made an incongruous couple, the King and Monck, with Charles towering over the stocky general as they walked to a waiting carriage. But the two of them symbolised the importance of the moment: the rough soldier whose strong hand rescued England from anarchy deferring to the manicured sovereign who would restore the mystery of kingship and the missing element of hierarchy required for Parliament and state to function.

During the years when Royalist agents had tried to win Monck over to their cause, vast sums had been offered secretly by way of reward. When Charles II returned, Monck wasted little time in collecting his due – both financial and by extending a personal web of patronage. He was quickly created Duke of Albemarle, made Lord General, or Commander-in-Chief, of the Army, and laden with other honours.

In his correspondence with Charles prior to their meeting in Dover that May, Monck had set only one precondition for how the King should rule. Making himself the soldiers' champion, Monck had insisted that the army's arrears of pay be settled as a prelude to its disbandment. This involved demobilising 18 regiments of foot, 15 of horse and dozens of garrison parties scattered about the land, totalling around 50,000 men. Parliament and sovereign had to agree a huge programme of taxation in order to buy off the soldiers, preventing the emergence of another Lambert (the general himself languished in the Tower) who might seize power. Under the new assessments, £70,000 extra per month for eighteen months was to be raised to pay off all of those regiments.

Although plans were set in train for the complete disbandment of what had once been Fairfax's New Model Army, it may be surmised that both Monck and the King thought some soldiers might be required to act as police, maintaining internal security. There were plans to keep a few troops of cavalry to protect the people of London against thieves and the mob. Also, the future of a regiment of Royal Guards, who had accompanied Charles on his return from the Low Countries, remained uncertain.

Matters were brought to a head in January 1661, when a crowd of several hundred Fifth Monarchy Men marched to Kenwood on Highgate Hill and declared a sort of divinely inspired insurrection. Monck quickly scattered the zealots with his forces. Much of the old Parliamentary army had already been paid off, but one or two regiments, critically Monck's own – the core of his Coldstreamers – were still under arms.

On the 14th of the same month, Monck's regiment of foot and his troop of horse marched to Tower Hill. At about 10 a.m., a carriage appeared, bearing commissioners appointed by Parliament to oversee the disbandment of the army. As they got out, the troops formed a circle around them. Colonel King, one of the commissioners, addressed the men, an eyewitness recording:

That God had highly honoured them in the eyes and hearts of the King and kingdom; yea, and made them renowned throughout the world and to all posterity, in stirring them up to be eminently instrumental in the happy Restoration of his Majesty to his royal throne, the Parliament to their privileges, and our whole kingdoms to their antient laws, liberties, and government, without any battle or bloodshed: for which signal services his Majesty and the whole kingdom returned them not only their verbal but real thanks.

The troops were invited to lay down their pikes and muskets. No sooner had they done so than they took a new oath to serve the King as 'an extraordinary Guard to his Royal Person', marched forward, picked up the weapons discarded minutes before, and began shouting, 'God save King Charles the Second!' Some men threw their hats in the air, others primed their muskets and began a *feu de joie*.

With this ceremony, the modern British Army was born. It was formed from troops that had previously been enemies – a pattern applied by the British themselves in nation-building missions hundreds of years later from Sierra Leone to Iraq. Monck's men and a further regiment of Parliamentary cavalry (Colonel Unton Crook's horse) were combined with some Royalist battalions brought by Charles from the Netherlands and, a few months later, with some newly raised troops. The precedence of these different regiments was considered too delicate an issue to be tackled in Monck's lifetime, but Charles's returnees were later designated the 1st Foot Guards and Monck's old regiment the 2nd, or Coldstream, Guards. Even today their rivalry lives on, the Coldstreamers adopting the motto 'Second to None'. Monck's troop of horse and two of the King's household were combined into the Lifeguards; Crook's old Ironside regiment became the Royal Horse Guards, or the Blues.

These arrangements were in place for only a few months before the King's acquisition, through marriage, of a colonial possession (Tangier in modern Morocco) required a garrison to be raised. Within a couple of years, the army, which had fallen as low as 3,000 men, was restored to a strength of around 8,500.

Fairfax's New Model, it is true, was the first British professional military force, in the sense that its men were not paid off after each campaign and were properly trained. Ultimately, though, the New Model or Parliamentary army came to represent a sectarian instrument of military rule. It was infiltrated by various extreme religious groups, eventually fracturing along lines of loyalty to different commanders. It was for this reason that Fairfax's army, or its remnant, was almost entirely disbanded in 1660–2. Monck's men (and indeed Charles's Guards regiment) were the nucleus of a modern standing army not just because their regiments have served continuously since February 1661 but because they represented the unification of what had been the Civil War factions. Even so, their constitutional status remained unclear for many years.

Until the 1689 Mutiny Act, which set out a code of military discipline, the notion of a regular army was not to be found in any statutory form. In the meantime, the Guards were paid with budgetary sleight of hand, as part of the King's household. It was to take centuries for British soldiers to stop thinking of themselves as servants of the Crown. Indeed, some still do.

Such was the novelty of a standing army that there were no quarters or barracks for them. The men of the new Guards regiments had to be billeted, as the Parliamentary troops had been, in various places where paid lodgings might be found. An order in Monck's regiment mentions 'inns, victualling-houses, taverns, and alehouses', where the men were meant to provide for their stay, food and boozing from their daily pay. This was set at ten pence a day for privates while actually guarding the King; eight pence under other circumstances. The Coldstream Guards for many years were thus scattered about, living in pubs and inns in an area of London that now comprises Clerkenwell, Aldgate, Islington and Holborn – a thoroughly agreeable existence, one imagines, for men who had recently spent years fighting Highlanders in Scotland.

Since the arrangements for raising and paying troops during the 1660s and 1670s were not subject to specific Parliamentary consent, many in the Commons frequently voiced opposition to the notion of a standing army, regarding it as an instrument that might be used by a king to rule by force. The Royalists, meanwhile, had seen in the experience of Cromwell and his generals a lesson that religious extremists should not be allowed to run the country in a similarly arbitrary way. Each side saw in the other's pronouncements a desire to gain control of a powerful standing army as an instrument of internal repression.

Monck had believed in the need for regular military forces for many years. He and Fairfax seemed to have drawn common lessons from their campaigns in the Netherlands in the 1630s. Each had tried to apply these ideas during the Civil War, with Fairfax succeeding and Monck seeing his suggestions for such a force ignored by Charles I. Under Charles II, Monck finally found himself as lord general of a professional army. He believed that one of the principal hedges against such an army being used as an instrument of tyranny was that it should be commanded by a strong, independent figure, i.e. himself. And while, as Duke of Albemarle, he played the part of courtier to Charles II with alacrity, it is evident that the Civil War had left Monck with the belief that no monarch or royal house could regard their position as a right to be upheld, regardless of conduct. Monck's treatise *Observations upon Military and Political Affairs* contained the sentence, 'You ought not to perpetuate any Government, neither to families nor yet for life.' This might fit easily with his earlier refusal to go along with Cromwell's plans to pass power to his son, but it was a bombshell coming from the man who had restored the Stuart monarchy.

Charles II was evidently shrewd enough to recognise in Monck the kind of independence of spirit that required careful handling. He not only larded the Duke with honours and money, but used Monck as a troubleshooter during the Great Plague, after the Fire of London and, reverting to his position as naval commander, during renewed naval hostilities with the Dutch. This second tour as an admiral was not a success for Monck, however, for he was defeated in battle by the Dutch fleet, a stain on his reputation in later life.

The final period of his service brought Monck into frequent contact with Samuel Pepys, one of the clerks running the navy. Pepys certainly paints a less than flattering picture of Monck in this period, recording at one point, 'he is grown a drunken sot'. Others were scathing about abuses of patronage by Monck and his wife, with one noting, 'both of them asked and sold all that was in their reach, nothing being denied them for some time'. Pepys also considered Monck rather dim. At the same time, though, he was perceptive enough to recognise both his popularity and his standing with the King. When Monck returned from fighting the Dutch in October 1667, he received a vote of thanks from Parliament in spite of the defeat. A perplexed Pepys wrote, 'I know not how, the blockhead Albemarle [i.e. Monck] hath strange luck to be loved, though he be (and every man must know it) the heaviest man in the world, but stout and honest to his country.'

On 2 January 1670, Monck died while sitting in a chair at home. The King immediately ordered that he be embalmed by royal physicians, prior to lying in state at Somerset House. The obsequies observed at this time dictated a lengthy period on display, allowing worthies the opportunity to travel to London from various parts of the country. The dead general was thus exhibited for weeks, suitably prepared by the doctors so that his remains did not visibly deteriorate or prove too offensive to the mourners' nostrils.

The character left to posterity by most of those contemporaries who wrote about him was of 'honest George Monck'. He was the archetype of the reliable soldier who eschewed courtly sophistication and spoke about things as he found them. Even someone like Pepys, whose patron was a rival of Monck's for the King's favour, had to concede these traits.

It would be fatal to conclude from this, though, that Pepys was right when he called Monck a 'blockhead', since there is much evidence to the contrary. It is Monck's seizure of power in 1660 – the key drama of his life – that shows what a calculating and ruthless man he could be when he thought that the interests of England and, obviously, his own family demanded it. Monck's plain, thickset appearance, his refusal to use flowery language and even his West Country accent may all have caused people to underestimate his intelligence.

When Thomas Hobbes published *Behemoth, or the Long Parliament* in 1671, the tract in which he tried to digest the experience of that national madness that was the Civil War and find its deeper meaning, he chose to place the march from Coldstream at the very end of his story. *Behemoth* concludes with the words, 'You have told me little of the General till now in the end: but truly, I think the bringing of his little army entire out of Scotland up to London, was the greatest stratagem that is extant in history.'

In giving this powerful testimony to the significance of Monck's coup, Hobbes played the same trick on his readers as the general had played on his rivals – of writing him off, allowing him to remain on 'remote stages' until the moment of his own choosing. In describing the march as the 'greatest stratagem', Hobbes also acknowledged that Monck had cloaked his real intentions, sometimes wrongfooting his rivals with lies.

There can be no doubt, though, that the general acted with cunning and calculation in 1660: he maintained a network of secret contacts in order to gain the most timely intelligence of what his rivals were doing; he neutralised his army rivals; once in London, he marshalled sufficient secluded Members of the Commons to produce at the key moment in Parliament as his coup moved towards its unstated climax, Restoration.

The quality of his thinking is also shown in the book *Observations upon Military and Political Affairs*, ostensibly written by him in 1644–5, while a prisoner in the Tower, but evidently amended later in life and finally published in 1671, after his death. In formulating general principles about the conduct of war, *Observations* showed an intellectual ambition to which the vast majority of British officers through the ages would never have aspired. It would be overstating it to say that Monck's treatise made him an English Machiavelli or Clausewitz, but it was not a lack of merit that ensured Monck's book circulated little in the decades after his death. Rather, it seems that a British officer corps that would rank among the poorest read in Europe (the French were the unquestioned champions of military theory) was not much interested in the reflections of a man who had done so much to shape the country.

Monck's book combined much of what was to become standard in such works – advice about the concentration of force or qualities of decisive generalship – with some fresh ideas that seem part of our modern age, such as the vital importance of intelligence gathering in order to wage successful war. His reflections on relations between generals and their political masters are of greatest interest, though. In his advice that 'you ought not to perpetuate any Government', Monck showed that the relationship between England and the Monarch had been permanently altered by the Civil War, and that the Restoration was not simply handing the country back to the Stuarts to do with it what they liked. Indeed, the overthrow of James II just a few years later would underline Monck's conviction that no king had a God-given right to continue his rule, regardless of his behaviour.

As for success in war, Monck stated that it needed underlying economic strength as well as military professionalism: 'I account a Rich Publick Treasure, providently provided before-hand, and a people well trained in Martial Affairs, to be two of the only Pillars (next under God) that will preserve a Kingdom or State from ruine and danger.' Monck argued for moderation in waging war: 'It is an excellent property of a good and wise Prince to use War, as he doth Physick, carefully, unwillingly, and seasonably.' As for the role of generals in launching conflict or defining its aims, he believed, 'It is a dangerous thing for a General to make himself chief in pursuading a Prince, or State to any weighty and important resolution, so that the counsel thereof be wholly imputed to him, which belongs to many.'

In these last two points Monck did much to define the British Army and its style of generalship for the next two hundred years. First, any blatant adventurism was to be eschewed. Second, responsibility for going to war must always be seen by the wider public as the decision of a government rather than its generals.

In an age of modern liberal democracy, many regard the armed forces as 'apolitical'. But there should be no doubt about it, Britain's post-Civil War settlement was made possible by a military coup in 1660. Furthermore, in the two centuries that followed Monck's action, the army that he founded would often find itself up to its neck in politics. The knack for aspiring 'political generals', as Monck had shown, was to intervene in civilian counsels only occasionally, and to be very careful about cloaking their intentions. In foreign wars, senior officers were bound to have strong views about the feasibility or righteousness of military plans, but they needed to use wisdom and guile to bend civilian opponents to their way of thinking.

Monck's coup, though, was such an unarguably political act that his historical reputation became the subject of partisan dispute. Tories would see him as a man loyal to his rightful sovereign who rescued England from the madness of its 'state of nature' following the execution of Charles I. Their ideological opponents – later known as Whig historians – tended to see Monck as a cynical adventurer who changed sides too many times, betrayed Cromwell and ultimately sold out the Commonwealth in order to enrich his family.

As to the significance of his actions, though, there is less dispute. Monck had other options, after all: he might have consolidated his personal power and made himself Protector, as some urged him to do; conversely, he could have allowed the election of a new Parliament, without the return of Charles II, thereby producing a true republic. Instead, he took the key step in the creation of a constitutional monarchy, and founded a professional army.

The procession from Somerset House to Westminster Abbey on 30 April 1670 was a splendid one, paid for by the King. Atop the coffin was an effigy of the Lord General, Duke of Albemarle, dressed in armour. As the carriage carrying it made its way up the Strand, it was watched by two regiments of City Militia, who were lining the route. The 1st Foot Guards followed on; then Monck's old regiment, the Coldstreamers. Behind this military parade came Monck's son and the other mourners. Ann had died a fortnight after her husband, but, with no lying in state necessary for her, had beaten him to their vault in Westminster Abbey. While some contemporaries liked to look down on her for her lowly origins, her death testified to the depth of her love for the general, and, as one modern biographer has noted, 'No breath of scandal was to hurt either of them at the bawdy court of the restored Stuart king.'

Circumstances had cast Monck not as the victor of epic battles but in the role of kingmaker. This gave him a more significant legacy than the greatest master of the battlefield of his own age, Oliver Cromwell.

Even so, the army that Monck had founded was, at the time he left it, a small enterprise: several thousand men who figured little in the calculations of European statesmen. The task of getting the wider world to sit up and take notice of this new power would eventually fall to a tall young ensign who walked behind the general's coffin on that day in April 1670. His name was John Churchill.

John Churchill

1650–1722

The name of him is better than ten thousand men.
CORPORAL MATTHEW BISHOP

THE SERVANTS AT Nonsuch House had grown used to the sounds of lovemaking. They had become blasé, too, about the bewildering procession of gentlemen that their lady took to her bed. But on that particular day her adventures took a most unexpected and possibly dangerous turn. As Barbara Villiers entertained young Lieutenant Churchill of the Foot Guards another of her lovers had arrived at the front door unexpectedly and with the greatest drama. For this admirer, striding into the house with his fine robes and cascade of curling locks flowing behind, realised full well that she had been inconstant to him, and was none other than King Charles II.

By the time the King burst in, Mr Churchill had hidden himself in the wardrobe, but it did not take the King long to smoke him out. Moments later, the three breathless protagonists were eyeing one another. The French Ambassador gleefully reported the whole scandal back to his king Louis XIV. John Churchill was twenty years old, the son of a Devon Cavalier repressed by the Roundheads, tall, fresh faced and strikingly handsome. The King, who at this point had passed fifty, was also over six feet tall, but his sybaritic habits and advanced years had taken their toll on his once refined features, which had filled out in puffy middle age. Barbara Villiers, twenty-seven, looking tiny between them, with her piercing blue eyes and auburn hair held these two men (and several others) in her thrall.

At last the King turned to Churchill. 'You are a rascal', he told the young officer, 'but I forgive you because you do it to get your bread.' With a wave of the royal hand, Lieutenant Churchill was dismissed.

There were no repercussions. Charles II was not a hypocrite – not in matters of sexual jealousy at least. He pursued tarts and aristocrats alike with such abandon that he did not begrudge Barbara Villiers her own amusement. The King's mistress, also known as Lady Castlemaine and the Duchess of Cleveland, was, in the words of one contemporary, 'lewdest of the royal concubines'. Lord Macaulay, writing for the Victorian public in 1858, called her 'the most profuse, imperious, and shameless of harlots', and damned John Churchill for being 'kept' by her.

That Churchill was her hired plaything is quite clear, but the King had understood in an instant during their bedroom encounter that the young Guards officer really had no other means of making his way in the world. In our modern age we may indeed even see something touching or empowering in the fact that Barbara Villiers accepted fortunes from the old men who panted and gasped on top of her but reserved her own generosity for the boy seven years her junior whom she certainly loved deeply. A contemporary (and hostile) account of their liaison described it thus: 'The Dutchess was enchanted with the pleasures of her new and innocent Lover, a Lover whom she had made such, and who first sigh'd and felt, in favour of her, those amiable Disorders and transporting Joys, that attend the possession of early Love; she presented him with unlimited Bounty.'

This was just one of the many rumours that surrounded the relationship of Villiers and Churchill. Some suggested that she seduced him when he was just sixteen, not long after he appeared as a page at court, and that she bought him his first commission in the army. In 1674, a few years after the incident at Nonsuch, the Duchess certainly gave him an outright gift of £4,500 – a fortune that Churchill invested wisely to give himself an income of £500 a year. She may also have procured his promotion to captain the following year.

Churchill's decision to secure his future with her gift rather than give in to the obvious temptations of court high living was quite typical. He had tasted humiliation and poverty during his childhood in the West Country, the consequence of heavy fines imposed by Parliament on Royalist sympathisers, his father having been a Cavalier. General Monck's restoration of the Stuarts revived the Churchill family's fortunes, but they could not be considered wealthy. Their credentials as loyalists who had suffered for their beliefs, however, gave the family access to the Stuart court, something which they exploited shamelessly.

John's older sister went there as a lady-in-waiting but soon became mistress to James, Duke of York (later James II), and she was thus able to introduce her brother into royal circles. Such was the spirit of these times that John was also rumoured to be the lover of the Duchess of York, spurned wife of his own sister's lover.

The young John Churchill's fortunes at this stage were inextricably linked to those of his patrons, the Duke of York (via the agency of his sister) and the Duchess of Cleveland. These relationships also defined his early progress in the army. His first spell of foreign service, in the English garrison of Tangier from 1668 to 1670, may have been the result of the Duke of York's desire to send Churchill as far away as possible from his wife. Certainly, the years as a *beau sabreur* resulted in all kinds of insinuations and gossip attaching to his name. Although he often displayed great self-control and tact, it is apparent that the sexual jealousies of the Caroline court were sometimes too much for him. During a few months in 1671, Churchill fought two duels – sustaining superficial sword wounds in both. It may well be that his second period of military service overseas, like that in Tangier, resulted from his patrons' desire either to save his life or avert the scandal of him killing an opponent.

Churchill's promotion in 1674 in an English regiment in the service of France was a product of the close ties between the Duke of York and Louis XIV. Continued haggling between Parliament and the Crown over the cost of maintaining standing forces meant that the Stuarts resorted to the expedient of keeping several regiments of English troops overseas. In a crisis they could be returned to England or Ireland, but in the meantime they had effectively been rented out to the 'Sun King', whose ambitions for France required huge armies.

In his early twenties John Churchill thus served a French master and learned the art of war in the world's most advanced army. France could field 100,000 troops, and its generals, men such as Vauban, Conde and Turenne, were rapidly establishing themselves as great captains, theorists and teachers for the rest of Europe. England, having standing forces that did not exceed 10,000 throughout the 1670s, counted as a third-rate military power. Young gentlemen did not expect to learn the career of arms in England; rather, France was the magnet for them.

During fighting at the siege of Maastricht in 1673 and at Enzheim the following year, Churchill's French commander commended 'the handsome Englishman'. He had shown great bravery in these actions, but it is important to note that the terms in which he was complimented alluded to his popularity with the ladies rather than to any military genius.

The story of John Churchill is, above all else, one of reputation. By his mid-twenties, the young officer had acquired renown not as a soldier or a statesman but as a gigolo, duellist and social climber. Thus, in 1676, when Louis XIV's War Minister was asked to consider appointing him to the lieutenant colonelcy of a French army regiment, he rejected Churchill with the damning assessment that he would give 'more satisfaction to a rich and faded mistress, than to a monarch who did not want to have dishonourable and dishonoured carpet knights in his armies'.

The sails that blossomed on the horizon off Torbay early on the morning of Guy Fawkes' Day 1688 were too numerous to count. As the Dutch fleet stood in to shore and transports slipped into the harbour, it became clear that it was an armament of hundreds of vessels. William of Orange, carried by the 'Protestant wind', brought with him 60 naval ships and 500 tranports; his armada disgorged 10,600 infantry and 3,600 cavalry. They were invading by invitation of the English gentry; or, to be more precise, that section of it that regarded James II as a French stooge who was trying to drag the nation towards despotism and popery.

Lieutenant General John Churchill was by now thirty-nine years old and a senior figure in the army. He responded quickly to orders to join the corps forming on Salisbury Plain under the King's banner. James had more than doubled the size of England's army during his brief reign, and within a fortnight of William landing had 25,000 troops ready to oppose the Dutchman. But the King's inner circle knew things were not quite that simple. Despite James's attempts to pack the army with Catholics and other loyalists, certain regiments had already melted away. The army's Commander-in-Chief suspected Lieutenant General Churchill of treason and urged James to sack him forthwith, but the King did not believe it possible that a man who owed everything to royal patronage would betray him at this moment. After all, Churchill had stood by the Crown in a similar crisis three years earlier, when the Duke of Monmouth (one of Charles II's bastards) raised a revolt in the West Country that was crushed at Sedgemoor.

On 23 November 1688, the King called his generals together for a council of war at their camp. Lieutenant General Churchill urged an immediate attack on William's forces. James vacillated throughout the remainder of that day, for he understood that his grip on the loyalty of many subjects had weakened since Sedgemoor. Not long after dusk, Churchill defected, taking 400 sympathisers with him to Axminster, where William had raised his standard.

This move did not surprise the Prince of Orange in the least, since he had received a secret letter from Churchill weeks before his invasion fleet had set sail. William had even relied on the general to win over many influential army commanders. Whatever Churchill may have owed James (and it was a great deal), he considered his duty to his (Protestant) faith to be greater. The King's advisers were not surprised either, for they had long believed the general sympathised with the party that denounced James for turning England into a satellite of Louis XIV's France. Only the King himself, it seems, was stunned by the betrayal.

Churchill, by this point in his life, was such an accomplished courtier that he attempted, even at the point of rupture, to cover his bets with the monarch. He wrote a farewell letter to James, trying to explain his actions: 'This, Sir could proceed from nothing but the inviolable dictates of my conscience, and a necessary concern for my religion.' Even after James accepted that he had been outmanoeuvred and went into exile, Churchill maintained confidential contacts and secret correspondence with him, the tenor of which was 'no hard feelings'. The general seems to have rationalised that the wheel of fortune might turn yet again, bringing James back to power.

On Christmas Day, William made his triumphal entry into London, accompanied by noisy acclaim from mob and gentry alike. He had saved England from devilish popish designs, after all, and secured for himself the most phenomenal prize. It was dubbed the 'Glorious Revolution'.

The Prince of Orange knew that Westminster's balance of power between legislature and sovereign gave him a great deal more latitude than that in the United Provinces of the Netherlands. But in uniting the functions of Dutch Stadtholder and King of England, William would embody a new axis against his hated foe, Louis XIV. William was delighted, then, to break France's cosy relationship with James II's England, and to add its fleets and armies to a new grouping of Protestant nations.

It did not take long for the soldiers of England's little army to appreciate the shocking implications of this shift. William arrived with several battalions of Dutch household troops, who took the place of the 1st Foot Guards and Coldstreamers. The British Guards were later ordered unceremoniously out of London. William feared what we would now call a military coup: 'he remembered General Monck,' as Winston Churchill put it.

This was far from the end of it, though. An ageing German general of the Dutch service, Marshal Schomberg, was made Commander-in-Chief, the only time in the history of Britain's standing army that a foreigner held the post. The Prince of Orange, becoming William III, had made it quite clear how little he thought of English generals and their poorly trained troops.

In seeking an English confederate for his reforms, William had little trouble in deciding on John Churchill. Raised to the peerage as the Earl of Marlborough, he became Schomberg's number two, the necessary Englishman in the military set-up. These were royal rewards for pulling the rug from beneath James II and a recognition of his skills of organisation and persuasion.

So the newly made Earl had evolved from a trouserless player in Restoration bedroom romps into a man of substance. One of William's Dutch generals described Marlborough thus: 'His features without fault, fine, sparkling eyes, good teeth, and his complexion such a mixture of white and red as the fairer sex might envy: in brief, except for his legs, which are too thin, one of the handsomest men ever seen.'

Noble title, appearance and attributes guaranteed the Earl a pre-eminent role in the new structure of power, and, just as importantly, a place of influence for his wife. Marlborough had ditched his other great patron, the Duchess of Cleveland, more than a dozen years before, making his alliance with a singularly strong-willed woman called Sarah Jennings. In his epic four-volume biography of Marlborough, published in 1933, Winston Churchill described Sarah pithily as 'a spitfire and a termagant'. She shared John's craving for power and wealth, often going about it with greater directness and less scruple than he did.

In middle age, Marlborough had managed to convert his reputation into something more respectable than the lothario of his youth. But while he and his wife became important figures, a power couple in the salons, he had yet to make his name in command of an army on the battlefield. In that sense, even as he turned forty, Marlborough was still the 'carpet knight'.

Louis XIV, though, would soon give the general his opportunity. The French King did not intend to accept his reversal of fortunes in England. Rather, France and the Netherlands were now locked into a twenty-year sequence of wars. England, under her new monarch, was embroiled in it too, and Marlborough would soon see action.

When Marshal d'Humieres attacked the British outposts on the morning of 25 August 1689, he intended to give his enemy a sound beating. The crackle of musketry soon announced that French cavalry had fallen on the redcoats of Colonel Hodges' regiment. The British soldiers who stood in front of an allied army at Walcourt were its lookouts, and Marlborough had ordered them to buy him time by contesting the ground while he pushed his other regiments into line, ready to receive the French at defensive positions in front of the town itself.

The enemy cavaliers did not press their attack with vigour, instead riding up to Hodges' men, and discharging their cavalry pistols from a few dozen yards away, producing billowing smoke but few casualties. The 600 English infantry, although heavily outnumbered, fell back in an ordered way, delaying the enemy advance for two hours. As long as the foot soldiers remained steady, kept up their fire and formation, they would be all right. All the while, as the colonel's picket fell back through the trees, Marlborough prepared a couple of batteries of guns, ready to cut through the French ranks if they pushed on to Walcourt itself.

The little English army of 8,000 fighting on the border of the Spanish Netherlands (modern Belgium) and France in the summer of 1689 was Marlborough's first proper command. It had been subsumed within a larger force under the overall direction of the Prince of Waldeck, another of William's favoured generals of the Dutch service. The English general acted as second-in-command to Waldeck and was in control of the King's national contingent.

Prince Waldeck had been quite dubious about the English infantry when they had joined his army four months before. 'The English suffer from sickness, temperament, nonchallance, wretched clothing and the worst of shoes,' he had written, adding that they were ill-disciplined and their ranks contained too many men who were openly sympathetic to the ousted James II. Waldeck had been satisfied to see the English regiments licked into shape by Marlborough that summer, but evidently still felt unsure of how they would respond in their first real battle.

Walcourt was surrounded by an old defensive wall, which was lined by English and Dutch infantry. Marlborough's regiments of foot were on the defenders' left of the town, with his guns further out in the same direction, and his cavalry covering the extreme wing of the position. Having put these troops in order, and seeing that the French were bringing up their own artillery, Marlborough finally ordered Colonel Hodge's regiment to break off the fight and get themselves behind the defensive works.

Despite the strength of this position, and the caution inculcated by Louis XIV in many of his generals, Marshal d'Humieres decided to force Walcourt's defences by frontal assault. So, that afternoon, he dressed the ranks of eight battalions of infantry and threw them forward, drums beating and flags fluttering in the summer breeze. For several hours the French troops tried to break into the town, as allied infantry, occupying the walls, poured musket fire onto their heads. All the time, English batteries, cleverly sited by Marlborough so that they would be able to shoot down the lines of an attacker, bowled over the French with cannon shot. The thumping fire of these batteries billowed smoke in great clouds across the field, frequently wreathing everything in confusion. It was clear enough, though, by the late afternoon, that the attackers had taken heavy casualties: 500 dead and wounded Frenchmen lay littered about the town's defences.

At 6 p.m., Waldeck ordered a simultaneous attack from both flanks. Marlborough led the Life Guards and Blues forward in person, trotting down towards the enemy's disordered ranks. Realising that his foot were exhausted and in danger of being surrounded, Marshal d'Humieres ordered a general retreat, but even before this tricky manoeuvre could be accomplished, the English cavalry fell on some infantry on the French right, sabring them mercilessly. The failed attack showed every sign of developing into a rout. Only the arrival of the French cavalry, rushed into place as a rearguard, prevented complete disaster for d'Humieres. They held back the allied horse while the shattered remnants of several French infantry battalions streamed away from Walcourt. By the time the engagement was finished, early that evening, it had cost the Marshal six guns and 2,000 troops.

Waldeck reacted with the gratitude of a man whose battle had been crowned by unexpected glory. Making his official dispatch to the States General (the Dutch parliament) in the Hague, he told them, 'the English who were engaged in this action particularly behaved themselves very well'. To Marlborough himself, he wrote, 'I am happy that my troops behaved so well in the affair of Walcourt. It is to you that this advantage is principally owing.' The comments of this Dutch officer evidently went beyond the polite formalities observed after a successful engagement, and his letters to William III began to give the King notion of Marlborough's skill as a field commander. The campaign of 1689 in the Low Countries was, however, a sideshow, for the serious fight was to develop in Ireland, where a large French-backed army under James II was to do battle with William, leading to the Battle of the Boyne in 1690.

The stakes were enormous in this Irish campaign. For Louis XIV, backing James II, it was an attempt to restore the European balance of power that had existed before William's 'Glorious Revolution' in England. For the powerful Protestant families of England's landowning class, victory was essential to consolidate the new (post-1688) balance of power in London and prevent the return of James and any kind of absolutist project. For the Irish themselves, the Boyne was to prove a – or perhaps *the* – defining moment in the power relationship between indigenous Catholics and Protestant settlers.

It was only on 3 October 1690, at 1 a.m. in Cork harbour, that Marlborough was finally able to make his debut in Ireland, when he arrived at the head of an independent force. More than 6,000 troops came ashore in long boats, securing the landing place as the heavy guns needed to crack Cork's walls followed.

James had already been heavily defeated at the Boyne, and by the time of Marlborough's descent on the west coast, the former King had left Ireland. William's forces were essentially engaged in mopping-up operations. The fact that Marlborough would not have to take to the field against his erstwhile patron in either the Low Countries or Ireland may have weighed significantly with William III when he finally agreed to the expedition against remnants of the Catholic armies occupying the ports of Cork and Kinsale. It is apparent that England's Dutch King was not yet completely sure that Marlborough had escaped James's spell.

William need not have worried, though, for Marlborough went about the business of besieging Cork with great urgency. Three days after the initial landing, English siege guns opened up on the city walls, beginning the process by which great breaches would be made in them so that the place might be stormed.

Marlborough's celerity may have been connected to the knowledge that another of William's armies was close by and would soon join the operation, leading to questions about who should be in overall command. This happened within hours of the siege guns beginning their violent chorus when another of the King's armies, under the Duke of Wurttemberg, appeared, claiming the right to take over the operation. Marlborough managed to negotiate the diplomatically elegant but militarily nonsensical solution that he and Wurttemberg should take turns being in charge on successive days.

In the event, the battering proceeded for only two days before Marlborough, taking his turn in command, led a storming party under heavy fire to a position close to the main breach on 8 October. Seeing their likely fate, the garrison commander sent his drummers up to the walls to beat out the signal for a parley, the discussion of surrender terms. In doing so, he wished to spare his men and the town all of the outrages that might follow if the besiegers stormed Cork. So Marlborough concluded a siege with few losses. Within a week he had moved on to Kinsale and captured it as well.

During 1689–90, Marlborough had at last showed his practical skills: organising a complex operation like the landings and siege of Cork; reconciling tricky military/political issues when dealing with allied generals; and inspiring his troops to perform well in front of allies who still harboured doubts about the military value of the English Army. William III was well pleased, but many have detected in his compliment to Marlborough after these events a patronising tone that still showed him to be dubious about the English general's professionalism: 'no officer living, who has seen so little service as my Lord Marlborough, is so fit for great commands'.

The King and his old Dutch campaigners may still have been sceptical about the the quality of England's senior officers and troops, but it was in this period, throughout the 1690s, that a reformed English Army really acquired its national character. The quality of this reformed force was not yet appreciated in France, nor even in Westminster, and as the seventeenth century ended it would be true to say that the English Army was still regarded by most European military *savants* as a third-rate force of small size; ahead of the Danes, perhaps, but well behind Sweden, the United Provinces and, of course, France.

We might call this embryonic organisation 'the borrowers', a term that has been used to describe British armies in more recent times. In the 1690s, though, Marshal Schomberg and Marlborough were not scrounging kit but ideas for their regiments. The most important of these were tactical principles. English regiments were retrained, from a French system of firing their muskets in which several ranks of men were formed up, each line of troops stepping forward in turn to deliver their fire, to one devised by the Swedes and developed by the Dutch. Under this 'platoon fire' concept, a battalion of troops was formed thinner – say, three ranks deep, instead of five or six for the French – and the firearms were loaded by subdivisions of the unit along its line, platoons, rather than by ranks. If performed well, the platoon firing drill meant that a devastating initial salvo could be delivered because a far higher proportion of the Dutch or English battalion could actually fire (the French formation was too deep for men in the rear ranks to manage it). Furthermore, if the firefight went on despite this shattering initial volley, by dividing the fire along the frontage of the entire unit a relentless barrage of shot could be maintained, whereas the French battalion fell into a hiatus as each rank changed places to deliver its fire.

Platoon firing required considerable discipline and stoicism if it was to be maintained under a hot enemy fusillade. Happily, Marlborough and others had discovered that these were qualities their soldiers possessed in abundance. It was the Dutch who had really made this system work, but from the beginning of the eighteenth century it would be the English who reaped the reputation for delivering devastating fire. The thinner, more extended lines of troops produced by these drills would also become associated with the British Army in the age of the musket, even though the British did not invent it.

In its staff work and organisation, William III's army borrowed much from the French. The King's letters to Marlborough were written in that language, as were many of those between him and his Dutch allies. Since Louis XIV's armies were so much larger than anybody else's, many of the leading officers of this period, regardless of nationality, served in them, finding them the best places to learn the arts of manoeuvring, marching or feeding a force of anything more than a few regiments.

As for the tactics used by the cavalry, this was one area where the English made more of a contribution, for Cromwell had gained a reputation in Europe as an officer who used the sword rather than the pistol. Marlborough's charge at Walcourt may therefore be considered in the Cromwellian style. However, despite this distinctive English contribution to cavalry tactics, the Dutch continued to be influenced by Swedish ideas that had been around for almost a century and which were fed back into William's regiments of horse.

The English Army was therefore the bastard child of several military cultures that were regarded as more advanced at the time. It did manage to distinguish itself in one detail, though: with red coats. Many regiments had worn them since the English Civil War, and indeed Monck's Coldstreamers were described as such, but by no means all troops wore them after the Restoration. Even at the Boyne, William's army had contained several English regiments in blue coats. It had been necessary for them still to wear armbands for identification purposes. But in the later 1690s, red finally became a standard colour and a national signature. True, some foreign units of Guards also wore it, as well as various Swiss regiments, but it can truly be said that it was around the year 1700 that the 'redcoat' was finally born.

Around the same time the army of the musket era developed a form that would survive for 150 years. The pikemen of Cromwell's era disappeared from the ranks of the English infantry, each soldier having been given a bayonet with which to assault his foe on foot or to withstand enemy cavalry. At first these plugged into the barrel, turning the musket into a spear but making it impossible to load or fire at the same time. Later, they slid over the muzzle, making it possible to perform these tasks while keeping their bayonets fixed.

Another important advance concerned the arrival of field artillery. When Marlborough's campaigns began, artillery pieces were either too heavy to move in battle or purpose-built light 'battalion' (or 'galloper') guns that a handful of men could wheel forward to accompany the infantry. Marlborough would take bold steps in moving heavier guns during the battle, to support the footsloggers with much more punch. However, it took a while for the ordnance boards of Europe to produce new weapons that would combine the bigger shot of a 6-, 9- or 12-pounder with a lighter construction that allowed them to be moved forward as part of the offensive battle.

The carriage bearing Marlborough clattering through the streets of the Hague on 1 May 1704 was taking him to one of the most important meetings of his life. The general had reached his mid-fifties and his fine coat bore the gem-encrusted stars of his various honours and titles.

Beneath the tricorne hat and his fashionable wig though, the general sat in pain. He was on his way to meet the oligarchs who ruled the United Provinces, having reached a moment of such extreme frustration and personal angst that on this day his usually inscrutable exterior would crumble. In the ten days since he had arrived in the Dutch capital, his mood had progressively darkened. The journey across the Channel had been blighted by his wife's parting letter. It does not survive, but it is clear that in it she addressed her loving husband with all the coldness and anger that many others attributed to her. On 29 April, the despairing general had written to his Sarah, 'I have had more melancholy thoughts and spleen at what you said in that paper than I am able to express.'

This vexation was compounded with each new day in the Hague. For two campaigns he had commanded English troops alongside their Dutch allies against Louis XIV in the War of the Spanish Succession. This conflict had been triggered by the death of the Spanish King, without an heir, leaving a French prince with the strongest claim on the throne. It caused much of the rest of Europe, already deeply nervous about the burgeoning power of France, to combine against Louis XIV, lest his new dynastic tie with Spain create an all-powerful condominium. The problem for the 'Grand Alliance' was that being anti-French was about the only thing that held it together. William III had died in 1702 and been succeeded by Queen Anne (James II's daughter by his first wife) so the English were no longer taking their orders from a Dutchman.

During the opening campaigns of this war, the States General had allowed Marlborough to lead a combined allied army in the Low Countries, but only under the most stringent supervision of Dutch generals and political representatives. On several occasions, the innate caution of these gentlemen, derided by one of Marlborough's staff as 'herring-sellers', had frustrated the Earl's bold manoeuvres and prevented the destruction of the French armies. The senior Dutch commander, given the title Earl of Athlone by William III, often stood in the English general's way.

One Dutch politico, visiting field headquarters during the 1702 campaign, had reported back to his bosses, 'it is impossible to describe the scorn with which [Marlborough] judges Lord Athlone, his irresolution, his weakness of opening himself up to nobodies and following their advice in the teeth of decisions definitely taken'. At the end of the

1703 campaign, this Dutch 'Athlone' penned the following damning *mea culpa* about his struggles with Marlborough: 'the success of this campaign is solely due to this incomparable chief, since I confess that I, serving as second in command, opposed in all circumstances his opinions and proposals'.

The root of this Dutch intransigence lay in the desire of the political bosses – the deputies and pensionaries of the States General – to keep their army close to its homeland, to minimise expenditure and therefore to avoid risking costly battles. Marlborough recognised that in order to defeat Louis's vast army (which had swollen by this year to a quarter of a million men under arms), the polyglot alliance would have to be fleet of foot, strategically opportunistic and above all aggressive.

As the 1704 campaign was about to start, the whole anti-French axis was tottering, since French successes in Bavaria had opened the possibility of a march on Vienna, knocking the Austrians out of the coalition. Marlborough judged that only a bold strategic manoeuvre could save the situation. His consultations in the Hague, however, had convinced him that the Dutch politicians wanted no such thing. All of this dismal news, on top of Sarah's cruelty, had produced terrible headaches that further oppressed him.

When the coach arrived at the Grand Pensionary's house, Marlborough summoned up his inner reserves of strength, stepped down and girded himself for the argument ahead. In support, he had three Dutch generals who had served with him during the previous campaigns and who stood ready to back him in this confrontation with their countrymen. Those who met them were deputies representing each of the provinces in the Committee of Secret Affairs.

Marlborough began by telling them that it was his definite view that France intended to reinforce its success in Bavaria, threatening Austria and the whole Grand Alliance. They must agree to moving a combined Anglo-Dutch army from the Low Countries, where it was currently quartered, to the Moselle, about halfway to Bavaria, in order to take the pressure off the Austrians. The deputies for Guelders, Groningen, Zeeland and Utrecht were most dubious about this idea. They insisted that any army that went with Marlborough into Germany must be subject to instant recall. Furthermore, the States General decreed that no more than 15,000 troops might be marched this far away from the Netherlands.

As the argument continued with these sallow, stingy, narrow-minded men, Marlborough's patience and tact finally gave out. He told them plainly that they could agree to his terms – a march south to the Moselle by a *powerful* allied army – or he would take the English troops with him, leaving the Dutch behind alone. He brandished a warrant signed by Queen Anne, empowering him to do just that. They could play a cautious game, putting their own interests first, but he was simply not prepared to allow any of the troops paid for by the English Parliament to do the same: they were heading south, come what may. Leaving them to mull over the bitter revelation of the imminent collapse of Anglo-Dutch military cooperation, Marlborough bid them good day and left.

That evening, exhausted, the Earl sat down to write to his old friend Sidney Godolphin, who held the high office of Lord Treasurer back in London. Godolphin knew something that the general had concealed from the Dutch deputies, since he was sure they would never agree to his real design. He did not intend to march their army 100 miles south to the Moselle. His plan was to take it more than 250 miles, all the way to Bavaria itself. Marlborough admitted, 'I am very sensible that I take a great deal upon me. But should I act otherwise, [Austria] would be undone, and consequently the confederacy.'

The following day, 2 May 1704, Marlborough returned to hear the verdict of the Dutch deputies. They accepted his plan. This was welcome news indeed, although, of course, the deputies did not realise where Marlborough really intended to take the Dutch army they had just released to him. That evening, he wrote home again, this time to Sarah, announcing his success: 'I intend to go higher up into Germany, which I am forced as yet to keep here a secret, for these people would be apprehensive about letting their troops go so far.'

With the cloud over him starting to lift, Marlborough finally received another letter from his wife on 5 May, expressing contrition for her previous harshness. Marlborough's happiness was once more complete, and he wrote back to Sarah immediately, telling her, 'I do this minute love you better than I ever did before . . . 'till I had this letter I have been very indifferent of what should become of myself. I have pressed this business of carrying an army into Germany in order to leave a good name behind me, wishing for nothing else but good success. I shall now add, that of a long life, that I may be happy with you.'

The Anglo-Dutch army was in motion at last. At the end of the first week in May thousands of troops broke camp, assembling in the southern Netherlands, along with great trains of baggage and masses of cavalry. The host that set off to march hundreds of miles was only 21,000 strong when it left, but it had reached 40,000 by the time it arrived in Bavaria six weeks later. Of these, just 19,000 were men of the English Army (with even this figure including some units of foreign mercenaries). It is true to say, however, that this small corps, with its march south, embarked on one of the greatest gambles in English military history. Certainly, defeat would mean ignominy for its commander and would undermine the country's willingness to involve itself seriously in the land campaign against Louis XIV. The transfer of one of its armies inland for 250 miles was unique in modern English military history. But such was his experience in his many campaigns prior to 1704 that Marlborough had made skilful preparations. When the footsore men reached Heidelberg, a couple of weeks into their journey, a stockpile of thousands of new shoes awaited them. Some 1,700 supply wagons accompanied them on the way south, carrying provisions and tents. Marlborough was aided in his logistic preparations by England's wealth, which guaranteed plentiful credit wherever he went. The key thing about the trek to the Danube, though, is that it should be remembered for its effect on European opinion. In the first place, the march itself, taking an army southwards, passing three separate French corps, was a bold strategic manoeuvre. It paralysed each of these forces along France's eastern frontier, as Louis and his advisers tried to work out where Marlborough would change course and attack them. The dishonest story in the Hague about marching to the Moselle had, of course, been picked up by French spies, aiding this deception.

Such was the success of the redeployment that, even before battle was joined in upper Germany, it had created a sensation around Marlborough. It did not just force people to admit the general's skill. The march to the Danube also underlined that England had become a serious military player in Europe. Most of the country's campaigns before or indeed after 1704 were confined to nearby battlefields in northern France, Belgium and the Netherlands. Commanders from Henry V to the twentieth century fought over the same places, from Picardy to Mons or Lille. But Marlborough's march to Bavaria in support of Austria's Habsburg rulers showed that England would

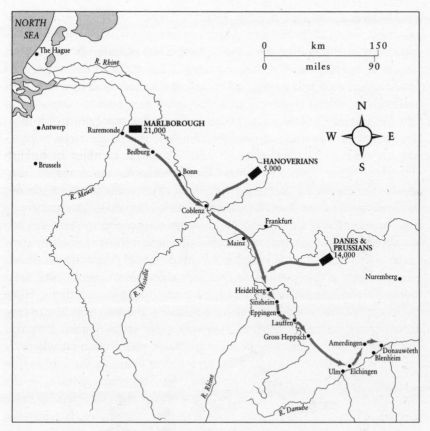

Marlborough's march to the Danube, 1704

intervene, if necessary, in the heart of Europe to preserve the continent's balance of power.

In late June and July 1704 there was in fact a certain sense of anticlimax in the Allied armies. Marlborough had stolen a march, quite literally, on the French, changing the balance of forces in Bavaria. But as weeks passed without a decisive engagement, the French managed to recover their position somewhat. On 2 July, Marlborough had hurled his troops forward in a tough fight over a citadel guarding a crossing of the Danube at Donauwörth. He needed this battle in order to allow him to manoeuvre on either side of that great river and to maintain pressure on the French. But victory was won at the expense of heavy casualties, something none of the rulers who had contributed to the allied armies liked, since new recruits were expensive to raise.

[47]

The Austrian field commander, Prince Eugene of Savoy, commented after the battle that his ally Marlborough seemed daunted by the scale of what he had undertaken in Germany, and that 'he would be ruined in England if he returned empty-handed'. But neither Eugene nor Marlborough had to wait much longer for a decisive trial with the French.

A little before 9 a.m. on 13 August 1704 Marshal Tallard, his ally the Elector of Bavaria and another general climbed the rickety steps into the steeple of Blenheim's church. These senior officers moved gingerly in their finery across the rafters to a point where they could look to the north. To their right was the Danube, securing the right of the Franco-Bavarian line. A tributary, the Nebel, met the great river near by, stretching up and across to their left, covering the front of almost all of Tallard's troops. Patches of fog still hung in the hollows about the Nebel, vapour rising from the swampy ground around the stream. To the generals' far right, covering their other flank, was higher, forested ground.

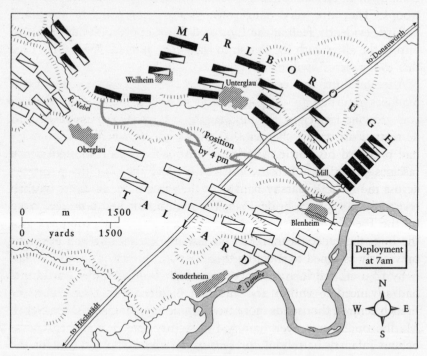

The battle of Blenheim, 1706

By the time Tallard went aloft to try to see what was going on, allied troops had already been under arms for almost seven hours. Great masses of Marlborough's army (now of 55,000 troops) had arrayed themselves along the line of the Nebel, in readiness to cross it. The French commander could see some of this, but mist and the smoke of cannon fire obscured much of the picture. Tallard had not been expecting an attack. It was due to his own prudence that his army was nevertheless strongly posted; both of its flanks were secured and two villages in his line (Blenheim and Oberglau) had been fortified, turning them into strongpoints. Although he could not see much of Marlborough's disposition, he was confident that the allied troops would disorder themselves crossing the squelching bog about the Nebel, opening them to a vigorous French counter-attack later in the morning.

The Elector of Bavaria, hearing the Marshal's plan to allow thousands of allied troops to advance before he launched his counter stroke, was uneasy, having seen Marlborough's men in action at Donauwörth. He cautioned his Commander-in-Chief: 'Beware of these troops. They are very dangerous: you cannot concede anything.' Tallard, evidently feeling the Elector did not appreciate the genius of hitting the allies with the marsh to their rear, replied, 'Well then, I see that today victory will be my own.'

After finishing this conference, Tallard and the other senior commanders returned to their posts, mindful that the din of artillery was growing louder by the minute. What he had not appreciated, as he trotted off on his charger, was the degree to which Marlborough had prepared his battle. The leading British troops had carried 700 fascines – bundles of brushwood – with which they laid five pathways across the Nebel's marshy banks. At the same time, artificers worked feverishly to repair a bridge over the stream that had been destroyed by the French. So, instead of losing their shoes and composure in the bog, the redcoats marched confidently across into the positions previously assigned to them by their chief.

By 10 a.m., a British column of several battalions under Lord Cutts had advanced to within 200 yards of Blenheim. To their right (the French centre), thousands more troops began moving across the Nebel. Marlborough's men were jammed into this sector, cavalry regiments behind infantry battalions, presenting a deep, packed target for the French guns. 'We were very excited by the extraordinary effects produced by our fire,' an officer accompanying the French artillery commander recorded, 'and from the very order in which the enemy were posted, every shot told.' Hundreds of men were being bowled over by the shot smacking into the English ranks. Arms, heads and equipment went spinning into the air as the balls continued to strike for hour after hour. In order to ease this horrible punishment, Marlborough ordered the infantry to lie down and the cavalry to dismount. Even so, the losses were piling up, as the general waited for Prince Eugene, in command of the allied right, to signal that he was ready to begin his coordinated advance.

Of course, Marlborough had not marched his men into this killing ground and halted them there for the pleasure of it. His plan relied on these troops pinning the French right and centre, so that none of these troops could be moved to resist Eugene when he finally pressed forward. Throughout, Marlborough maintained control of his army through trusted subordinates, bound to him by ties of kinship (his brother was the senior English infantry general) or several previous campaigns fought together. The allied army at Blenheim was steady under the terrible fire of that morning because its chief and his men had gained confidence in one another during two previous seasons' campaigning.

It was about 12.30 when the longed-for news came that Eugene had begun his attack. A general advance along the allied line began, with Cutts's men launching a furious assault into Blenheim. At the outskirts, redcoat pioneers tried desperately to hack away palisades of sharpened stakes with their axes, all the time watching comrades dropping under the hail of French shot.

Witnessing the ferocity of an attack by troops whose ardour he had assumed would be blunted by three hours of close-range artillery bombardment, the French commander in Blenheim, the Marquis de Clerambault, became unnerved. He knew that he had to retain control of the village, lest Marshal Tallard's whole disposition be threatened with ruin, so he gave a series of orders for reserves to move into the village.

Cutts's initial assault on Blenheim failed to break in, but he renewed the attack several times during the afternoon. Within a few hours, 27 French battalions, totalling about 12,000 troops, had been drawn into the fight for the village. Marlborough achieved this with 16 of his own battalions, denuding the French centre of any reserves. One of

Tallard's commanders, witnessing the maelstrom all around him, recorded, 'from one end of the armies to the other every one was at grips and fighting at once – a feature very rare in battles'. This was all part of Marlborough's design, that a general engagement should trigger the committal of French reserves while his own second echelon, in his centre, remained untouched.

As Marlborough began to develop his main thrust in the French centre, Tallard therefore had no alternative but to throw in his last picked troops – the mounted gendarmes. English cavalry moved through the ranks of their infantry and matched sabres with their enemy, bringing on a fierce cavalry mêlée. Eventually, the French horsemen lost heart and began streaming back. Watching this scene, the Elector of Bavaria was shocked, exclaiming, 'What! There is the *Gendarmerie* running away! Is it possible?'

At this moment, around 4.30 p.m., Marlborough began to drive on the deep formations of troops in his centre, pushing cavalry forward to exploit their initial success against the gendarmes. Several French battalions, seeing the hordes of redcoats in front, and knowing there were only green fields and baggage trains behind, ignoring the curses of their sergeants, began to leave the ranks and make a run for it. Tallard's centre collapsed.

With his regiments now advancing boldly, Marlborough's centre ploughed past Blenheim, where a sanguinary contest still raged, on and on until the Marquis de Clerambault and his 12,000 men, blinded by the ferocity of their own battle, realised that they had been surrounded, hemmed in against the Danube. A further welcome report then reached Marlborough – that Marshal Tallard himself had been captured by the allied cavalry. The French C-in-C was soon brought among some English generals, where victor treated vanquished with the customary courtesy, as the din of battle still sounded all around them. Realising the catastrophic position of the troops in Blenheim, Tallard sent word to Marlborough, pleading with him to allow a French withdrawal. This request brought the following reply from Marlborough: 'Inform Monsieur Tallard that in the position in which he now is, he has no command.'

With darkness beginning to fall on the battlefield, and the full awfulness of their predicament apparent to the Blenheim garrison, the Marquis de Clerambault hurled himself into the inky waters of the Danube. Some believed it suicide, others that he had been trying to swim to safety. Legend has it that hundreds, perhaps thousands, of French cavaliers lost their lives in the same river when their mounts stampeded away from the English cannon. English officers sent forward their representatives to demand a surrender.

That night, the enormity of what had happened was evident to everyone on the field of Blenheim. Louis XIV's army had suffered its first major defeat in forty years. Marlborough's chaplain, Dr Francis Hare, recorded the dejection among the captured French officers:

Some were blaming the conduct of their own generals, others walked with their arms folded, others were laid down, lamenting their hard fortune and complaining for want of refreshment, till at last, abandoning all reflections of this nature, their chief concern was for their King, abundance of these muttering and plainly saying 'Oh que dira le Roy!' [Oh, what will the King say!]

That same evening, Marlborough and Tallard met. The French commander told his captor, 'I congratulate you on defeating the best soldiers in the world.' The English general replied, 'Your Lordship, I presume, excepts those who had the honour to beat them.' Marlborough's pleasure in achieving the victory with an army he had honed during fifteen years of hard labour was evident.

Allied casualties were between 12,000 and 13,000; French, including the prisoners, something like 20,000. But the victory was far from over. In the days that followed, Marlborough pursued his enemy out of Bavaria, taking thousands more Frenchmen, as regiments broke apart in the chaos of retreat.

With the destruction of Tallard's army, shock waves spread through the palaces of Europe and the officer class, most particularly that of France. 'I should never have believed that the consequences of [Blenheim] would be so disastrous as they now show themselves to be,' one French general wrote to another, as their retreat continued a month after that great battle. 'The change is very perturbing and alarming for those unaccustomed to such great upheavals.'

Blenheim was without doubt a victory of a very rare kind, for it encompassed: a decisive result on the field; the ignominious capture of the enemy C-in-C; and a resolute pursuit after the action leading to the complete destruction of the defeated field army. But what were its actual consequences and are any visible even today?

Winston Churchill credited his illustrious ancestor with rescuing Europe from French domination, because Blenheim saved Austria's

Habsburg monarchy from defeat. This is not quite credible. It is highly unlikely that Louis XIV would have deposed the Habsburgs; even Napoleon, who had them at his mercy not once but three times, never did that. Rather the Sun King would have annexed some Habsburg lands and forced them out of the Grand Alliance. All in all, the business of eighteenth-century warfare was far too civilised for contests of annihilation.

Blenheim, however, for a fleeting moment, transcended the divisions of the allied command, and unblocked the stasis of what was largely positional or siege-based warfare. Its prime consequence – and, as always, this is the critical thing with Marlborough – was reputation. It showed a Europe accustomed to regarding England as an offshore trading outpost debilitated by centuries of internal conflict that this country could produce great captains, great troops and great effect on the Continental balance of power.

England was not used to sustained campaigning in Europe, and in order to do it used some techniques that were to become hallmarks of its military interventions. In the first place, it bought soldiers from petty principalities – like Hesse, Hanover, Luneberg and Zell. Other monies and diplomatic persuasion were used to put Marlborough in a commanding position over allied field armies, such as the Dutch (although they never formally accepted him as their commander). After Blenheim, Marlborough's reputation sufficed to ensure he retained the overall direction of the key allied armies. All of this meant that on 13 August 1704 only 14 of 66 infantry battalions in the victorious army were English regiments. Marlborough, like Wellington and Montgomery after him, was thus placed at the head of a large and successful force consisting largely of foreigners. This strategic sleight of hand, in which Britain would direct large armies in war but not pay for their upkeep in times of peace, began under Marlborough.

If the victory did not transform the overall course of the War of the Spanish Succession, it certainly changed the fortunes of the Churchill family for ever. Queen Anne gave Marlborough an estate at Woodstock and financed the construction of a vast palace there to be named after his great success. He was also upgraded from an earl to a duke. The general achieved a centralisation of power unmatched in modern Britain, being Commander-in-Chief for the Army and Master of the Ordnance (a separate department of state responsible for the artillery and engineers). At times, he even ran foreign policy as a whole.

All the while, as he managed England's alliances and armies overseas, his wife Sarah held a commanding position in Queen Anne's court. One consequence of their power was an accumulation of sinecures, pensions and plums that made them enormously wealthy – certainly billionaires in modern terms. What powers they did not grasp were in large part soaked up by Marlborough's old friend Sidney Godolphin.

Important as the Marlboroughs and Godolphin were, however, they did not direct affairs in a vacuum. The Glorious Revolution had given Parliament control over military spending in what was eventually formalised as an annual vote. A part of Marlborough's year, during the winter months when there was no campaigning, was thus spent shmoozing various landowners in Westminster in order to guarantee their continued support for the war.

It was during this period that the two political tendencies – Whig and Tory – came to dominate Parliamentary debate. These were not parties in the modern sense, with whips to ensure voting loyalty or a machine to propagate a particular political message across many constituencies. Rather they reflected the broad division of society that remained even a generation after the Civil War. 'I can't see much difference between them,' Sarah Churchill wrote, when trying to define the opposing political camps. 'The Whiggs had this Advantage that their pretended Principle was for Liberty and the Good of their Country. The Tories was for [Divine Right] by which I suppose they imagined they should have all the power and places of advantage divided among themselves.' When the Duchess's husband was off campaigning, the management of Parliament in support of the war policy was done largely by the Lord Treasurer, Godolphin, and it could be said that those around him formed a separate party in the House.

The marshalling of Parliamentary majorities might therefore be added to the extraordinary list of duties undertaken by the general with such skill. However, Marlborough's case eventually showed the dangers of amassing so much power and wealth under the emerging democratic system. He became too closely associated with the faction that favoured perpetuating the wars against France, so when the popularity of this particular ministry waned in the country (for all sorts of reasons, many unconnected with the war), Marlborough himself became an obvious target.

The atmosphere on London's streets on the evening of 17 November 1711 was combustible. A shift in power had created the potential for strife. It had been more than a year since the treacherous tides of faction and party politics had forced the resignation of Sidney Godolphin, Marlborough's staunchest ally. The general told his old friend, 'The folly and ingratitude of the Queen make me sick and weary of everything,' but he had continued to serve on through a sense of obligation to the Grand Alliance and his sovereign. And the fact that he was still serving seven years after Blenheim tells its own story: he had won great victories at Ramillies, Oudenaarde and Malplaquet, garnishing his reputation further, but although he could achieve great tactical results, he had been unable to deliver victory at the strategic level and thereby bring an end to war.

The British electorate (for that's what it had become as a result of the 1707 Act of Union between England and Scotland) was tiring of paying for the war: 75 per cent of public spending, which totalled about £8.5 million a year at this time, was going on the army and navy. General elections in 1710 had brought a huge House of Commons majority for the faction seeking peace. By November 1711, the Queen was preparing herself for a further shift in power. She herself was actively seeking an end to the war, negotiating with the French but keeping this secret from her C-in-C. The final eclipse of the 'war party' was expected imminently – with the sacking of the Duke and Duchess of Marlborough. Those who viewed developments as a sell-out to popery and French hegemony prepared on the 17th to march after dark through the streets of London with blazing torches. The protesters had chosen the anniversary of the Protestant Gloriana's, Elizabeth I's, accession for their demonstration. They carried effigies of the Pope, the Stuart Pretender and of the Parliamentary leaders who had ousted the war party. These they intended to burn in Westminster while singing Protestant hymns and denouncing those who now mesmerised the Queen. The atmosphere of bitter partisanship had been whipped up by news-sheets supporting the two factions; a riot was expected at any moment.

The Ministry – the new group that surrounded Anne – was extremely nervous. That evening, it ordered the Guards and the militia onto the streets of London. The arrival of Marlborough from Holland was expected hourly (he landed that afternoon, the 17th, in Greenwich). Was he about to play the role of General Monck? A proclamation was issued: that evening's procession was banned and the marchers ordered to disperse.

Sensing the ministry's panic, Marlborough judged it prudent not to enter the City. Instead, he spent the night at Greenwich Hospital, where, the following day, Queen Anne appeared in person. Her interview with Marlborough was conducted with icy formality, and she came away satisfied that he was not planning to seize power, reporting to the leader of the Parliamentary peace faction that '[Marlborough] made a great many of his usual professions of duty and affection to me'.

Satisfied that she could proceed, the Queen brought matters to a head in Parliament. A few days later she opened a new session and entered a House of Lords packed with peers expecting high drama. They knew they would not be disappointed when they heard the opening words of the Queen's Speech: 'I am glad that I can now tell you that notwithstanding the arts of those who delight in war, both place and time are appointed for opening the Treaty of a general peace.' The reference to 'those who delight in war' was an obvious dig at Marlborough and the war party. After her speech, Anne sat in the chamber, where she heard the debate that followed. Lord Ormonde rammed home her message: 'We might have enjoyed that blessing [peace] soon after the battle of Ramillies, if it had not been put off by some persons whose interest it was to prolong the war.' Ormonde, also a general, thereby made himself an active partisan of the ministry.

'I was ever desirous of a safe, honourable and lasting peace,' said Marlborough in response. He was now in his sixty-second year, and added that he wanted to retire from the rigours of campaigning and enjoy his prodigious wealth: 'I have not the least motive to desire the continuance of the war, having been so generously rewarded and had honours and riches heaped upon me.' This explanation of his personal circumstances added force to the Duke's protestations that it was not yet time to make peace with France, and his oratory was sufficiently persuasive that the opposition rejected the draft peace treaty, despite it having received the sovereign's endorsement. This produced a Parliamentary crisis, which was resolved during the following days as the ministry achieved victory in the Commons, then created twelve new peers in order to force the treaty through the Lords. Queen Anne had got her way and Marlborough was finished.

At the end of 1711 the tide of resentment, distrust and enmity that had been rising about Marlborough for the previous couple of years finally engulfed him. His critics were numerous and their charges ran the gamut of moral crime: in 1709 a novelistic account of the vice of Charles II's court had appeared under the title *The New Atlantis*, making public all the rumours about Marlborough and Barbara Villiers (it quickly reached six editions); writers attacked his military reputation, in particular the very costly action of Malplaquet (fought in September 1709); and in 1711 he was accused of creaming off £343,000 from army contracts and subsidies to allies.

Was Marlborough the immoral crook his opponents made him out to be? In short: he was not guilty of the corruption charges, but evidently he had slept his way to prominence. But it is in the field of his military name that the effect of all this mud-slinging was most interesting. One article about Marlborough's costliest battle, from the *New Examiner*, a Whig news-sheet in which Daniel Defoe, among others, excoriated the war party, is typical: 'Amidst this torture thousands expired that might have been preserved if the General had not sunk the Money designed for Medicines and Surgeons. No Age, no Country, how barbarous so ever, hath ever given us such an instance of Cruelty and Avarice.' The claim that ordinary soldiers suffered lingering deaths because their Commander-in-Chief had plundered the medical budget seems shockingly modern.

One lesson to be drawn from this is that almost as soon as its army came into being, Britain's generals found themselves savaged in Parliament and press alike. There is no doubt that this noisy, irreverent style of democracy protected the country very well against tyranny, militarism and corruption. The problem was that so much of this comment was utterly coloured, in 1712 as in so many times since, by party prejudice. Marlborough's achievements were thus being argued about before he left office and have been ever since by adherents of the different factions. That someone of such diplomatic and military skill received this treatment is all the evidence we need to establish the case that the reputations – good or bad – of so many British generals have been defined from the outset by wider political arguments. Since such views are usually opinions of the cheapest and least reliable kind, it is always better to rely on the assessments of those who slogged across the same battlefields as their leader. This includes both comrades in arms and enemies, who, by their experience, gain authority in calculating the real worth of these men.

On New Year's Day 1712, Marlborough replied to Queen Anne's letter of the previous day, which had sacked him from all of his posts.

'I am very sensible of the honour your majesty does me in dismissing me from your service by a letter of your own hand,' he wrote, utterly in earnest, 'though I find by it that my enemies have been able to prevail with your majesty to do it in a manner that is most injurious to me.' He went on to warn her of the dangers of making a separate peace with France. Louis XIV's verdict on these events in London was simple and pungent: 'the affair of displacing the Duke of Marlborough will do all for us we desire.'

The reactions of Marlborough's old soldiers, by contrast, were terrible. When it became public that Britain had made its separate peace with France, redcoat regiments had to be withdrawn from the allied lines in the Low Countries, where Dutch and other contingents continued to fight the French. Many of the British soldiers had campaigned for years under the impression that final victory would bring them into the rich *paysage* of northern France, where loot and pillage would reward them for their sufferings. With Marlborough's dismissal, and peace declared with France, this chimera finally vanished.

In the village of Molain, close to the Belgian border, 600 redcoats crossed into France, determined to sack the place. The locals put up a fight, so the British troops locked them inside a church. 'But as they fired again from thence,' Captain Parker records, 'in their fury they set fire to the church, burnt it to the ground, and upwards of four hundred persons perished in the flames.' This incident, without doubt, constituted one of the worst crimes in the history of the British Army. A few months later, there was more trouble, when several regiments withdrawn from the line mutinied in Ghent. A general slump in morale and discipline pervaded the regiments once they realised they were to be paid off. Corporal Matthew Bishop wrote that 'it proceeded as much from the ill conduct of the Officers, as from the Imprudence of the Men'.

Both of the old soldiers quoted above had previously regarded Marlborough's mere presence as a harbinger of victory. Captain Parker wrote of one bitterly contested action in 1711, 'It is quite impossible for me to express the joy which the sight of this man gave me at this very critical moment . . . for he never led us on to any one action that we did not succeed in.' Corporal Bishop gave this tribute: 'I have often said to our Men, by way of Encouragement, *that the name of him is better than ten thousand men* [original emphasis].'

In December 1712, Marlborough boarded the packet boat from Dover to Ostend to begin almost two years of voluntary exile. His friends said that he had grown tired of the calumnies of his political enemies, and sought to calm the political fever by removing himself from the scene. Others claimed the flight was necessary to escape an imminent trial on embezzlement charges. Marlborough waited until after Queen Anne's death to return to England, where he himself passed away on 16 June 1722, aged seventy-three.

Winston Churchill, in his monumental biography, sought to end any argument about Marlborough's historical importance: 'He was not only the foremost of English soldiers, but in the first rank of statesmen of our history . . . he was a virtuous and benevolent being, eminently serviceable to his age and country.' Only the last claim is debatable, for the thousands of Marlborough letters that survive give very little substance to the modern idea that he was motivated by the idea of 'service to his country'. Instead, he usually invoked the interest of his religion, sovereign or family.

It is important, then, to see Marlborough in the context of the early eighteenth century, when a sort of transfer market of eminent generals existed between various European armies, and modern nationalism had not been invented. If we strip away such anachronistic concepts, then many of the attributes for which historians like Churchill felt they had to apologise become far more understandable: his constant pursuit of wealth; his correspondence with his old patron James II, as well as with others in France when England was at war with Louis XIV; and his tireless seeking of the title 'Captain General for Life', which was an attempt to guarantee his powers that alienated almost everyone.

A desire to paint a saintly picture of Marlborough also fails to convey a ruthless streak that was central to his success as a diplomat when persuading the Dutch oligarchs to send their army into Germany in 1704 and on many other occasions. One Dutch officer wrote this acute description of Marlborough's darker side: 'The Duke is a profound dissembler, all the more dangerous that his manner and his words give the impression of frankness itself. His ambition knows no bounds, and an avarice that I can only call sordid, guides his entire conduct.' Once we embrace the fact that Marlborough was a relentlessly driven *arriviste*, ready to do almost anything to succeed, then we can see the salient features of his legacy a little more clearly.

To Britons, he was an inspiration. His life can be seen as the most complete fulfilment of the male fantasy: he led immense armies to victory in battle; was on intimate terms with half the sovereigns in Europe; became one of the world's richest men; and received youthful training in the arts of the boudoir from a veritable sexual Olympian. His trajectory, starting as an impoverished youth in Devon and closing with a fall from power and final redemption, may be seen as an archetype for the picaresque novels that became so popular in the mid-eighteenth century. Marlborough showed the way to thousands of young men for hundreds of years: the army was a social escalator, the 'profession of arms' the way to make good a life otherwise stifled by considerations of class or money. At the same time, he showed his country that British soldiers, when properly led, could defeat the French. This gave politicians in the eighteenth and nineteenth centuries the confidence to intervene in the affairs of Continental Europe.

We must, though, also consider his effect on Britain's likely allies and foes. In his lifetime, Marlborough played a critical role in convincing the Dutch that their role as the pre-eminent Protestant power was finished. But it was the French who became fixated with him. Early biographies in French stress his status as a European statesman worthy of study, but there was a darker subtext, one of deep resentment for the man who had prevented France achieving its destiny under Louis XIV. This only became overt during the latter part of the eighteenth century, after the revolution, when France defined itself in nationalistic terms. 'Marlbrouck' became a popular lullaby and a marching song during those years. It is described by some as a kind of exorcism for the defeat at Blenheim, a repetitive refrain, testifying to how deeply the British bogeyman had penetrated the French psyche. A biography of Marlborough published in Paris in 1808, at the height of the Napoleonic Wars, gives further insight into French resentment. Blenheim, it says, 'was celebrated in the expectation of British domination. The three kingdoms [England, Scotland and Ireland] could allow themselves a feeling of pride when they learned of a success that would carry the glory of their arms to the ends of the earth.'

So the Marlburian legacy was largely about Britain's place in the world. David Chandler, the most eminent modern biographer, has said Marlborough laid the foundations for 'two centuries of British greatness'.

Marlborough's spell certainly lasted long after his death: he frightened the French and proved that the British Army had to be taken seriously. It is also true that the War of the Spanish Succession, in which he fought for so long, achieved something of substance. The treaties that ended it forced the Spanish monarchy to renounce any claim on the French throne; they made the Bourbons recognise the succession of the Hanoverian George I to the English throne, ending support for the Stuart Pretender; and, crucially, they gave substantial trading rights to Britain in the Americas.

Britain defined itself increasingly as a trading empire, and it was to be on the other side of the Atlantic that another general, not yet alive when Marlborough died, was to make his mark on history.

William Howe

1729–1814

Search the vast volumes of history through,
and I much question whether a case similar to ours is to be found.
GEORGE WASHINGTON ON HIMSELF AND HOWE

THE MEN WHO SET OFF in rowing boats at about 9 p.m. on 12 September 1759 knew that the odds were stacked against them. In fact, it was almost a suicide mission. Their orders were to scale the cliffs upriver from Quebec in the teeth of French opposition. The first couple of boats contained a party of two dozen picked troops under Colonel William Howe.

For weeks, their commander, Major General James Wolfe, had tried to find a way to seize the centre of enemy power in Canada. His opponent, the Marquis de Montcalm, had made every preparation to protect the city, which sat on a rocky promontory overlooking the Saint Lawrence. Quebec was surrounded on three sides by precipitous heights and could be approached only by road from the south-west, across ground called the Plains of Abraham. Montcalm had protected this obvious avenue of approach and kept a strong defence on the bay just downstream of the city which most authorities regarded as the obvious landing place.

On this night, however, the British longboats were rowed a couple of miles upstream of the city. They were to land at L'Anse de Foulon, a small cove of shingle at the foot of cliffs. A steep shepherd's path rose almost 200 feet up from this place to the Plains of Abraham above. A local had told Wolfe about this precipitous route, and he knew it to be guarded by French sentries. About one mile beyond L'Anse de Foulon, atop the cliffs in the gardens of a mansion built for the Bishop of Samos, the French had installed a battery of four cannon which could hit the landing force as it came up the Saint Lawrence.

In the early hours of 13 September, the first boats were being paddled gingerly, right under the guns of the Samos battery. The

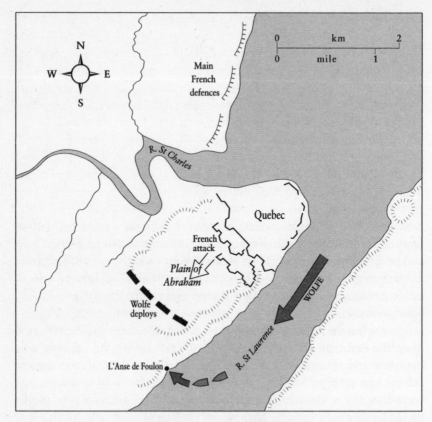

The attack on Quebec, 1759

coxswains strained their eyes in the darkness to see their landing place. Once they were confident they had passed it, they steered out of the centre of the channel and towards the land, letting the tidal flow of the Saint Lawrence carry them to the beach with as little splashing of oars as possible. Every sound must have been nerve jangling.

When the first boat was close to the shingle the moment they had dreaded materialised. A French sentry shouted, '*Qui vive!*' and cocked his weapon. Captain Donald MacDonald, a Scottish soldier of fortune, was ready for this moment. Without pausing a beat, having himself served in the French Army some years before, he shouted back in the sentry's native tongue: 'Be quiet, you fool, I am bringing reinforcements!' The first light infantry were soon among the small sentry party, overwhelming them in an instant.

As Howe's men jumped onto the shingle, he knew that a heavy burden of responsibility rested on his shoulders. If the French were alarmed, then a handful of determined men standing at the top of the cliffs would be able to keep Wolfe's entire army at bay, for the route up was only two men wide. It was not for nothing that the first British party had been called by the same name used in storms of fortresses: the Forlorn Hope. Wolfe's orders at Quebec had told them that, 'a vigorous blow struck by the army at this juncture may determine the fate of Canada', but did the general himself know how scaling the cliffs would possibly deliver him the capital of the French colony? His subordinate brigadiers had been given almost no specifics. Some believed that Wolfe, close to nervous collapse, riddled with consumption and possessed of a strong presentiment that this battle would be his last, wanted to do nothing more than die in one last glorious gesture.

The first few redcoats began their climb, with Captain MacDonald at their head. Howe was a few feet behind. The colonel, thirty years old, was a big man, at least six feet tall, with broad shoulders and dark good looks. He was an officer of few words – or few unnecessary ones, at least – but enough to earn him the compliment from Wolfe of running 'the best trained battalion in all America'. Howe had the physical presence and reputation for courage that made it easy for his men to follow him up the cliffs. He was one of those men who in those times were thought to have been bred to lead; just seventeen months earlier his older brother George had fallen at the head of a similar party, engaged in a desperate enterprise at Fort Ticonderoga.

At the top of Quebec's cliffs, there was a further confrontation with a French picket. This time it was bloodier, the leading redcoats giving the French cold steel in preference to anything noisier. Some of the defenders managed to scramble away into the night, shouting the alarm. With the top of the path secure, it wasn't long before Wolfe himself appeared, just as the first light of dawn brightened the horizon. Congratulating Howe on his coup, he ordered him to take several dozen men off to the left, along the clifftop, to silence the Samos battery. Now that the French were alarmed, there wasn't a moment to lose. Dozens of British longboats were queuing up on the Saint Lawrence to disgorge their men.

When the light infantry reached the French gun position, their enemy had already turned one of the cannon about, so it faced inland, and soon it was spewing out grapeshot, scores of metal balls that gave it the scatter-gun power to mow down infantry at close quarters. Howe's men took cover and began returning fire, trying to pick off the gunners.

The light infantry battalion was itself an innovation for the British Army, formed from bright, active men picked from Wolfe's different regiments, to be used when the tactics of standing in line and delivering volleys of musketry had to be set aside in favour of something which looked more like the infantry fighting of today, with small groups of men using cover, fire and manoeuvre.

Soon enough, the French defenders began to break, realising that they had little hope of holding out indefinitely against enemy infantry who pelted them with musket balls from just a few yards away as they tried to work their guns. The battery was silenced.

Arriving at the clifftop a couple of hours later, a captain in one of Wolfe's regular infantry battalions noted: 'As soon as we gained the summit, all was quiet, and not a shot heard, owing to the excellent conduct of the light infantry under Colonel Howe; it was by this time clear day-light.' Thousands of men were now collecting on the Plains of Abraham. Having succeeded with this stunning *coup de main*, Wolfe's original orders had been fulfilled. The commanders of this little army looked to him, as they still had no notion of what to do next.

By choosing to approach by the cliff path, Wolfe had denied himself the use of any heavy guns. Two field pieces were being hauled up the face by block and tackle, but that was the limit of his artillery. These cannon could give some supporting fire to the infantry but were quite inadequate against Quebec's walls. On these defences, there were numerous heavy cannon, and they would speak against the British as soon as they approached. Wolfe must have realised that counter-attack from the garrison was also a possibility, for he ordered his troops to form a line across the Plains of Abraham, from one rocky edge to another.

Seeing his enemy by daylight in this extraordinary position, Montcalm's consternation can be easily imagined. He knew certain things that Wolfe did not: Quebec had almost no supplies, as Montcalm had sent them upstream or inland, to keep them away from the British. But Wolfe's army was now sitting between the city and the French stores. The French general estimated that his own force of about 4,500 troops was equal to the British one, but knew that the longer he waited, the stronger his enemy would become. He quickly resolved to leave his defences and attack the British in the open field, hoping that other French troops, several miles to the south-west, would hear his attack on Wolfe and join in to assail the British from the rear.

The French regiments filed out of the city gates: Sarre, Languedoc, Béarn and Guienne, fine regular battalions in their off-white coats, as well as several hundred Canadian militia. While the battalions deployed into battle line, the French artillery began playing upon Wolfe's troops. The British, though, had formed their men very loose: just two ranks deep and with three feet between each pair or file of soldiers. This formation, which stretched the battalion even longer and thinner than those in Marlborough's day, was the innovation of General Sir Jeffrey Amherst, C-in-C of America, who knew it would suit this New World theatre of operations: allowing troops to pass through woods without breaking formation; maximising the battalion's fire against its enemy; and presenting a less dense target. Such flimsy formations would have been very risky in the face of cavalry, but there were hardly any troops of that species in America.

Amherst, though, was not on the Plains of Abraham on 13 September 1759 to see the vindication of his system, but over a hundred miles away, fighting his way up the Hudson valley towards Canada. It was to be Wolfe who would witness the revelation of what happened when Montcalm's battalions met this thin line of redcoats.

With drums beating, the French infantry moved to about 150 yards from the British. The battalions halted, presented their muskets and fired a volley. A few men, including Wolfe himself, were hit. But Montcalm's men had let fly much too early. The smooth-bore musket was such an inaccurate weapon that anything more than 100 yards was hopeless. British commanders preferred to hold their fire until far closer than that, so Wolfe's men waited. The French regiments delivered a little more desultory musketry and resumed their course, trudging towards the redcoat line. The British had double shotted their muskets, an unusual procedure. It would deliver twice the volley, even if it made the Brown Bess kick like a mule and reduced the effective range even further. But, as the Languedoc and Béarn tramped towards them, those impassive redcoats knew of the terrible surprise that they had in store.

When the French were no more than forty yards away, the order to fire was given at last. Hundreds were felled by the shower of shot. Captain Knox of the 43rd recalled:

Well might the French officers say, that they never opposed such a shock as they received from the centre of our line, or that they believed every ball took place, and such regularity and discipline they had not experienced before; our troops in general, and particularly the central corps, having levelled and fired – *comme un coup de cannon*–'ereupon they gave way, and fled with precipitation, so that, by the time the cloud of smoke was vanished, our men were again loaded, and, profiting by the advantage we had over them, pursued them almost to the gates of the town.

Running after the fleeing French, Wolfe's battalions began to break up. The 78th, Fraser's Highlanders, went into a kind of bloodlust, scything down their running foes with claymores. Other regiments, too, showed no mercy to the disintegrating enemy. In this pell-mell both Wolfe and Montcalm received their mortal wounds. When the surviving French officers relived their shocking defeat later inside the city, nobody had sufficient seniority or confidence to take command. They capitulated.

Wolfe's victory, and martyr's fate, defined Quebec as an epic, stirring a nation that was just starting to savour its identity. It became the subject of excited conversation beside many a hearth, and a potent mythology arose around it. The final conquest of Canada had to wait another year, when General Amherst proved his strategic dispositions as wise as his tactical ones.

Colonel Howe benefited enormously from his role in the attack. Wolfe, an old friend, left him £1,000 in his will – and since Howe was not short of friends or interest either, his career lifted off. He became a brigadier, commanding picked troops in three subsequent campaigns.

Howe had also attained a degree of celebrity from Quebec, becoming what fashionable Londoners considered a fine representative of a military dynasty. Another of his brothers, Richard, was destined to become an admiral. Their mother came from a distinguished Hanoverian military family, and, rumour had it, their father was an illegitimate son of George I. By the mid-eighteenth century, the army had emerged as an important source of patronage for the sons of Britain's landed classes. Those at the top of the tree saw it as a distinguished way for them to do something of value, serving the Crown, and, by recommending the sons of lesser families for commissions, as a means to command loyalty in the shires. This system of power defined William Howe to a considerable extent and, it would transpire, shaped both his qualities and his limitations.

The fight at Quebec formed part of the Seven Years War (1755–62), a general conflagration between the European powers. Britain ended it with vastly expanded imperial possessions – in the Caribbean and India as well as America. Some see 1759 as an *annus mirabilis*, in which Britain transformed itself into a world power. Why then concentrate on William Howe, a heroic but nevertheless bit-part player in this triumph, rather than Jeffrey Amherst, a gifted general and architect of events? The answer is that much of what Amherst and others gained around the world was to be threatened a little over twenty years later, and no single general would bear a greater responsibility for trying to defend what had been achieved in 1759 than William Howe.

The prospect greeting the general as he leapt out of a longboat on 17 June 1775 must have seemed infinitely less daunting than the cliffs of Quebec. The sailors had put Howe ashore on the southern tip of the Charlestown peninsula which jutted into Boston harbour. Immediately to his front, serried ranks of redcoats; the picked troops of the British Army in North America were once more under his hand. A battalion of light infantry, one of grenadiers and a couple of other battalions of the line totalled more than 1,000 men. Several other British battalions were present, but their brigadiers were inferior in rank to Howe, who would end up trying to co-ordinate the whole attack, albeit to a plan of someone else's devising. On a little knoll just to his right, gunners were positioning several 12-pounders, heavy guns. Beyond the British soldiers, about half a mile directly to his front, he could see the works thrown up by the enemy on Breed's Hill. This did not rise much over 100 feet, but the rebels had spent the day and a half since they occupied the peninsula constructing a redoubt on its crown. They had done well, given the short time, piling up earth and stone behind timber stays to give themselves good cover, even from cannon fire.

Howe's orders from his Commander-in-Chief were to take the hill and crush the rebels. The Commander-in-Chief had rejected the option of simply using boats to land behind Breed's Hill and cut off the Americans' retreat; he wanted to meet them in open battle. Major General Henry Clinton, another senior officer present that day, summed up the mood at British HQ: 'The general idea was the redoubt was only a redan [i.e. a smaller fortification], that the hill was open and easy of ascent and in short that it would be easily carried.' More than that, they wanted to teach a lesson to the ingrates whom they had protected

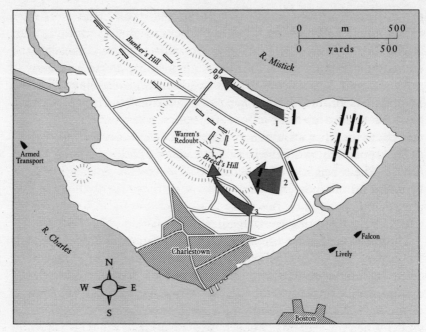

The battle of Bunker Hill, 1775

against the French in the Seven Years War but who now called George III a tyrant. The army had already been nettled by the so-called minutemen, who shot redcoats from behind trees and walls and then ran away when charged. This was a chance to stick them with the bayonet.

In looking up at his objective, Howe knew it was best not to underestimate those manning the redoubt. Their commander, Major General Israel Putnam, was someone Howe knew personally: he had campaigned in Amherst's force on the Hudson in 1759 and with Howe himself in the Caribbean two years later. So Howe understood that the ragtag force peering over its trenches on Breed's Hill was led by a man who knew his business. Howe looked, as every good commander did when faced by such a strongpoint, for a way to go around one of its flanks. Glancing up to the left of the hill, he could see a jumble of gardens and houses, the settlement of Charlestown itself. This was not good ground for manoeuvring troops, and in any case the Royal Navy had begun firing carcass (or incendiary shells) into the timber buildings in order to deny them to the rebels. So Howe's choice seemed to be a head on attack or one to the right. There, on lower ground, and perhaps 200 yards behind the rebel redoubt, was a fence where the enemy militia had piled up brush and stones to create another barrier. It wouldn't be easily taken, but it was certainly less of an obstacle than the redoubt itself. Howe led his light infantry forward to attack it.

As the redcoats moved closer to the fence, the music of the 12-pounders behind them ringing in their ears, they gradually saw more of a third element of the American defence: connecting the redoubt to the fence – and running at right angles to both – was a series of firing positions, probably behind piled logs, that the engineers called *flèches*. The rebels had been all too aware that the redoubt might be bypassed on this side of Breed's Hill and had put the *flèches* there to prevent this possibility. But these positions would also have another effect, as the light infantry were about to discover.

The rebels held their fire admirably. (This was the battle in which the order 'Don't fire until you see the whites of their eyes' was given. Although witnesses agree that such words were used, there is disagreement over whether they came from the lips of General Putnam or Colonel William Prescott, the rebel commander on Breed's Hill itself.) When the lead finally began to fly, with the leading British a few dozen yards from the fence, its effects were horrible, just as they had been against the French at Quebec. Worse, the militia in the *flèches* were able to enfilade the redcoats, shooting along the British line from one end to another as it approached the fence. Howe's light infantry simply couldn't take it: after suffering heavy casualties they broke and ran. Howe's own survival was remarkably fortunate, two of his staff being shot down beside him.

Next, the British attacked the redoubt head on. Colonel Prescott watched them come on. He later recalled: 'After a considerable Time finding our Amunition was almost spent I commanded a sessation till the Enemy advanced within 30 yards when we gave them such a hot fire, that they were obliged to retire nearly 150 yards before they could Rally and come again to the Attack.' The second British assault was therefore also beaten back.

The third attack came on the left, channelling troops in column past the smouldering ruins of Charlestown and into the redoubt. Lieutenant Waller of the 1st Battalion of Marines took part in the battle's climax: 'I cannot pretend to describe the Horror of the Scene within the Redoubt when we enter'd it, 'twas streaming with Blood & strew'd with dead & dying Men the Soldiers stabbing some and dashing out the Brains of others was a sight too dreadful for me to dwell any longer on.'

The British finally had their height – and the one behind it, Bunker Hill – but at a terrible cost. They had suffered 1,150 casualties, around 40 per cent of the troops involved. Howe called it 'this unhappy day'; others commented caustically that the British Army could not afford another such 'victory'. The rebels, thrilled by their success, redoubled their efforts to drive out their enemy.

The enemy that William Howe faced in 1775 was of a very different stamp to the one he had overcome in 1759. Defeating this new opponent would require political subtlety, strategic vision and great personal drive. The daring young colonel of 1759 had accumulated a good deal more experience of war since then, but age was catching up with him, too. However, he had not lost his soldier's eye for ground, nor his grasp of the tactics needed to fight in the American backwoods and indeed, these qualifications caused the Ministry to choose him for this service.

Many British veterans of the Seven Years War in America were ambivalent about serving against the rebels. This was a quarrel between Englishmen; it mirrored that between the Whigs and the Tories at home. Many of the troublemakers were brothers in arms from Quebec and other campaigns. These issues would have been very familiar to a Monck or a Marlborough; it was yet another instalment of the struggle to balance liberty with loyalty to Crown. If a further civil war had been avoided in Britain over such questions, it was in part due to the fact that the most prickly advocates of personal freedom – religious nonconformists – had been 'encouraged' after the Restoration to emigrate to the colonies, where, in 1775, long-smouldering tensions had finally caused a conflagration.

The American loyalists (Tories) and rebels (Whigs) had their own vocal partisans in Westminster. As war broke out, a generation of army officers – more than sixty of them were Members of Parliament at this time – belatedly discovered that sitting in the Commons was not the straightforward proposition they had imagined it to be. They had been drawn into the Palace of Westminster by a desire to make contacts, lobby for high command and represent their families' landed connections. In 1775, however, those who were in the pocket of Britain's great Whig families were under intense pressure to refuse a command in America.

Ministers only approached Howe because General Amherst had already declined the Commander-in-Chief's job. As for Howe himself he too was an MP tied to the Whigs, and had foolishly promised electors in his borough that he would not serve against the American rebels. His ambition for advancement, though, proved greater than his loyalty to a principle, so he went. He knew what he had done, of course, and feelings of guilt about breaking his word were probably eating away at him before he had even reached Boston.

Deep divisions did not just define personal responses to the rebellion. It was impossible to make war without the support of Parliament, which had to vote the necessary money. The American war was unpopular from the outset with most Whigs and many Tories. Despite these sentiments, though, sufficient MPs agreed to vote an expansion of the army from around 35,000 in the early 1770s to a peak, by mid-1778, of 120,000 (40,000 of whom were in America, comprising redcoat regulars, mercenary contingents hired from Germany and 'provincial' regiments of loyal Americans).

In any case, by October 1775 Howe had become Commander-in-Chief of British troops in America. Hemmed in by rebel brigades all around Boston, he resolved to do nothing until he received major reinforcements. Realistically, this would not be before the spring of 1776, so, from his first moment in command, he was open to accusations of inactivity, indecision and funk. These came not only from ambitious subordinates like Major General Clinton, who wanted to displace him, but from his enemy on the other side of the city.

Lieutenant General George Washington regarded the difficulties of the rebel army as dwarfing any that Howe faced. During that first winter, surrounding Boston, most of the militia troops under Washington's command simply packed up and went home when their short enlistments expired. No amount of pleading or exhortation by the general could stop them. By January 1776, he had only 5,800 men present for the siege – fewer than Howe commanded inside Boston. The Continental Congress, which now directed the rebellion, could offer Washington almost no money, little ammunition and no uniforms for his troops as the bitter winter progressed.

'Search the vast volumes of history through, and I much question whether a case similar to ours is to be found,' wrote Washington, marvelling at Howe's inactivity, 'to wit, to maintain a post against the flower of the British troops for six months altogether, without powder, and at the end of them to have one army disbanded and another to raise within the same distance of a reinforced enemy.' The American general knew how close the rebellion had come to collapse that winter, but it was to be just the first of many occasions when Howe's failure to move decisively would puzzle his enemy.

It would be wrong to pretend that Howe had a straightforward task in subduing the Thirteen Colonies; far from it. There were enormous logistical difficulties in sustaining an army in America, with items even as basic as bread being shipped by sea and often taking months to arrive. The enemy had a vast hinterland in which to take refuge, while it was very hard for the British to operate away from the coast and major rivers because of the great difficulties in moving supplies and artillery inland. The King's troops also found themselves up against a strong and resilient ideology: the revolutionary propagandists could dismiss any reverse as the result of merciless brutality by the monarch's 'bloody lobsters', whereas any coup by the 'liberty boys' was celebrated as evidence that revolutionary zeal could triumph over professional soldiery.

There is, though, plenty of evidence to support the idea that a well-led British Army, striking hard against the revolution in its first two years, could have altered the course of history. We cannot be sure that the rebellion would have been defeated altogether – although quite a few reputable historians have made such claims. Rather, the shape or course of the revolt could have been altered, switching it back from a military struggle to one primarily of politics and economics.

Those directing the revolt thought its outcome very dubious during the first two campaigns. Washington, as we have seen in relation to the siege of Boston, often considered the whole business close to collapse. The Continental Congress itself did not have the temerity to declare independence until 4 July 1776. Before then, it clung to the line that it was open to reconciliation with George III. Finally, there was the question of popular support, which was not solidly behind the revolution: probably about one-third were committed to it, another third ardently loyal to the Crown and the remainder unsure.

Ministers in London and many in the Congress considered that if the British could divide the American states in two by taking New York and going north, via the Hudson valley, to Canada, this would be a heavy, possibly mortal, blow. This, then, was the strategic 'big idea' of 1775–7. Lord North, the British Prime Minister, supported the war but freely confessed his ignorance of military matters. The official in London most closely involved with war policy was therefore Lord Germain, the American Secretary. In appointing Howe as C-in-C, Germain made it clear that ministers back home could not manage the war in detail. Letters took six weeks at best to cross the Atlantic, so Howe would have to decide many matters independently. A Marlborough, or indeed an Amherst, would have regarded this as giving him considerable latitude to fight an aggressive campaign in the way of his own choosing. Howe, though, was a very different creature.

The sight greeting Washington's lookouts on 22 August 1776 was as alarming as it could be. The boats in Gravesend Bay, on the south side of Long Island, quickly grew too numerous to count. On board the flagship *Eagle*, General Howe's brother, Admiral Lord Richard Howe, began directing the most ambitious and largest amphibious landing ever attempted by the Royal Navy. In all, 350 sailing ships would disembark 25,000 soldiers. Wave upon wave of longboats departed the transports, carrying redcoats packed knee to knee, naval officers signalling by coloured flags as the different divisions formed up. By noon, they had got 15,000 men and 40 guns ashore. While the *avant garde* of the army picked its way through the fields and orchards of Long Island, on the beach beating drums rallied regiments to their colours one by one.

In all, Howe would have nearly 25,000 troops fit for the Battle of New York. His opponents could muster only 19,000. What was more, the geography of the port meant the American troops were scattered about, covering many landing places and the routes by which the redcoats might approach the city on the tip of Manhattan Island. There was every chance of Washington's troops being defeated in detail. The rebels understood the dangers but felt they could not simply concede the city: New York was far too important as a trading centre, and was the key to the Hudson valley. Washington had resolved to defend it on Long Island; not on its beaches, which were taken without contest, but on Gowanus Heights, a ridge of high ground which dominated Brooklyn and the north shore of the island, facing Manhattan. To this end, he had deployed 10,000 troops in prepared positions there.

The complex logistical preparations for the British landings, vicissitudes of the trade winds and wait for reinforcements mean that Howe

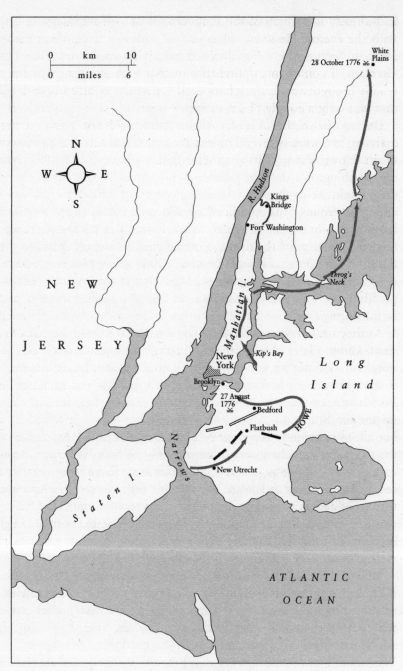

The New York Campaign, 1776

[78]

had already lost much of the summer of 1776 before he got to grips with the enemy. He knew what he had to do – break Washington's army in open battle – but doubted his ability to do it, telling Lord Germain, 'I confess my apprehensions that such an event will not be readily brought about.' As it happened, a perfect opportunity to do just that was only a couple of days away.

During the night of 26/7 August, thousands of British troops marched in darkness several miles to the east, and then a couple to the north. Howe was preparing to seize Jamaica Pass, the key to bypassing Washington's defensive lines on Gowanus Heights and turning their flank. At daybreak, a smaller division of British troops would appear in front of the American lines, opening a lively artillery bombardment, pinning the defenders while Howe and Clinton, accompanied by the elite of the army, went around to cut off Washington's line of withdrawal. This plan – and Howe must receive credit for adopting it, even if it was suggested by Clinton – carried the exciting possibility of avoiding another Bunker Hill and dealing a heavy blow to the enemy.

As they neared the end of their night march, reaching Jamaica Pass itself, Clinton later noted bitterly that their Commander-in-Chief 'did not seem to know we were there'. However, nor did the Americans, as it soon became clear that the flank march had succeeded. When the British attack went in behind many of the Americans manning the lines on the heights, mass panic broke out. Washington had posted thirty battalions to defend these positions, but the Americans streamed down the slope towards the lower ridge overlooking Brooklyn, much closer to the water, where a further line of redoubts had been prepared to secure the crossing point to Manhattan. British grenadiers pursued them, but at this point Howe ordered them to stop and come back. 'I was not without hopes', wrote Clinton, 'that His Excellency . . . might be tempted to march directly down the road to the ferry, by which if we succeeded, everything on the island must have been ours.'

Howe, though, had lost his nerve when he saw the fresh line of defences on Brooklyn Heights. 'I would not risk the loss that might be sustained by the assault,' he said later. Clinton and many other officers felt that there would have been little risk in forcing it while the Americans were in such confusion. The Battle of Long Island cost Washington more than 1,000 casualties and prisoners, including three generals. Ministers in London were delighted when they heard about the victory (British casualties were fewer than 400), and knighted Howe for his feat, but officers in the army itself were flabbergasted that a far greater opportunity had been lost.

During 28 and 29 August, Washington made good use of the breather given him by Howe. A fleet of small boats evacuated his army from Brooklyn to Manhattan. He thereby saved himself and more than 8,000 troops to fight another day.

Although Washington had eluded capture, there was still everything to play for. Much of the enemy army was now on Manhattan, which was connected to the mainland by just two bridges, close together, on the island's northern tip. A skilful use of British naval and military power might trap them. Yet, from 29 August to 15 September, the British Army did not move. There were some valid reasons (the difficulty of navigating the waters around Manhattan due to tidal flows, batteries and sandbanks) and some less impressive ones (bringing up the creature comforts for the soldiers in camp), but Washington gained another breather.

When Howe finally moved on 15 September, he landed not on the mainland, where Clinton had suggested that he could cut off most of Washington's army on Manhattan, but on that island itself, just above New York at Kip's Bay. Operations, once again, developed at a leisurely pace and the Americans gained another lease of life. Howe waited nearly another month, until 12 October, before launching an amphibious operation, which marked the third failure to trap the main body of Washington's army, this time on the northern part of Manhattan.

The fourth missed chance took place one week later, when Washington stood and faced Howe at White Plains, north of New York. The Americans had prepared elaborate fortifications, but Howe cleverly spotted that a hill to the west of them would allow the whole position to be turned. This was done by a division of Hessian (i.e. German mercenary) and British troops, but Howe did not then exploit his success to hit the main part of the enemy position.

Reviewing Howe's actions from the Battle of Long Island onwards, one modern historian comments: 'to have destroyed or captured this substantial force personally led by Washington would have dealt the Americans an irreparable blow. Had such a stroke been followed by a prompt landing on the northern part of Manhattan, the war would no doubt have been over.' It may be over-egging it to say that Howe could have won the war, but, as subsequent events would show, the months following the landings of 22 August on Long Island certainly represented the best – and perhaps the only – chance that Britain had to break the back of the American rebellion by force. Howe was too dilatory and unimaginative to seize it.

There is no unfair use of hindsight here. In the late summer of 1776 friend and foe alike were baffled by Howe's failure. The American Major General Israel Putnam wrote after Long Island, 'General Howe is either our friend or no general . . . had he instantly followed up his victory, the consequence to the cause of liberty must have been dreadful.' Some have tried to build historical castles on suggestions like Putnam's – often made rhetorically – that Howe's insipid campaign resulted from his own desire for reconciliation between Whig and Tory brothers in America. Although his personal beliefs may have given rise to some conflict, this theory holds little water, for it is apparent that Howe saw the humiliation of Washington's army in battle as an aid rather than an obstacle to that goal. Rather, the failures of his campaign can be seen as the product of excessive caution, and a complete inability to grasp the strategic opportunities that opened with the victory of Long Island.

Washington was criticised by many of his countrymen for mistakes of his own during this period, with one arguing that he showed 'little genius and not much natural aptitude for war'. The American C-in-C only really paid for one of his misjudgements, though: leaving behind a large garrison in Manhattan at Fort Washington appropriately enough. When Howe captured it in November 1776, he secured a consolation prize of 2,800 American prisoners and 146 cannon.

Many advantages accrued from holding New York: it cut the rebels from their principal port; proved a rallying point for loyalist Americans (of whom there were plenty in the city and its environs); could form a base for operations up the Hudson; and gave the Royal Navy a vital anchorage. There were considerable costs, too, though. Holding the city soaked up thousands of troops from an army that could ill afford such detachments. The outposts needed to secure waterways leading to the city attracted constant enemy raids.

In garrisoning these outposts, British commanders saw the limitations of their troops. The army found recruitment very tough indeed during the late 1770s. In England and Ireland these were times of relative prosperity, so few sturdy farm lads were interested in taking the King's shilling. Recruiting parties were often reduced to throwing criminals and invalids into uniform. (It was better in Scotland, where the Highland gentry, keen to atone for the 1745 rebellion, curried favour by raising new regiments.) Manpower problems sapped the usual quality of the British infantry and had many implications for Howe. He feared costly battles. There were constant courts martial of deserters, thieves and rapists, leading to much friction with locals and presenting a gift to rebel propagandists. Finally, the problems filling the ranks led the government to hire thousands of foreign troops, mainly from Hesse-Kassel.

The extended dispositions occupied by Howe in New Jersey in late 1776 provided Washington with a chance to end the year's campaign with a daring coup. The rebel general's attack on a Hessian brigade encamped near Trenton on 26 December represented a last desperate throw of the dice, a chance to win back the faith of his people at the end of a miserable year. Washington's regulars, his Continentals, advanced in driving snow, catching the Germans unawares. In the confusion that followed, 918 Hessians were taken prisoner. Fewer escaped, shamefaced, to tell the tale of their surprise by the enemy.

Howe cannot be blamed for the poor precautions taken by the German commander. He can be held responsible for taking up such long lines in New Jersey in the first place, though, and for ordering his troops into winter quarters (i.e. to stop fighting) without realising that his enemy could not be relied upon to play by such gentlemanly European conventions. 'Due to this affair at Trenton,' wrote Hessian Captain Johann Ewald in his journal, 'such a fright came over the army that if Washington had used this opportunity we would have flown to our ships and let him have all of America. Since we had thus far underestimated our enemy, from this unhappy day onward we saw everything through a magnifying glass.' Ewald even went as far as to claim that the psychological reversal of fortunes caused by the capture of substantial numbers of George III's troops 'surely caused the utter loss of the thirteen splendid provinces of the Crown of England'.

Of course, those around the King or the Prime Minister did not see things in quite such bleak or portentous terms. But at the end of 1776 the conflict had in fact reached a tipping point. The British had taken their best shot – for reasons we will see, they were never again able to concentrate similar numbers of troops against the main enemy army. The American citizenry had seen what the Ministry could do, and

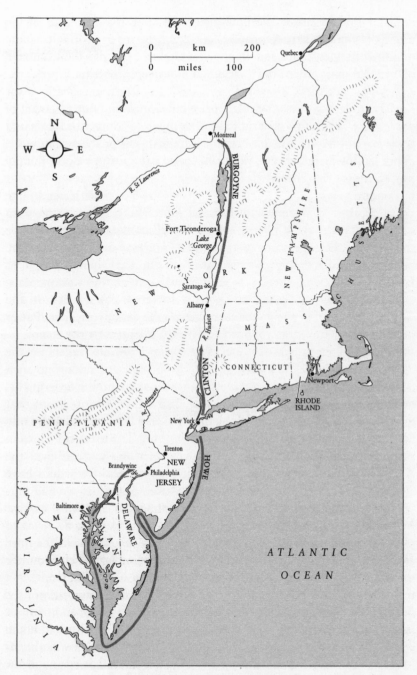

British Strategic Plan for 1776

it had failed to break Washington's army. Far from it, even in the midst of winter his troops had rebounded from a series of defeats and humbled the professional soldiers. It would not be until the campaign of 1777, though, that affairs assumed a decisive character.

Fort Ticonderoga was a strategic prize enveloped in a thick blanket of wilderness. When this post on Lake Champlain – sitting astride the key route to and from Canada – changed hands, people wanted to know about it. But Ticonderoga's position, so far from Europe's corridors of power, meant that knowledge took an agonisingly long time to arrive in London.

On 7 July 1777, Lieutenant General John Burgoyne became master of the fortress, having placed guns on a hill commanding the works, thus forcing the Americans to abandon it. The ease of Burgoyne's coup finally dented Ticonderoga's reputation as the 'Gibraltar of America'. It marked a hopeful opening to Burgoyne's campaign to advance deep into the colony of New York with a force of 10,000 British and German troops. For the victorious general, the capture of Ticonderoga bolstered his ambition to push down to Albany, driving rebels to one side and the other, opening most of the 300-mile route between Montreal and New York City.

The events on the banks of Lake Champlain convinced Burgoyne that he could advance away from the water, and his line of supply, into the interior of New York, while all the time thousands of rebel militia gathered from across New England to oppose him. The third British campaign had thus begun in earnest, and was entering a dangerous phase. A serious attempt was being made to implement London's strategy of cleaving apart the rebellious Thirteen States.

Howe simply couldn't decide what part to play in this. Between November 1776 and April 1777 he had sent three completely different plans of campaign to London. Finally, he had resolved to take the rebel capital, Philadelphia, while sending a smaller force up the Hudson valley from New York in order to lend Burgoyne a hand. But this meant that there would be several British armies in being simultaneously: Burgoyne's coming south from Canada; a garrison of 3,000 in Rhode Island, where Howe had sent them to secure a naval anchorage late in 1776; the garrison of several thousand needed to hold New York; the force Howe intended to send up the Hudson from that city; and the main expeditionary force, heading for Philadelphia, under Howe's own hand. This was such an obvious violation of the military principle of concentrating force – exposing each of these five armies to defeat in detail by the Americans – that many officers simply could not believe their C-in-C was about to do it.

On 5 July, Henry Clinton returned to New York from London. There he had discussed strategy for the year ahead with Lord Germain, other ministers and the King himself. He was fully aware of Burgoyne's expedition and believed that it made obvious strategic sense for the main army, under Howe, to move towards Burgoyne, crushing any Americans who offered battle in between. At the first of several difficult meetings in headquarters, Clinton tried to pursuade Howe to abandon any idea of going to Philadelphia, or at least to postpone such a move. Instead, Clinton, in his own words, 'with all deference suggested the many great and superior advantages . . . from a cooperation of his whole force with General Burgoyne on the River Hudson'.

That same week, Washington, collating snippets of intelligence from spies about the embarkation of various regiments on transport vessels in New York, reasoned, like Clinton, 'there is the strongest reason to conclude that General Howe will push up the river immediately to cooperate with the army from Canada'. Both the rebel C-in-C and the British second-in-command understood that a two-pronged movement of this kind would bring together 25,000 redcoats and most likely crush the American Army.

Clinton thought he had convinced Howe, but on 18 July the latter informed him that he would shortly set sail with the substantial fleet (now carrying 15,000 troops) that had gathered in New York harbour and that Clinton should assume command of the New York garrison. Three days later, a messenger arrived and told them that Burgoyne had taken Ticonderoga. Both Clinton and Howe therefore knew the thrust from the north had begun in earnest.

Howe's fleet finally sailed on 23 July, on a course for the south. 'I could not to the very last bring myself to believe it,' Clinton wrote later. 'I was persuaded he intended to deceive us all.' Finally, the scales fell from Clinton's eyes: going south was no clever ruse prior to turning about and sailing the fleet up the Hudson; Howe was taking his army in the opposite direction to Burgoyne.

The distance overland from New York to Philadelphia is roughly 100 miles. A man on a good horse could cover it in a few days. But Howe's sea journey, complicated by contrary winds and his own indecision, took a whole month. Cooped up on board their smelly transports, short of rations and information, many of Howe's officers worried about wider events. One Hessian colonel wrote home to Germany:

If I dared to tell you what I think of our present situation. I should say outright that our expedition into these parts of the south is not to my liking. For if, instead of coming here, we had set sail for New England and joined Burgoyne's army, we should without fail have forced that province and its capitol to their duty before the end of the month ... we should have had one of the most glorious campaigns, and perhaps peace before the end of it.

This letter was addressed to the Prince of Prussia, and it is important to note how closely the American events were being watched in every European capital. When news of Ticonderoga's fall finally reached Paris, it stymied the vocal war party there. The French, anxious to gain revenge for the loss of Canada eighteen years earlier, had been supplying the Americans with muskets, cannon and powder. Many 'volunteers', professional officers, had also crossed the Atlantic in order to help Washington's army. Even so, there was a reluctance to wage all-out war against Britain. They had no intention of doing it – with all the risks that war entailed – if Howe's forces were about to crush the rebellion. Everything depended upon the 1777 campaign. In Spain and the Netherlands, too, those who felt the time was ripe to relieve George III of some of his colonial possessions awaited news.

It was early September before Clinton, in New York, received further word of Burgoyne's progress. Messages had to be smuggled through the forests, and the information, in a letter dated 6 August, was already a month old. Burgoyne had begun the most difficult part of his advance – the inland stage – south of Lake Champlain, through the forested back country, towards the Hudson. This passage of just a few dozen miles had not been easy for Amherst in 1759 and was proving even less so for Burgoyne. Rebel militias were swarming about the British column and had started a process of blocking and flooding the route south. Even so, Burgoyne's message did not yet show signs of alarm. Clinton replied to him on 11 September that he hoped by the 21st to set off from New York up the Hudson with the long-promised diversionary push towards Albany.

On the same day Clinton wrote, Howe succeeded in his aim of getting Washington to stand a general action in defence of Philadelphia. The

American C-in-C had taken up a defensive position along Brandywine Creek, a river about twenty-five miles south-west of Philadelphia. Howe later justified his strategy for 1777 by saying that striking at the rebel capital would force Washington to fight, and that 'the defeat of the rebel regular army is the surest road to peace'.

Washington's dispositions that morning exploited the defensive value of the creek, with cannon and infantry ready to attack any British who crossed one of several fords. The weakness of his position was that, even though he extended his divisions over several miles, there were fords on his flanks that he could not cover. The rolling ground, with thick copses between the the fields, made it very difficult for either C-in-C to have a good idea what was going on outside his immediate environ.

Howe exploited this by using 8,000 troops (just over half his men) to march in the early hours around Washington's right flank. Meanwhile, the remainder of the army moved up to the front of the American positions, beginning a heavy bombardment to convince them that the main British assault would come in the obvious place. Howe's manoeuvre – very similar to that of Long Island – succeeded admirably, and when his larger division attacked Washington's flank that afternoon, the American army was thrown into confusion. Late in the day, Washington struggled to stabilise his right, while disengaging his army in order to save it. In the end, he succeeded, as once again Howe's failure to pursue his fleeing enemy denied him the full benefits of victory.

The British C-in-C lacked vigour and aggression. One civilian who saw him on the morning of the battle recorded: 'He was a large, portly man, of coarse features. He appeared to have lost his teeth, as his mouth had fallen in.' This was what had become of the dashing light infantry officer who had stormed the Plains of Abraham. Howe at Brandywine was forty-eight years old. He was worn out and struggled to find a way to win. Some of those officers who were most frustrated by these failings spread rumours that his lethargy resulted from too much drinking and too much time in bed with his mistress.

When the British Army entered Philadelphia just over a fortnight later, Howe gained his objective for the 1777 campaign. It had taken him two months to get there from New York. Although his move on Philadelphia had produced the hoped-for general action, it had not been decisive. Congress had evacuated the city, and Washington was to make his camp near by. But what of Clinton and Burgoyne's progress?

Between the Battle of Brandywine and Howe's capture of Philadelphia, Burgoyne had been fought to a standstill on the banks of the Hudson near Saratoga. He was still well short of Albany, with the New England militias closing in on all sides. Burgoyne should have tried to fight his way out of the trap and back towards Lake Champlain, but instead gambled that he might still be able to get through to Albany, and sent a message to New York to that effect. Clinton had finally set out from New York on 3 October and managed, with the small force he could scrape together without exposing New York to capture, to take some key rebel fortresses guarding the Hudson River. By 16 October, his force was just forty-five miles south of Albany, but on that very day Burgoyne, beaten, surrounded and outnumbered, surrendered. Nearly 6,000 troops under his command went into captivity.

J.F.C. Fuller, an officer whom we shall meet again later, estimated the Saratoga capitulation as one of the decisive battles of world history. That might seem odd given the small numbers of troops involved and the remote scene of the action, but news of Burgoyne's surrender triggered the French declaration of war, which was followed by similar announcements by Spain and the Netherlands. In Britain, the humiliating defeat destroyed the Parliamentary majority in favour of a vigorous prosecution of the war. After 1777, it became impossible to fund large-scale reinforcements to America. Such was the sympathy among Whigs for the American struggle for liberty and their *schadenfreude* at George III's problems that fashionable ladies attended London parties dressed as Washington's soldiers.

Between 1778 and 1783, Britain thus faced a worldwide onslaught against its interests from the combined forces of America, France, Spain and the Netherlands. Despite shipping thousands of troops from America to the Caribbean (further weakening the Crown's war against the rebels), Britain lost most of its rich island possessions there to the French, as well as Florida and Minorca to the Spanish. Across the globe, the French were able to assemble powerful fleets and landing forces, which also succeeded in throwing Britain out of Senegal and southern India. It has been described as the loss of the first British Empire.

Eventually, caught out by the shuttling of French squadrons between the Caribbean and the eastern seaboard, this wider conflict also cost

George III the Thirteen Colonies of America: a surrounded British force in Virginia was cut off from rescue by the Royal Navy and surrendered at Yorktown in 1781.

On the night of 18 May 1778, Philadelphia witnessed one of the strangest spectacles in its history. Processions of British officers dressed as knights, and young women as medieval damsels, celebrated a party. In a city gripped by war, there were tables groaning with food, fireworks and mock tournaments, and poetry was declaimed in the night air. This themed event, called the Mischianza, was staged as a ceremonial send-off for William Howe following his resignation. In accounts published at the time, it was described as an affectionate gesture from the officers who had served under him.

Leaving aside the fact that the British Army has always jumped at the chance to throw a party, it is interesting and only fair to point out that Howe was popular among many of his people right until the end of his command. He was correct and affable with the regimental officers he met on the march, and the soldiers appreciated his concern for their comfort.

Even as he sailed home, though, there was plenty of whispering that Howe was a failure. On his return he demanded a board of inquiry which he hoped would vindicate him. There were hearings for many months, but in the end there was no official report or 'closure' to the whole affair. The more people looked into his command, the more self-serving and feeble his excuses sounded: it was too cold to do anything in the winters of 1775/6 and 1776/7; it was too hot to do anything for much of the summer of 1777; the troops were too tired to finish off Washington after the Battle of Long Island; and so on.

Among those who had worked with the general most closely, there was plenty of criticism. One staff officer wrote probably the fairest assessment during the 1777 campaign: 'Brave he certainly is and would make a very good executive officer under another's command, but he is not by any means equal to C-in-C.' The leader of a loyalist regiment heavily engaged at Brandywine was tougher: 'His manners were sullen and ungracious, with a dislike to business, and a propensity to pleasure. His staff officers were in general below mediocrity.' The most bitter but acute appraisal was made by Henry Clinton. In life the two men managed to maintain cordial relations, even though Clinton made clear that he held Howe responsible for missing many opportunities in 1776 and for a misguided strategy in 1777. However, a note later discovered in Clinton's papers read: 'Had [Howe] gone to the Devil before he was sent to America, it had been the saving of infamy to himself and indelible dishonour to his country.'

History, for some reason, treated Howe very leniently for at least 150 years. Much of what was written blamed others, notably Lord Germain. The American Secretary was regarded with particular distaste by many of the generals, because he had previously served in the army and been disgraced for cowardice at the Battle of Minden in 1759. But Piers Mackesy, in *The War for America 1775–1783* (1964) managed a pretty credible vindication of Germain, based on the most comprehensive examination by any scholar of the state papers relating to the strategic direction of this war. Mackesy showed Germain to have been an effective mobiliser of the vast armies and fleets required for global war, whereas Howe and Clinton (succeeding as C-in-C) were described as 'members of a stable political community who had arrived and could not be shaken from their perch . . . their fertility of invention was spent in devising reasons for inaction'.

Too many of Britain's generals had turned into the same kind of highly paid 'play it safe' bureaucrats that officered the French Army of Marlborough's time. The divisions over America among Britain's landowning oligarchs had undermined the ability of their institutions – Parliament and the army – to win the war.

Howe was without doubt the person responsible for failing to crush Washington in 1776, when Britain had its best chance. The American victory at Trenton convinced the rebels that it was worth fighting on. Howe then failed to formulate a coherent strategy for the 1777 campaign, sending instead confusing alternatives over a period of months to London. Germain was guilty of errors, no doubt, but had the Commander-in-Chief in America been capable of thinking and acting like someone worthy of this lofty title, Germain's influence on the strategy pursued during that pivotal year would have been kept to a minimum.

As for the disaster of Saratoga, clearly Burgoyne should have doubled back when it became clear how serious his predicament was. He alone got himself into the mess. Equally, though, Howe was the only person who could have got him out of it. Instead, the C-in-C ignored advice and took himself off to Philadelphia, having his number two with insufficient force to make a meaningful push on Albany. Clinton's critique is hard to dispute: had Howe instead moved with his main army up the Hudson in July 1777, there would have been time enough to open the way to Albany before moving on to Philadelphia later. Such a plan would probably have saved Burgoyne, kept British forces more concentrated, and still forced Washington to give battle either in upstate New York or, eventually, near Philadelphia.

It is arguable whether Britain ever could have won a complete military victory in America. But I do think that Howe's mismanagement of the command allowed the rebellion to grow and emboldened Britain's enemies to wage a global war that was disastrous to its interests. Had the general 'gone to the Devil' before he ever took up the American command, there can be little doubt that the map of the world could look quite different today. Howe was not a completely useless general, since he had a very sound tactical touch (for example, at Long Island and Brandywine). He was, however, somebody without the faintest idea of strategy.

Victory could have been defined in 1776–7 as breaking Washington's Continental Army, capturing or killing him and scattering resistance into guerrilla bands. Had this been done, France would not have intervened. The historical alternatives then become mind-boggling: the global French campaigns of 1778–83 bankrupted the country and led directly to the Revolution. A successful British general in America during 1775–7 might thus have forestalled those tumultuous events and thereby the consequent rise of Napoleon.

There can be no doubt, though, that the emergence of a militant revolutionary state in France, something Howe witnessed in his old age, was to present Britain with a threat of an altogether higher order. In the 1770s and 1780s it had been a fight for empire. In the 1790s and 1800s it was to be a struggle for national survival.

Prince Frederick, Duke of York

1763–1827

Big, burly, loud, jolly, cursing, courageous.
WILLIAM MAKEPEACE THACKERAY

The YORK-MINUET.

THERE REACHED A POINT in many of the young Prince's games where the number of servants available for duty on the lawn proved insufficient for the lesson at hand. Frederick, fifteen years of age during the summer of 1778, as General Howe relinquished the American command, heartily enjoyed his practical military education. 'The grounds of Kew House were transformed into the terrain of the Seven Years War,' one contemporary observed. In his enthusiasm, the Prince herded gardeners, maids and footmen into lines of troops. His war games were overseen by his military tutors and followed much study of European campaigns, in particular those of the Prussian King after whom George III had named his son. The Prince of Wales, just one year older than Frederick, occasionally played along in these sessions, but even at this early stage of their lives, it was his younger brother who relished the part of soldier.

George had encouraged his sons to cultivate a *ferme ornée* at Kew, a place where, following the aristocratic fashion of the day, they could till the soil and learn the simple pleasures of farming and good oeconomy. Alas, the growing shoots were often trampled underfoot by phalanxes of servants, as Frederick, captivated by his namesake's Seven Years War victories, strove to re-enact battles like Rossbach and Leuthen.

For the Prince, schooling in generalship began with classroom study of great generals from Julius Caesar to the King of Prussia. The early manoeuvres at Kew in turn gave way, late in the summer of 1780, to his departure from England, en route to the Continent to learn from the great generals of the day. Rumour suggested that the impregnation of one of the Kew milkmaids sped his departure. Frederick's itinerary, however, was designed with serious study in mind. He would remain overseas for seven years. That George III sent his son to learn warfare from the great German masters of the late eighteenth century (the Duke of Brunswick and, after this preparation, the Prince's idol, Frederick the Great of Prussia himself) may be seen as a sign that the achievements of Marlborough and in the Seven Years War had not lessened Britain's inferiority complex in matters of military science. The Duke of York had therefore been carefully schooled prior to assuming command and had benefited from a professional education more complete than almost any other British general who might be called upon to lead an expeditionary corps. But, of course, he lacked

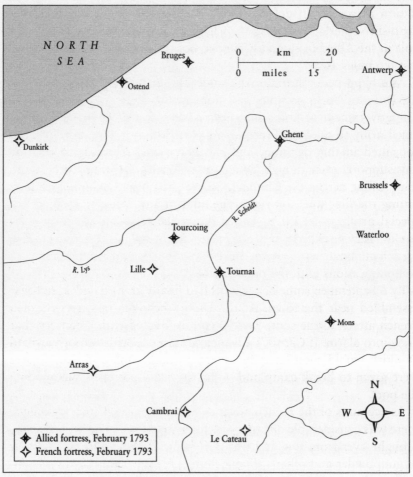

The Duke of York's battleground, 1793–9

practical experience or read regimental service, so when the chance finally appeared for him to lead an army in battle, nobody knew whether he could do so successfully.

The French attack of 6 September 1793 on the Austrian lines near Herzeele was typical of the Revolutionary Army. The phalanxes advanced, a riot of Jacobin fervour tempered by the experience of veteran cadres from the old Bourbon regiments. There was much shouting, cheering and general high spirits from the ragamuffin soldiers. They had been thrown forward by their general, Lazare Carnot, a man who would be dubbed 'the organiser of victory' for his vigorous mobilisation of society in defence of the Revolution. On this day in the Spanish Netherlands – modern Belgium – Carnot's troops punched a hole in the Allied front and headed almost due north, towards the sea, just ten miles away.

As it happened, a British army, under the command of Field Marshal the Duke of York, occupied positions in the dunes around Dunkirk. The government at home had ordered this British contingent of the allied army to take the French-held port. Military men had not been consulted in this decision, and the Navy was reluctant to provide any support, even though doing so would have entailed little more than sailing across the Channel. So the British had achieved nothing during the first week of their siege, and in any case had none of the special artillery needed to batter down the town's walls. Indeed, it could barely be called a siege, since the absence of naval support meant French gunboats harassed the British lines and kept open the garrison's communications with the outside world.

By 6 September, some heavy guns had finally arrived and were being assembled near the town. At the Duke's headquarters, reports of a French attack to the south were therefore treated with a concern that grew into alarm. If Carnot's advance continued, British troops around Dunkirk would soon have the enemy to their flank and rear. Orders were given to break camp and withdraw from positions surrounding the port.

As accounts of the French advance flew about the British regiments, there was considerable disorder and many panicked. The 30 siege guns brought over from England were left behind, along with 300 barrels of gunpowder and other valuable stores. A loss of this kind was considered disgraceful by professional soldiers; indeed, when something similar happened in Spain twenty years later, Wellington insisted the general responsible be court-martialled. But such a punishment would have been too embarrassing to King and Ministry to be countenanced. Instead, the Duke rallied his troops after the debacle. One of his staff officers wrote home: 'His good humour and spirits never forsake him, and he meets the unfortunate events that have happened with a degree of constancy and resolution that do him infinite honour.' The task of commanding the small field army that Britain could deploy in 1793 had been given to the Duke, in part, because it was assumed that being a prince would help in the difficult matters of diplomacy needed to bind together the polyglot forces of the anti-French alliance.

Frederick was only thirty years old at the time of Dunkirk. A striking figure, over six feet tall, broad chested (but increasingly stout), his shock of hair and straight nose gave him a bearing considered by many at the time to be the acme of noble good looks. He had also, prior to September 1793, demonstrated bravery in action and some skill at the head of his troops. Following Dunkirk, though, many officers serving in Flanders wrote accounts that suggested the Duke was an incompetent dilettante, more fond of wine and women than of grand strategy. These reports produced a rapid effect – much malicious gossip in the corridors of Westminster and a measure of public ridicule, including a caricature by the master, James Gillray, showing the Duke 'campaigning' with a whore astride his lap and a bottle in his hand. One courtier, visiting the Duke's headquarters a month after Dunkirk, wrote home, 'Some of the things reported in England may be true, but I am persuaded that he is both good natured and humane, although, by sometimes talking absurdly, he gets a contrary character.'

It was the Duke's habit of holding forth to his young staff that was at the root of these problems. One noble visitor (and politician) surveying the scene in Flanders told a confidant: 'He *talks* too much, and is careless to whom. I ventured to tell him so, and took an opportunity of recommending him to ask the superior officers to dinner; and, as he could not prevent their writing home, to try at least and furnish them by *his* conversation there with *materials* which would do *no harm* [original emphasis].' In terms of modern political management, Frederick's mistake was not briefing the right people with the right line.

There has been some debate about whether the 'Grand Old Duke of York' rhyme was a response to the events of 1793–4 in Flanders or to the brief campaign he led five years later in Holland, but the essential point is that early in his career the Prince became an irresistible target for popular lampoon. The King had sent one of his sons to lead an army fighting in defence of monarchy (so barbarously defiled by the French regicides). Failure was dangerous to that principle in Britain itself because the Jacobins had plenty of sympathisers there, even in Parliament. In our own era the shocking defeat of an army led by the King's son would obviously create a huge news story. We should not be surprised, then, that it caused a sensation in London more than two centuries ago, for even then irreverence, republicanism and merciless satire were widespread.

After the shock of September, the campaign settled down somewhat in the latter part of 1793. The armies contesting the Low Countries found themselves in a predicament very similar to that faced during Marlborough's time. So many troops had used these open lands as their thoroughfare during the preceding centuries that a dense network of fortresses and defensive barriers had evolved. These checked rapid progress by either side and demanded constant resort to siege warfare. During the marches between strongpoints the British contingent recovered some of its equilibrium, and in April 1794, for example, the Duke received widespread praise for planning a brilliant cavalry attack at Beaumont. But grand designs to smash the French were to be rudely discomfited just a few weeks later.

On 17 and 18 May, the protagonists fought the Battle of Tourcoing. It consisted of an attempt by the Duke of York to concert multiple attacks on 40,000 men of the French Armée du Nord, which held an exposed portion of the line. Frederick's British corps was not large enough to mount this attack on its own, so allied cooperation was the order of the day. The Austrians were brought into the fight – and in such strength that command of the whole devolved to an Austrian field marshal. The battle turned into a dismal fracas because York's plan relied on several different columns marching with equal determination to envelop the French Army to their front. Once the various columns had begun their trek, their commanders began to hesitate and the whole design felt apart. During the second day, the French pressed home counter-attacks and the allies lost 4,000 men killed or wounded and 1,500 captured.

Following Tourcoing, the coalition campaign in the Low Countries fell apart. The Austrians decided, after a year of see-saw fighting, that their province was more trouble than it was worth and effectively gave up trying to defend it. Once the largest contingents in this multinational army had begun to abandon it, in the second half of 1794, the other allies had no choice but to join their retreat into the Netherlands. There were scenes of much confusion and disorder during these marches, and cooperation between the nations effectively collapsed amid mutual recriminations.

This saga is important mainly because it showed the British Army struggling to make a good show of itself. From its dispatch the previous year, a bewildering array of shortcomings had been exposed on the battlefield. There were one or two chapters where a single brigade of horse or foot distinguished itself, it is true, but overall, taking to the field ten years after America had won its independence, the organisation had displayed every symptom of an atrophied, inefficient, peacetime army. Although the army had shrunk somewhat in the 1780s, it still remained substantially larger than it had been before the American rebellion. However, its need for recruits outstripped the supply of fit young men, largely because the economy was still so healthy, with emergent industries skimming surplus men off the land. Those who tried to fill the ranks thus often relied on 'crimping', or cheating of various kinds: signing up the old or patently unfit; taking men who were re-enlisting having already deserted; and doing deals with local magistrates to put convicted felons into uniform.

Towards the end of 1794's marching up to the top of various hills and marching down again, Lieutenant Colonel Harry Calvert, one of York's most trusted staff officers, wrote to an old friend, a major general, in England. His letter reveals the extent of this army's deficiencies or 'wants' and the rage that such military incapacity aroused in a keen young colonel:

We want artillerymen, we want a general officer at the head of the artillery, we want drivers and smiths; we want three major generals of infantry; we want a commanding engineer of rank and experience; we want a total reform in our hospital; we want at least two out of the four brigades of mounted artillery with which his Grace of Richmond is amusing himself in England; we want a total stop put to that most pernicious mode of bestowing rank on officers without even the form of recommendation, merely for raising (by means of crimps) a certain number of men, to restore to the army those independent disinterested feelings, and those high principles which should actuate a soldier, and form the basis of the military discipline of a free country, and to relieve deserving officers from the intolerable grievance of seeing men without merit, without family, or the smallest pretension to any military ability, pass over their heads and arrive at a very high, and till now a very respectable rank in the army, solely through the means of a rascally crimp.

Without going into every particular of Calvert's invective, the key shortcoming that he identified was in the leadership of Britain's army – both at the level of hopeless regimental officers who owed their position to political patronage and in the inability to find any capable superior officers who had exercised higher command. These failings in George III's army were just as apparent to Britain's allies. 'Even more disadvantageous for the English infantry was their rare knowledge and intercourse of the company-officers with their men,' wrote one Brunswick officer, adding: 'It happened often that one could notice whole regiments on the march, of which the officers followed only hours later, when they had finished breakfast at leisure.' Under such circumstances, the regiment turned out under the command of its non-commissioned officers. The same was true of drill at home, where the absence of officers also often led to sergeants running the show. This unfortunate pattern did at least produce one good side-effect: Britain entered the Napoleonic Wars with a cadre of skilled NCOs, and certainly they provided the disciplinary backbone for its army.

Officers' amateurism was matched at national level by the ignorance of Britain's political leaders about how to make best use of their armed forces, a shortcoming that produced the bungled siege of Dunkirk. During the first decade of struggle against the French revolutionaries, the desire to 'do something' while hazarding little and staying close to the sea, ready for evacuation by the Royal Navy, was a defining characteristic of British policy. This led one French authority to comment derisively: 'To doubt the defeat of an army sent by the British Ministry to any part of the Continent to contend against our troops would have been imputed to disaffection.'

Of course, not everything was woe: the redcoats did show certain impressive qualities during the fighting of 1793–4. The cavalry managed some dashing charges, which was a little surprising, perhaps, given that the mounted arm was later considered one of the weaker parts of the machine, but their successes were due in part to the strength and breeding of their horses. A quality bloodline – some indescribable quantum of grit or determination – was also evident in the British foot-soldier, who frequently stood in situations where others would have broken. Lastly, although the officer corps in general was sadly lacking in professionalism, some zealous, impressive men emerged in middle tiers of the army in the Low Countries: Calvert himself, later a key member of the army's higher staff; Colonel John Moore, who commanded a brigade under York; Lieutenant Colonel Arthur Wellesley, later the Duke of Wellington, who led the 33rd Foot; and John Le Marchant, who distinguished himself as a cavalry officer and would later become an important military educator.

During 1793–4, the legions of France withstood the attempts of *ancien régime* Europe to throttle their new society. In these campaigns the Jacobins taught grim lessons to the professional soldiers of many other countries. French armies attacked with an alacrity and creativity that old Austrian or Prussian generals accustomed to stately eighteenth-century warfare found very hard to counter. Carnot and Jourdan, another Armée du Nord commander, crafted new decrees that created in France the world's first true mass army – one of conscripts from the breadth of society. Not only did this produce vast numbers of recruits but it brought artisans, intellectuals even, into the ranks, whereas Britain struggled to recruit volunteers of quality.

All in all then, by late 1794, the members of the first great anti-French coalition were smarting from lessons learned in the Low Countries and were keen to end hostilities as soon as it could be done in a dignified way. For the British Prime Minister, there was an added problem. William Pitt knew that the continued presence of the Duke of York at the head of this battered army afforded the opposition an irresistible handle both against the Ministry and the King. It therefore finally fell to Pitt to write to George III requesting that the Duke be recalled. His letter, dated 23 November 1794, is a long and difficult read, because in it Pitt had to tell the King just how problematic his son's continued command had become, while surrounding this distasteful message with sugary expressions of loyalty and courtly courtesy. 'It is indeed impossible that the zeal and meritorious exertions of the Duke of York should be disputed by anyone who has the opportunity of being accurately informed of his personal conduct,' noted Pitt before slipping in the dagger: 'but the general impression is formed on other grounds . . . the want of experience and of habits of detail may have made it impossible for him to discharge all of the duties of his situation, and effectually to prevent or remedy abuses and evils which have crept into the service.' The Prime Minister noted how difficult 'the impression' of this incapacity made it for the Duke to carry on leading the army in the Netherlands before alluding to the bigger underlying issue: 'it is impossible to say how far this impression, if it is not removed, may operate in Parliament and in the Public to the disadvantage of Your Majesty's Government . . . it will be impossible to prevent this subject from being brought into Parliamentary discussion.'

In a single lifetime, that of George III, the presence of a king or royal prince at the head of an army had changed its symbolic role dramatically. His father, George II, had in 1743 been the last British sovereign to lead his armies into battle, at a time when such a gesture was still seen as an expression of commitment and statesmanship. But by the end of Frederick's command in Flanders, it was clear that the political costs of associating the royal house so closely with a failed expedition were too great to stomach. Pitt's letter thus marks a turning point in the relationship between army and society in Britain. In Russia, Austria or Prussia, sovereigns and princes continued to lead the campaigns against France in person, for they did not have a raucous democracy like Westminster's to contend with, one in which they would be held accountable for failure.

Removing the Duke required considerable delicacy, and for several weeks after his recall to England he remained in a sort of official limbo. He was still a young man who expected some active employment in life, but there were precious few posts appropriate for someone with the exalted rank of field marshal. In a rather distracted way, ministers decided to offer him the post of C-in-C, in place of the septuagenarian, inactive Lord Amherst (of Seven Years War fame), who had held on to the position for years like some military bed-blocker. The C-in-C, who occupied offices on London's Horse Guards Parade, was at this stage a sort of inspector-general who tried (often unsuccessfully) to instil some sort of common standards among the scattered regiments of the British Army.

So, a tactic devised by Pitt and his colleagues to relieve the Duke of York of his field command ended up producing spectacular dividends. For it did not take long after the Field Marshal started work at Horse Guards in February 1795 for the great advantages of this scheme to make themselves felt. First, his role in the Flanders campaign, with all its problems, had made him an excellent person to diagnose the army's ills. His youth and feelings of anger at those recent transactions also energised him to his new task. Finally, the very royal pedigree that had become a liability in his field command proved a vital asset when scaling the mountain of army reform, for it placed him and his mission above petty political vendettas. Virtually any other general who could have been considered for the post would have soon attracted the label of 'Whig' or 'Tory'.

The first general order issued on 14 February 1795, as the Duke took up his new office, announced, 'all matters respecting His Majesty's Military Service, excepting what may relate to the Foot Guards, should pass through His Royal Highness' hands'. Leaving aside the usual awkwardness of the Guards, this order gave the Duke a plenipotentiary mission to reform the army. Such a broad rubric might have caused paralysis in someone too indecisive to use it, but York and the small team he had with him were determined to wreak change. Not only did the pride of the army demand it, but the threat of French invasion and national catastrophe appeared increasingly real.

In 1795, the army headquarters at Horse Guards consisted of about 35 people. The Duke had brought with him four picked officers (including the fulminant Colonel Calvert) to act as his troubleshooters. Apart from the Commander-in-Chief and his office, there were two principal branches of the staff: the Adjutant General (dealing with personnel and legal matters) and the Quarter Master General (whose task was to sustain the army). The whole amounted to about twenty officers and a dozen or so secretaries and clerks. The army of 1795 could hardly, then, be accused of being overmanaged or carrying a vast retinue of civil servants. This may well have helped the new C-in-C in his great mission, since it made it easier to grip the machine and turn it to his purpose, and in the years following his appointment, the staff were in a continual frenzy: firing off directives, general orders and circular letters. Someone had taken charge at last.

Early in May 1799, the Antelope, an inn near High Wycombe, to the west of London, received an unusual group of visitors. The dozen or so men in their twenties and thirties were the first ever class of a new, as yet untitled academy. (In 1801, as a result of the Commander-in-Chief's patronage, it was finally christened the Royal Military College.) The class of 1799 arrived with their trunks, portmanteaus and valises, banging about the inn's narrow corridors, each vying for the best quarters. Their stay in Wycombe was intended to last for a year, and during that time they would be taught the skills needed to organise an army on operations: everything from map-making to finding forage and making proper reports to generals.

This small nucleus of men was part of a broader drive for military education being forced through by the Duke of York. In Flanders, six years earlier, there were simply no British officers qualified for service as staff officers for the Quarter Master General, so the five men chosen for this duty had been foreigners. The principal lecturer at the Royal Military College was General Francis Jarry, a distinguished old Frenchman who had served both his own sovereign and Frederick the Great. This business of organising an army, it will be noted, could only really be learned from a foreigner; Jarry was a *savant* of some renown in Europe and therefore considered quite a catch by the college's sponsors. Classes began (in rooms at the Antelope) on 4 May 1799, with the lessons given in French, which soon exposed the poor education of some of the students.

Colonel John Le Marchant, who attributed many of the French successes on the Continent to superior headquarters organisation, was the leading figure in the creation of this first British staff college. The task of launching the RMC was full of petty frustrations, though, and Le Marchant wrote to one friend demanding, 'How can we be so absurd as to oppose that, neglecting as we do all instruction and the aid of science in our military enterprises, we are to be victorious over troops that possess those advantages in the highest degree of perfection?'

York and those around him at Horse Guards had set the improvement of professional standards in the officer corps as one of their main objectives during his first three years as Commander-in-Chief. Military education was evidently critical. In 1802 the RMC opened a much larger junior division to prepare hundreds of teenagers for commissioning as officers; this was the beginning of Sandhurst. In 1803 the Duke of York's School was also established, giving a basic education to more than 1,200 boys.

Whatever measures were taken to instruct the officer corps, it was well understood that time would be needed for these new establishments to have an effect. It was also the case that this training, even of captains or majors in staff duties, was reform from the 'bottom up' that could not, particularly in 1795, when the Duke took over, solve the problem of there being so few senior officers who knew their business. Similarly, the system of promotion by seniority of the ranks above colonel made it extremely difficult for the Duke to put gifted officers like Moore and Wellesley in command of brigades as quickly as he'd like.

From the outset, therefore, there were attempts to force those in place to do their jobs better. In May 1795, for example, the head-quarters at Horse Guards issued a general order to the army demanding that regulations for the manoeuvring of troops 'be strictly followed and adhered to', and setting out a weekly training regime to be followed by all regiments. Monday and Friday were allocated for regimental training; on Tuesday and Saturday the regiments had to combine for brigade exercises; and Wednesday was set aside to put 'the whole line', what the French at this time were calling a division, through its paces. The aim of this was to encourage regimental, brigade and higher commanders to learn the basics of their craft: to see how long it took to effect certain formation changes on different types of ground; to observe how other regiments behaved; to encourage competition between them; and to understand how larger armies had to be organised in the field.

Each regiment was to be exercised 'under the personal direction of its own Commanding Officer', an allusion to their frequent absence and the woeful lack of commitment shown by many lieutenant colonels. The absenteeism noted by the Brunswick officer in Flanders permeated all levels of command. When regiments were posted to India or the Caribbean, where disease carried off so many, it was the norm for many officers to make their excuses and disappear. Often they exploited a loophole whereby a man commissioned or promoted into a regiment serving overseas had up to one year before having to present himself to his commanding officer. The staff at Horse Guards tried to tackle this problem with an angry letter to commanding officers in September 1795, threatening that those who did not report forthwith for embarkation to their regiments serving overseas would be 'reported to His Majesty and superseded'. The scale of these abuses can be deduced from the fact that the letter was addressed to the colonels of no fewer than thirty-nine regiments.

Threatening officers with 'supersession' meant putting them to the back of the promotion queue. This tactic shows how limited the Duke's options were in trying to force out men who held commissions purely because they were the idle sons of minor gentry owed a favour by someone of influence. Sacking or court-martialling them for dereliction of duty was almost impossible. In this and other matters, many of the Duke's early orders were only partially successful. The reputation and social standing of the army thus remained low, with one leading admiral even proposing that it could be scrapped and replaced with a larger force of marines.

Other methods were tried to lick the officer corps into shape. The practice of 'recruiting for rank', basically a medieval tradition whereby a man who raised enough men for the King could get a captain's or even a colonel's commission, was ended. This method put unqualified officers in charge of men who were often too old or crooked (in either sense) for service, the 'crimping' referred to by Calvert in his angry letter home from Flanders.

Within more established regiments the Duke tackled another abuse: the buying of commissions to advance a young man to the rank of major or even lieutenant colonel while still in his early twenties. Many of these transactions took place while the 'officers' were in their teens and still at school. New rules stipulated that promotion from ensign (or second lieutenant), the first officer rank, through lieutenant to captain required at least two years' regimental service. Those seeking to become majors had to have been soldiers for at least six years.

Changes to the commissioning and promotion system touched a nerve in British society. An officer's warrant was one of the most easily defined marks of gentility. Those with money and influence had become used to trading in such papers, buying respectability for their sons. They resented the change. Many openly opposed notions that merit should be the principal measure for promotion in the army.

To Britain's landed class, the army was part of a bargain. They paid tax and in return they got the vote and something for their family: a decent way for a son to earn a living. This same principle applied to the Navy, Church and magistracy. But by the end of the eighteenth century the army was the biggest source of patronage and enough of its commissioned class were also serving as Members of Parliament to make any radical change fraught with difficulty. Some 65 of the 558 MPs in the Parliament of 1796–1800 were army officers, making them the largest single occupational group.

In the battle for reform, the Duke brought a unique ability, as the King's favourite son, to steer such socially sensitive change. What higher loyalty could redcoated reactionaries espouse than devotion to the Crown? Sir Walter Scott noted: 'No rank short of that of the Duke of York – no courage and determination inferior to that of HRH – could have accomplished so great a change in so important a service but which was yet so unfavourable to the wealthy and powerful whose children and protégés had formerly found a brief way to promotion.' The C-in-C knew that reforming the officer corps was one of his most difficult tasks; it would take many years, and even the early steps made him some implacable enemies.

The Napoleonic Wars (and it is fair to call them such from this time, when Bonaparte had become the most powerful figure in the new republic) triggered many forms of social change in Europe, not least nationalism. In Britain, the very real threat of invasion accelerated this trend. The French landed in Ireland in 1798 to back a revolt there (it was eventually crushed with a certain brutal ineptitude). In preparing to meet this challenge in England itself, the government found that a boisterous anti-French patriotism brought people flocking to the colours of volunteer and militia regiments. This *rage militaire* even turned military encampments into places of fashion and society where the wives of those John Bulls who raised new bands of volunteers also disported themselves in uniform.

While the Duke of York thus tried to take the steps that would produce a regular army capable of fighting on the Continent in the long term, much attention was also given in the late 1790s to giving some sort of military bearing to the hundreds of thousands of volunteers being prepared for home defence. This was an urgent imperative, so whereas many years passed before the Duke appeared in person at the Royal Military College, he took the leading role in inspecting the new bands of citizen soldiers much sooner.

Some 15,000 volunteers were drawn up in Hyde Park for the King's Birthday Review in June 1799. Their regiments had names like Loyal Hackney and Royal Westminster. The Duke of York rode his charger down their line to ensure everything was in order before George III himself arrived in a carriage at 9 a.m. The guns of the Honourable Artillery Company boomed out a salute as the King's carriage was driven along the line of regiments that stretched from the Serpentine to Hyde Park Corner. The heady nationalistic atmosphere as he watched them loosing off a volley with their muskets may be gleaned from a report in the *Gazette*: 'After the firing, the whole waived their caps in the air and gave three hearty huzzas; which, joined to the sound of military music striking up at the same moment, and the various expressions of joy from the spectators, even the female part of them joining by waving of handkerchiefs, is said to have drawn tears of joy from their gracious sovereign.'

In these events the King and his family performed a service recognisable from the wars of the twentieth century: that of leading national mobilisation. There was a political point in this banging and hallooing by overenthusiastic volunteers, and it was rammed home in the official account, which described the scene as a 'splendid assemblage of citizen-soldiers, armed in defence of the best of sovereigns and the happiest, most perfect constitution upon earth'. Early jitters about Jacobinism and the future safety of Britain's royal house had passed.

At the King's Birthday Review, the Duke of York's older brother, the Prince of Wales, and two younger ones were also present in military attire. They acted, though, as spectators, unlike the C-in-C who was master of ceremonies. This disparity aroused the worst kind of princely sibling rivalry, which, ultimately, would threaten the Duke of York's reforms.

George III himself still played an important role in the armed forces, particularly in the promotion of admirals and generals. Frederick, widely regarded as his favourite son, was actually running the army, or at least its administration. He was strengthening the HQ at Horse Guards and its role in promoting regimental officers, making his own office increasingly important as a fount of patronage. The Prince of Wales, meanwhile, held only the rank of colonel. This was little more than a ceremonial bauble and he came to resent the fact that, as heir to the throne, he was of considerably inferior military rank to his younger brother. The Prince seemed to make little allowance for the fact that he was infinitely more interested in sybaritic pleasures than the tedium of the drill square. As for the Duke of Kent, one of York's younger brothers, he had devoted quite a few years to soldiering, but had proven a poor officer who bridled at tickings off from his superior, the C-in-C. Indeed, over time, Kent's dislike and envy of his older brother hardened into something quite dark and unpleasant.

These tensions found focus in army matters. They damaged sibling relations and those between the Prince of Wales and the King, who declined point-blank to take seriously his oldest son's pretensions to promotion. The King's oldest son resented his father's refusal to promote him, and as the sovereign became increasingly debilitated by his 'madness' their enmity worsened. So, while the Duke of York's career as C-in-C was generally a great boon to the army, there was a reverse to this particular medal for his growing power complicated the affairs of the royal family. With hindsight, it can be argued that such conflicts were inevitable until British royals, shorn of real authority, assumed a purely symbolic role in national mobilisation (as in the Second World War), but in 1799 there was still much real work for the Duke of York to do.

During the latter part of that year, with the prospect of an expedition to the Netherlands, the Duke sponsored legislation that finally allowed volunteering from reserve forces into the regulars on a substantial scale in return for a cash bounty. The army's thirst for manpower was immense. Its West Indian campaigns of 1793–6 had cost it 80,000 men dead or rendered unfit by sickness. Attempts to match France's new conscription laws had failed. Legislation passed in 1796 (the Quota Acts) had been intended to draw men from each county for military service, but Britain simply wasn't ready for large-scale military service on the French pattern and the new regulations were widely ignored or flouted. By putting forward the 1799 bill, Horse Guards returned to the fray, with the measure allowing more transfers from reserve forces providing a partial solution.

However, since the regular forces still needed huge numbers of volunteers, the C-in-C tried to make service more attractive. One of his first directives stopped the practice of powdering hair. The ritual of scraping the locks back and dusting them (often with flour!) was an irksome routine that had been forced on soldiers for decades as part of some eighteenth-century idea of what constituted a smart appearance. In addition, more practical uniforms were issued, improved barracks built and financial incentives improved, for example by reducing pay stoppages so the men ended up with more in their pockets. Such measures earned the Duke the sobriquet 'the soldier's friend'.

The dramatic expansion of the army in order to meet the threat of foreign invasion offered several vital possibilities for the reformers: it allowed incompetent senior officers to be shunted off to the task of home defence; it brought a new generation of men into the more junior commissioned ranks (most paid nothing for their commissions, thus representing a wider band of society, and many volunteers transferred into the regular army, where they formed a bloc striving for advancement); lastly, it created a large pool of trained manpower that allowed Britain to introduce a limited form of conscription – by drafting men from the reserves into regular regiments – that was to prove vital in sustaining an army large enough to fight Napoleon.

On 23 August 1804, the Commander-in-Chief appeared for yet another review, this time atop the cliffs near Hythe in Kent. There were a few superficial similarities with the event in Hyde Park of five years before: many of the 4,000 troops in front of him wore red coats and the Duke was on horseback again, attired in his formal regimentals. But much more was different.

After the initial inspection of troops and the firing of salutes, the brigade arrayed in front of the Duke came to life. They marched in slow time and then with the hurried pace prescribed for the new light infantry. They formed column and line, and all the time the redcoated regiments were protected by a screen of green jackets, riflemen of the 95th. Then the troops were guided through a mock battle, with the sharpshooters seeking concealed positions in hedges, the artillery firing numerous blanks and the infantry of the line showing how they could deliver a devastating volley. 'The whole of the review was conducted with the greatest order, no mistake occurred,' as one account trumpeted it.

The Duke had spent that August morning watching Major General John Moore's brigade being put through its paces, with that zealous officer proudly at its head. This force was undoubtedly the elite of the army in 1804, although one or two other regiments might have disputed that honour. They had undergone a summer of training in a new system of tactics and discipline at Shorncliffe Camp. Moore's machine had been refined and practised until it functioned very smoothly indeed. Following the brief peace of 1801–3, this new brigade stood guard at one of the likeliest landing points for any French army. Napoleon had anointed himself Emperor and gathered a huge, well-trained invasion army across the Channel at the so-called Camp of Boulogne. Landing boats were being collected in the French harbours, just as they would be in 1940. Britain's leaders faced the real possibility that the French enemy would overwhelm them.

Moore could justly take the credit for bringing his regiments to this pitch of preparation, but so much else was due to years of patient reform by the Duke. It was York who had ordered regular field training back in 1795. The creation of new light corps – both infantry regiments and the 95th Rifles – was another innovation nurtured by the C-in-C, for he had realised that these fast-moving, hard-hitting formations would form the vanguard of future Continental expeditions. The system of defence for southern England, complete with Martello towers and Moore's brigade, was another plan that had been overseen by the C-in-C. And, slowly but surely, the quality of both officers and men reaching frontline regiments like Moore's had been improved. The spectacle of Moore's brigade in full flow, then, was a powerful and tangible sign of how the Duke's reforms were bearing fruit. There were some less visible ones, too.

When Britain sent an expedition to Egypt in 1800, three officers from the first class of Royal Military College graduates had comprised part of its headquarters. This tiny but vital reinforcement had greatly helped in the organisation of the army. Improvements in the equipment and training of the soldiers had also been evident when the redcoats defeated the French at the Battle of the Pyramids in 1801. This British Army campaign in Egypt marked, in the view of Baron Jomini, one of Europe's leading military thinkers, 'the era of its regeneration'.

Years of military build-up had, by late 1804, created a vast force for the protection of Britain and its empire. When the wars had begun, a dozen years before, the army had about 50,000 troops. By the time of the Shorncliffe Camp, it was ten times that. Much of this vast figure was made up of volunteer civilians, enthusiastic amateurs of questionable military value, but armed and trained nevertheless. There were also the army's formal reserves – militia and yeomanry – financed by wily Parliamentarians on the condition that the troops were kept for home defence and thus unavailable for overseas expeditions. Of the full-time army, about 100,000 soldiers were needed to defend various imperial outposts, from Canada to India. This left Britain's political leaders with the ability to deploy an expeditionary army in Europe of anything up to 50,000 well-trained regular troops.

Between 1804 and 1809 there was much debate about how best to play this card in the game to defeat Napoleon. The aim was to find somewhere it might have great effect while at the same time being retained under British command, for it was still small compared to the forces of Continental powers like Russia and Austria. It took years for this conundrum to resolve itself; indeed William Pitt, the leading advocate of an energetic campaign against the French, died before it did. The key point, though, is that the decade of army reforms of the late 1790s and early 1800s secured the country from invasion and gave several prime ministers the option of becoming serious players in the business of Continental warfare.

During this decade, the Duke of York provided constant supervision and guidance. It must be remembered that at this time many a gentleman in trade or even on the army staff considered a working day of four or five hours (often just in the morning) to be an arduous office existence. The C-in-C's routine at Horse Guards began at 9 a.m. and rarely ended before 6 p.m. It was normal for him to respond to 300 letters in a day. Managing the business of officer careers proved to be a huge part of this workload and he set aside Tuesdays and Fridays (while Parliament was sitting) for interviews with men who felt they had been unfairly treated or merited promotion. He had taken steps to increase the role of commanding officers in assessing who should get a step up in rank and who should not. At the same time, he accepted that some commanding officer's vendetta or favouritism might prevent a deserving man from rising even under the improved system, so he made himself a one-man court of final appeal, encouraging those who felt hard done by to approach him at royal levees or even as he strode down Whitehall. The Duke's larger-than-life persona during this time of bustle and activity was later described by William Makepeace Thackeray as: 'Big, burly, loud, jolly, cursing, courageous; he had a most affectionate and lovable disposition, was noble and generous to a fault, and was never known to break a promise.'

It should come as no surprise that a man of such enormous energy also had outsize appetites. He consumed fine food and wine voraciously, requiring successive alterations to his uniform. The Duke spent virtually without limit, getting through his substantial income and frequently requiring credit. As for his sexual activities, Gillray had been on to something when he had caricatured the Duke a decade earlier. At the time of the Shorncliffe review, he had become besotted with a woman who would in time become a grave danger to him. Mary Anne Clarke had married a stonemason, taking his name, before moving on to live with a stockbroker and then an army agent. Some accounts described her as an actress, although it is fairer to say that she was a bright, attractive woman who perfected the knack of seducing men and living off them. One otherwise sober life of the Duke of York, published in 1827, noted rather bitterly, 'This prostitute had sufficient charms to attract the notice of a prince.'

For Frederick, stuck in the proverbially loveless royal marriage (to a Prussian princess), Mary Anne proved an excellent match: she was great fun and an exciting lover. So mesmerised was he by her that the Duke installed her in a beautiful house in Gloucester Place and gave her £1,000 a year. For some time, he maintained a routine of spending weekdays at his town house in Piccadilly and going to his country estate near Weybridge, where his wife lived, at weekends. However, such was the Duke's thirst for Mrs Clarke's company that he rented her a country house too, conveniently located near his rural abode. History does not record the excuses he gave his wife when popping off for his weekend amusement.

Mrs Clarke was also a person of gargantuan tastes – for dresses, shoes, furnishings and all other emblems of fashion. In time, she ran up huge debts with tradesmen, using the Duke's name to secure her credit. Their affair lasted something like three years before he ended it and agreed a deal whereby she would keep quiet about their relationship in return for £400 a year. Evidently, though, this was hardly enough to keep Mrs Clarke in the style to which she had become accustomed.

The House of Commons was in a state of nervous excitement on the morning of 27 January 1809. Reports were flying about London of the battle waged twelve days earlier at Corunna in Spain. General Sir John Moore had fought a gallant rearguard action against the French but had been mortally wounded on the field. Britain had at last found an arena where its army could make a difference, the Iberian peninsula, where Portugal and Spain were trying to fight off French domination. In the Members' lobby and corridors of the House there was discussion among Moore's partisans and his foes. Had the Ministry dispatched 33,000 troops to Spain with little prospect of success against the invading French, so dooming a brave general? Or was Moore himself guilty of bungling a chance to give Napoleon a poke in the eye?

Lieutenant General Sir Arthur Wellesley, always an acute judge of the political temperature, had weighed whether the latest expedition, ending in the Royal Navy's rescue of Moore's army, would rebound to the credit or debit of the government of the day. He concluded that Napoleon had obliged them, for, he wrote, 'I am convinced they could not have come off with honour if the French had not attacked.' Corunna could thus be added to a list of recent battles in

1 George Monck: a portrait in very typical seventeenth-century style with ceremonial armour and baton symbolising a general's rank. The scene in the background recalls Monck's prowess in siege warfare.

2 Cromwell at the head of his Ironsides at the battle of Dunbar in 1650. His principal contribution to military art was in the aggressive use of cavalry. Soon after this victory, he handed command in Scotland to Monck.

3 The key moment in the Restoration: Monck kisses Charles II's hand as he lands at Dover. For generations, historians viewed Monck's actions through the filter of Whig or Tory prejudice, seeing him respectively as a turncoat adventurer or someone who grasped that England's anarchy would go on indefinitely unless the King was returned from exile.

4 John Churchill, Duke of Marlborough painted in very much the same way as George Monck forty years earlier, the only difference being that by the early eighteenth century the fashion for spectacular wigs had become evident. Churchill loved the trappings of wealth and was notorious among his staff and officers as a freeloader.

5 An episode from the battle of Oudenaarde, the third of Marlborough's great victories in the War of the Spanish Succession. This vignette captures a key difference in cavalry tactics, with the French often preferring to use the pistol while the British, following Cromwell's example, preferred charging *à l'outrance*, with the sword.

6 The climax of Blenheim. The Danube can be seen on the right and the village of Blenheim itself in the centre, with British cavalry streaming past it, surrounding the French defenders. Marshal Tallard, captured as the centre of his line broke, can be seen on the left, wearing the grey coat.

7 Bunker Hill at the moment the King's troops finally broke into the rebel redoubt on 17 June 1775. British commanders learnt their lesson from the heavy losses suffered in this battle, and thereafter tried to avoid frontal assaults on American positions.

8 A modern depiction of General William Howe probably captures his ageing but distinguished demeanour better than any of the engravings done at the time. Many of his staff felt Howe was too passive in the prosecution of the war.

9 The Duke of York pictured in heroic fashion, wearing the uniform of his Guards regiment, as he would have appeared in his late twenties and early thirties.

10 Horse Guards (on the left with the clock tower) pictured in the mid-eighteenth century. In the early 1800s, with York as Commander-in-Chief, a global military establishment of hundreds of thousands of troops was run from here by a staff of fewer than three dozen people.

11 Wellington as Field Marshal, painted in 1814. He returned to London in the spring of that year after five years' overseas campaigning, during which he was transformed from a junior lieutenant general into one of Europe's leading figures.

12 The epic clash at Waterloo. Wellington's troops, including these Highlanders, formed in square in order to beat off a torrent of Napoleon's *cuirassiers*. Interestingly, this heroic feat was portrayed by a French artist, Felix Philippoteaux, with British artists lagging some decades behind in the depiction of such stirring scenes.

13 A photograph of Charles Gordon, taken in 1880 during his first stint as Governor General of Sudan. It captures the piercing gaze and haunted intensity of a man who, by this year, felt thwarted in his mission to bring civilisation to Sudan.

14 A French depiction of the moment when Gordon's severed head was presented to the Mahdi. Few details of the general's death can be confirmed with certainty, but there were numerous witnesses to the fact that his head was displayed at the Mahdi's camp.

15 By the late nineteenth century British artists were turning their hands to the kind of battle depictions that their French colleagues painted under Napoleon. The image of an impassive British square withstanding a frenzied onslaught by fanatical natives appealed to the public at home. Soldiers who were engaged in battles like Tamai and Abu Klea emerged, by contrast, with an admiration of their enemy's courage.

which the rebuilt British Army had made a very respectable showing of itself.

Wellesley's presence at Westminster that day was due to the vote of thanks he was due to receive from the Commons. Members wanted to record their gratitude for the victory won by the future Duke of Wellington several months earlier in Portugal. Wellesley's triumph had been of a less equivocal nature than Moore's: he had defeated a French army at the Battle of Vimiero and forced them to surrender Portugal. Having tasted this success, the government was determined to maintain a bridgehead in the peninsula. But if Wellesley thought that morning's business was all going to be plain sailing, a lap of honour for the conquering hero, he would be sorely disappointed.

The excitement stemmed less from Vimiero, which was already several months in the past, or from the contrary opinions about Moore's ultimate sacrifice, but from the mischief that Colonel Gwylym Lloyd Wardle, MP, was about to make. He had put down a motion one week earlier, so Members had been aware for several days that he was about to launch a spectacular blow against the administration. He was a Radical, part of a loose faction in the Commons that denounced the government and its war policy, and had gained a certain popularity among Britain's downtrodden citizens by attacking corruption, humbug and improper influence-peddling wherever they claimed to find it.

Wardle stood to speak, knowing the advance rumour had guaranteed the House would hang on his every word. He called for an urgent inquiry into the conduct of the Duke of York as Commander-in-Chief. As he spelled out his charges, and it became clear that the Duke's various enemies had coalesced against him, it must have been the stuff of York's nightmares.

Wardle owed his military rank to having recruited a certain number of men, a system since scrapped. His further progress had been checked by the army reforms. Now he stood ready to produce witnesses who would claim that their advancement had been blocked for the wrong reasons. But Wardle's star turn was to be Mary Anne Clarke, who would tell the spellbound Members that she had run a promotion racket whereby aspiring officers paid her to bring their names to the Duke of York's attention. In time, a further component of this conspiracy would emerge – clear evidence that Wardle, Clarke and the others had been incited and perhaps bankrolled by none other than the Duke of Kent, who resented his removal from the command of Gibraltar's garrison in 1803.

Some elements of this politically explosive cocktail had been apparent for some months. When the Duke of York had angled (with no chance of success) for a command in Spain in 1808, for example, a caricature was published showing a 'Female Junto' of stylishly dressed ladies pleading with him not to go, saying their concern was for his sake, 'not for *our* pensions'. This apparent reference to a string of paid-off mistresses had been sufficiently elliptical to amuse only those in the know. However, a pamphlet, also published in 1808, had drawn together some riotous misbehaviour by cadets at the Royal Military College with the circumstances surrounding the Duke of Kent being dismissed from Gibraltar into a clear *ad hominem* attack on the C-in-C.

Once charges that the King's son had kept Mrs Clarke in such lavish style and had been blatantly corrupt were made on the floor of the Commons, they inevitably caused uproar. The Secretary at War leapt up and promised an immediate inquiry, in which the whole House of Commons would sit in judgement; he insisted that the C-in-C would be found innocent. Lieutenant General Wellesley was next on his feet, immediately hazarding his Vimiero laurels in support of the Duke's good name. This defence gave Wellesley's direct recognition that fourteen years of patient reform by York had turned the army into something capable of facing the French 'masters' of war. But that, of course, was no answer in itself to the charges of influence-peddling.

During the weeks that followed Wardle's first speech, the Commons heard testimony from a variety of witnesses. As anticipated, Mrs Clarke was indeed the most sensational, providing juicy morsels about the Duke's private life as well as claims that she used her feminine wiles to get men promoted. Newspapers reported each twist and turn, every coffee house was abuzz with it, and the mob was in a state of febrile excitement, cheering Colonel Wardle whenever he appeared in public.

As the weeks wore on, though, there was a certain relief among ministers, because none of the witnesses (who gave their testimonies without taking any oath) was able to deliver a knockout punch. When it finally came to a division on Wardle's motion, on 16 March 1809, the charge that the C-in-C had behaved corruptly was defeated by a substantial margin (364 votes against Wardle; 123 for him). Most of the army officers – by this time they had reached an all-time peak of seventy-nine MPs – who were there agreed with Lieutenant General Wellesley's view rather than Colonel Wardle's.

This affair was the first modern British scandal in more ways than one. The Ministry was concerned that so many MPs had voted *with* Wardle. Although the evidence against the Duke never amounted to much – for there was no proof that anyone had gained anything by improper means – he was damaged by it. The *appearance* of wrong-doing scuppered him. A typically modern phenomenon, the curious consensus among backbenchers, press and mob, ultimately proved more important than the facts of the case. So, a couple of days later, the Duke of York stood down as Commander-in-Chief. Lieutenant General Wellesley, who, by this point, was about to set sail for Portugal with a new expedition, thought the Duke's treatment completely undeserved. This view was shared among many junior officers, emerging in their letters and journals.

Just a few months after the Duke's resignation those who had brought it about fell out with one another. Mary Anne Clarke, having failed to receive the money promised by Wardle (on behalf, she said, of the Duke of Kent), retracted her evidence, turning on her co-conspirators. She published her own account of the scandal in which she stated, 'My acquiantance with Colonel Wardle, and his associates, has convinced me that the garb of patriotic ardour conceals the most destructive passions and principles that can have no end but in *self-advancement*, power and honours [original emphasis].' Having emerged as the author of so much humbug, Wardle eventually left England. Two years after stepping down, a vindicated Duke of York was restored to his post of Commander-in-Chief, which he held for sixteen more years.

Although his latter period at Horse Guards also saw valuable reform, much of it directed at improving the ordinary soldier's lot, few remember the Duke for much more than the nursery rhyme. There are one or two other legacies, too. A handsome statue of him looks out across the Mall to Horse Guards. Less obviously, the number of 'Duke of York' pubs is a mark of soldierly affection for him, dating back to an era when retired redcoats often became publicans. It is interesting to note, by this crude standard of military respect, that there are more Duke of York pubs than there are boozers named after Wellington.

Certainly, the British Army before him was not rubbish. Also, it can be proven that the many reforms and directives spewed out by Horse

Guards from 1795 to 1809 were the work of a team. But all of the Duke's staff would have been powerless without the patronage of an engaged leader who brought to the bureaucratic battle the hitting power of being 'Field Marshal' and 'HRH'.

The class envy and latent republicanism of many Britons fed the scandal that brought him down in 1809 and later starved him of the historical reputation he deserved. Plenty of people still have trouble conceding that any member of royalty can achieve anything of substance, but the Duke was an indispensable figure at a pivotal time in history. For at the same moment that it became unacceptable for him, as a royal prince, to command an army in the field, it required a man of this pedigree to overhaul the institution of the British Army. There would be many subsequent moments, such as after the Crimean War, when the army would have benefited enormously from a similarly committed royal patron but lacked one.

One of the best eulogies to the Duke's reforms was made in the House of Commons in January 1809 by Arthur Wellesley, just as the Clarke scandal broke:

I can say from my own knowledge, as having been a lieutenant colonel in the army when HRH was appointed to command it, that it is materially improved in every respect; that the discipline of the soldiers is improved; that under the establishments formed under the direction of HRH, the officers are improved in knowledge; that the staff of the army is much better than it was; and much more complete than it was; that the cavalry is improved . . . and everything that relates to the military discipline of the soldiers and the military efficiency of the army has been greatly improved since HRH was appointed Commander-in-Chief.

As for the Duke of York's success in mastering the arcane ways of Whitehall in order to overwhelm politicians and get what he wanted for the army, the best estimate came from Lord Palmerston. 'A strong man; son of one king and brother of another,' the minister who had dealt with York on many matters said, 'heir presumptive, a political leader . . . he was always at the head of the army (except during a short interval) and took advantage of every opportunity to push on his encroachments.'

The situation on the eve of the Peninsular wars was well described by William Napier, an army officer who would fight in that conflict and write the first great history of it. Public opinion knew little of the Duke of York's great work to redress the organisation's failings which had been exposed in the Low Countries during the 1790s. Ironically, the prince found himself considered to be part of the problem rather than its solution. As Napier wrote:

England, both at home and abroad, was in 1808, scorned as a military power ... An ignorant contempt for the British soldiery had been long entertained, before the ill success of the expeditions in 1794 and 1799 appeared to justify the general prejudice, and the excellent discipline afterwards introduced and perfected by the Duke of York was despised.

These words succinctly sum up attitudes that were expressed in countless coffee houses, parliamentary debates or cruel caricatures during the early 1800s. Yet, as York resigned his office, public perception lagged behind reality: the organisation stood on the threshold of legendary victories.

There are many reasons why the Duke deserves a reputation as the greatest reformer in the history of the British Army. His success was to have an effect on everything from the survival of the British political system in the face of the French threat to the shaping of Europe after it had passed. He forged a shield to defend Britain against invasion, and then a sword that would be used to strike back at Napoleon. Ultimately, though, it was not the Duke of York but Wellington who would have the opportunity to plunge that weapon into the enemy.

Arthur Wellesley

1769–1852

*I am determined always to act according to the dictates of
my own judgement.*
THE DUKE OF WELLINGTON

On a September morning in 1803, Major General Arthur Wellesley was at the head of 5,000 British and native troops, marching in tropical heat. He was anxious. Having been sent by the Governor General of India to suppress a group of Marathas, princelings whose domains began 100 miles inland from Bombay, Wellesley was having trouble pinning them down. Such was the British general's uncertainty that, two days before, while passing through a valley to the south of the River Kaitna, he had divided his forces, sending another column by a parallel passage through the high ground in order to prevent his enemies coming south by one route while he was going north by the other. All the time, his efforts to discover more had been hampered by the swarms of enemy light horse who prevented British scouts from approaching.

Finding himself on the plain of the Kaitna on 23 September, at last Wellesley could see a vast host arrayed in front of him, along the opposite bank of the river. On the right and centre were something like 12,000 infantry, under the Rajah of Berar, extending up to the village of Assaye. Looking further to the left, protecting the enemy's other flank, they saw a great mass of horsemen – something in the order of 20,000, commanded by another princeling, Scindiah.

The Rajah's position was a strong one: not only did he have the river to his front, but there was a rocky gully between the Kaitna and the ridge occupied by his infantry, who had been smartly drilled by French officers. Scattered along his lines were many batteries of cannon – nearly 100 in all. The British general knew that he would have to face the Rajah at a huge numerical disadvantage, because, having divided his forces, he was not due to meet up with the other column until the following day. But Wellesley was not a man to be intimidated. Instead, he took the bull by the horns: 'I therefore determined upon the attack immediately,' he wrote, adding: 'it was certainly a most desperate one.'

He did not want to lose an opportunity to destroy the enemy army. But his decision to attack without waiting for the other British column to join him was a gamble.

Wellesley had come to India through the patronage of his older brother, who had been Governor General. They had grown up in Ireland, sons of a second-tier aristocrat and a mother who believed that young Arthur would never amount to anything. Wellesley the soldier had shown gallantry at the storm on Seringapatam in May 1799, and later been promoted to major general, but he had never won an important battle in an independent command, and many envious officers attributed his rise not to administrative efficiency or his fine tactical eye but to brotherly favouritism. On this dusty morning, he saw the chance to prove himself.

As Wellesley cantered about, concerting his plan of attack on Assaye, his fellow officers would have observed a man with a fine seat, an athletic, wiry physique and an intense look of concentration. His hair was close cropped, his nose prominent and slightly hooked. He spoke, as he wrote, with clipped economy, rarely with any sign of excitement or emotion.

Having discovered a ford across the Kaitna to his front right, the general issued orders for his troops to move down to it with all due celerity. Once across, they would deploy in two main battle lines, supported by a third of cavalry. Wellesley's grasp of the topography told him that the plan could yield great dividends, by bringing his army, concentrated, close to the right side of the enemy disposition. He hoped to fall on the flank of the enemy infantry, close to the village of Assaye.

As his two battalions of Highlanders and his four of sepoys (native Indians) formed into columns to pass the ford, their trudging feet kicked up clouds of dust that were observed by the Rajah. Many of those leading their men forward were inexperienced. A veteran officer of the 19th Light Dragoons, watching a young friend marching by with the East India Company artillery, called out, 'My lad, your maiden sword will be blooded today.' The fresh-faced subaltern recorded later: 'Not a whisper was heard through our ranks; our nerves were wound up to the proper pitch, and everyone seemed to know and to feel there was no alternative but death or victory.'

Wellesley's skirmishers splashed through the muddy waters of the
Kaitna, fanned out on the enemy bank and lay low while the serried
(i.e. with troops closely formed) ranks of redcoats formed behind them
in the two lines prescribed by their commander. But at this point, the
general's plan began to go wrong.

The enemy artillery, finding its range to the men packed together in
the ford, began making lethal practice. A ball missed Wellesley himself by just a couple of feet, carrying off the head of his orderly
dragoon and splattering everyone with its contents. What was more,
once across this obstacle, the general noticed that the whole enemy
army had begun to change its front, wheeling to face the new threat on
its left. British officers, seeing this unexpected display of soldierly skill
through the smoke and dust, damned the Rajah's French drill masters.
The British commanders seem to have been unaware that during this
redeployment of the Indian infantry, their cavalry began a bigger movement, trotting around from the right of the enemy line to behind it,
so they could reappear on the right, close to Assaye, where Wellesley's
advancing battalions would present their own vulnerable flank. In
the time it took the redcoat army to form its battle lines, and begin
moving towards the high ground and Assaye, the intensity of enemy

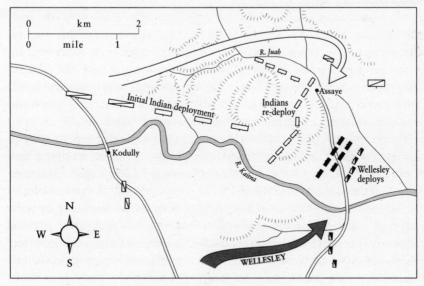

The battle of Assaye, 1803

artillery fire began to increase measurably. Once they came within a couple of hundred yards of the great, fire-belching Indian guns, they began hurling out grapeshot, carving into the advancing battalions.

Wellesley therefore faced a crisis. Many of the cannon he had relied upon to answer the enemy's fire with fire were now motionless, the bullocks who pulled them having been cut down by grape. Some of the sepoys began to leave the ranks, and seek safety behind the rocks of the gully that lay just in front of the enemy. 'The fire of the enemy's artillery became so destructive that no troops could long stand it,' according to one officer, 'indeed not a moment was to be lost in closing with the enemy.' Wellesley ordered his men to push on, trying to bring his left forward even more quickly, so as to leave his right flank a little more protected from the risk of cavalry attack. However, galled by the fire and the slaughter of so many comrades, the Scots and sepoys did not follow the general's orders precisely. Instead, they rushed onwards – the right as fast as the left – gave a single volley of their muskets and got stuck in with the bayonet. In moments all was chaos, as the redcoats wrought their revenge.

Seeing the order vanish from the British line and the exposed nature of its right, Scindiah, whose horsemen had completed their redeployment from the other end of the Maratha line, led a wave of his cavalry forward. They set spurs to their nimble mounts and fell into the ranks of the 74th Highlanders. The commanding officer of the 19th Light Dragoons could see that matters had become critical. He led his squadrons forward to drive off the Indian cavalry.

In the din of metal on metal and the cries of men, the 19th turned the great tide of enemy horse. As the cavalry mêlée continued, the infantry kept pushing forward, through captured guns, on the heels of the retreating enemy infantry. After a few more minutes the battle was effectively over. As the Rajah's men began to break and run, the British general would like to have unleashed his cavalry in pursuit, but it was not to be, for the 19th had been spent saving the Highlanders, and their commander lay dead on the field.

Major General Wellesley had shown what he could do in an independent command, displaying aggression and good judgement in equal measure. He defeated an enemy army five times as big as his own and captured all its guns. It was a better performance than most British major generals could have managed. However, the price was heavy indeed – 141 British and 224 sepoys killed, and so many wounded that the total casualties amounted to nearly four in every ten men who had marched that morning. Wellesley mourned the cost, for he was not as sanguine as Marlborough in paying the butcher's bill for his own advancement.

Among those who had lived through the Battle of Assaye, there was a sense of having witnessed military genius at work. Lieutenant Colin Campbell, a bright young Scot co-opted onto the general's staff, wrote home:

The general was in the thick of the action the whole time, and had a horse killed under him. No man could have shown a better example to the troops than he did. I never saw a man so cool and collected as he was the whole time, though I can assure you, till our troops got the order to advance, the fate of the day seemed doubtful; and if the numerous cavalry of the enemy had done their duty, I hardly think it possible that we would have succeeded.

Assaye possessed many of the features that would become hallmarks of the general's battles: a rapid and flawless tactical appreciation; orders given with clarity as well as economy; the determination to prevail, especially in a 'close-run thing'; and a willingness to place himself at the decisive point, regardless of risk. The battle showed some other sides to the man, too: his inability to pursue a broken enemy; and a cool sense of how to write a victory dispatch to the powers that be that explained away his heavy losses.

It was in India, then, that the army first glimpsed Wellesley's greatness. But it would be in Europe where it matured.

The general who left Parliament on 2 January 1809 had won more laurels since Assaye, having fought successfully during the brief Copenhagen campaign (1807) and in Portugal (1808). He had also become an accomplished political operator, building on years spent on the staff at Dublin Castle and his time dealing with complex diplomatic/military problems in India. As we have seen, his speech in defence of the Duke of York that morning had contained an encomium to the Prince's army reform. It had also allowed him to gratify his instinct, as a Tory and part of the Ministry, to defend a member of the royal house against the insinuations of upstart MPs seeking popularity with the mob. For all that, though, Wellesley must have been privately unsure as to whether the Duke was an obstacle to the next great plan of his life.

While in London, the general was lobbying leading members of the government to appoint him to the command of a new military expedition to the Iberian peninsula. In 1807, the Spanish had risen against the French occupying their country; Napoleon's troubles had later spread to Portugal. These events caught the imagination of many Britons, for Spanish popular resistance succeeded at first where all the *ancien régime* professional armies had failed over the previous fifteen years, bringing about the spectacular defeat of a French corps at Bailen in 1808. British support for the rebels was, in its simplest terms, a vote-winner for the government in London, even after the evacuation of Sir John Moore's army from Corunna.

By early March 1809, the issue of who should command the new expedition had become vexed. Wellesley penned a memo on the defence of Portugal which he circulated to leading members of the government. It began, 'I have always been of the opinion that Portugal might be defended whatever the result of the contest in Spain.' His document played brilliantly to the anxieties of the Ministry, while pushing his own credentials for the job.

The proposition was, simply that rebuilding the Portuguese Army, while making use of 30,000 British troops and exploiting the country's natural defences, would allow the government to maintain a Continental bridgehead against Napoleon. The Emperor would then face an unpleasant choice: allow the British to sit in their Portuguese sanctuary, stirring up all sorts of mischief in Spain, or invade and drive them out, a step which Wellesley estimated would require 100,000 French troops. Wellesley knew that politicians always worried about money (because raising it required unpopular taxes) so he concluded, 'It is probable that the expense of these measures will not this year exceed a million sterling. But if they should succeed, and the contest continue in Spain and Portugal, the benefit which will accrue from them will be more than adequate to the expense incurred.' By way of comparison, ministers agreed to pay Austria subsidies to fight the French that amounted to considerably more than this over the course of just three months in 1809. Wellesley's memo has rightly been praised as displaying remarkable foresight. He had spotted a great strategic opportunity and knew how to play for it.

When Cabinet discussed the issue that March there were a number of obstacles to be overcome, not least that the system of army seniority demanded that a longer-serving officer be given the command of

30,000 men. This was definitely the Duke of York's opinion, and some ministers suspected him of coveting the command for himself. Given the Duke's unfortunate experiences in the Low Countries in 1794–5 and 1799, nobody in the cabinet seriously backed that idea, but there were still any number of well-connected men ahead of Wellesley in the queue. (He was now the most junior of 130 lieutenant generals in the army list.) Nevertheless, George Canning, the Foreign Secretary, argued forcefully that Wellesley's unique abilities made him the right man for the job. At a meeting on 26 March 1809, Canning finally convinced his colleagues, leading George III to grumble about 'so young a Lieutenant General holding so distinguished a command while his seniors remained unemployed'.

The appointment of Wellesley marked an important victory in the struggle to place personal ability ahead of other characteristics when choosing a man for supreme command. Canning was jubilant at his success, writing to the British ambassador in Portugal just before the new man was sent out: 'In Wellesley . . . you will find everything that you can wish – frankness – temper – honesty – quickness – comprehensiveness – and military ability – and not only eminent beyond any other military commander that could be chosen – but perhaps possessed by him alone, of all our commanders, in a degree that qualifies for great undertakings.'

It was only on 27 September 1810, fully eighteen months after considering the defence of Portugal, that the quality of the general's calculations was demonstrated. Early that morning, Lord Wellington (for that is what Wellelsey had become, late in 1809) and his staff gazed down from the lofty heights of the Serra de Bussaco. The ridge occupied by his Anglo-Portuguese army was a formidable obstacle – so steep in places that the enemy would have to scramble up on all fours. But as they looked down at the dark columns of Marshal André Massena's army, it became clear that the French commander was about to join battle on precisely the unequal terms that Wellington had planned.

The Battle of Bussaco may be seen as a vindication of Wellington's judgement on every level. Starting at the highest, that of strategy, Massena's presence at this spot, at the head of 65,000 troops, was a huge distraction from Napoleon's plans for the subjugation of Spain. It was precisely the measure predicated in Wellington's memo.

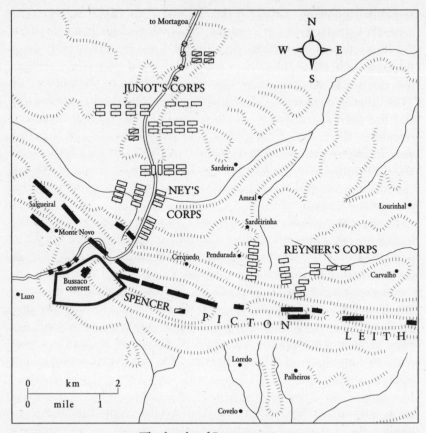

The battle of Bussaco, 1810

Portugal's army had been retrained, just as the general had advocated in that message, and now provided extra brigades in each division of redcoats. The British Army had thus been augmented by more than one-third.

Wellington's plan of campaign was also vindicated that morning. He had predicted that Massena would advance on Lisbon by either of two routes. Bussaco was his chosen battleground on one; but had the Marshal gone the other way, an alternative fighting ground, improved by extensive fieldworks, had been prepared there, too. Behind the Bussaco position, closer to the capital itself, a dense network of defensive works, the lines of Torres Vedras, had been laid out by the engineers in conditions of great secrecy. If Massena chose to follow him to Lisbon, Wellington was more than ready. It only remained, that

September morning, for the enemy to prove the quality of the British general's calculations at the lowest or tactical level. But having chosen the Bussaco position and keeping his main battle line hidden behind the crest itself, the dice had been loaded on that matter too. Wellington was not a man who saw any point in a fair fight.

Wellington's tactics for shielding his men from enemy observation and fire stemmed in part from a conviction that the political will to remain in Iberia was fragile. 'I suspect the Ministers in England are very indifferent to our operations in this country,' he wrote, shortly after returning to Portugal. The general thus sought to avoid heavy casualties, since these would attract unwelcome attention at home and prompt the expense of sending out reinforcements. In fact, at the time of Bussaco, the climate for keeping an expeditionary army in the region had improved a little in Westminster. If he was able to make the French pay a heavy price for this ridge, the Ministry might gain a little more support in Parliament for its war policy.

Massena's attempt to take the heights involved thrusts by two corps. On his left, General Reynier would lead one body up one of the steepest parts of the ridge to its highest point. The Marshal hoped that this blow at Wellington's centre would cause the British general to commit reserves to its defence. Marshal Ney would then strike further to the right, at a point where a road crossed the feature. Massena hoped that Ney would make the breakthrough. He knew that the troops would struggle up the ridge and was worried that the attack would become bogged down if they stopped to fire at the British, so he gave strict orders for them to maintain their progress in marching columns, deploying only when they reached the top.

Once Reynier's men were scaling the slope, the faults in the French plan soon manifested themselves. With French battalions advancing on a front only 20 or 30 men wide, but 12 or more ranks deep, well-aimed cannon shots could knock down whole files of men. The redcoats and Portuguese poured musket fire into the sides of the columns, too. Wellington had posted skirmishers on the forward slope of the Bussaco ridge, and hundreds of these men kept up a running fire against the French, knocking some down and galling the rest as they puffed and panted, powerless to respond. By throwing out thousands of sharpshooters, Wellington shrouded his main deployments, just as the Indian cavalry shielded his own foes before Assaye seven years earlier.

Remarkably, given these odds, some of Reynier's men made it to the top of the ridge and began deploying, ready to give the British a taste of their powder at last. At this moment, the battle reached a crisis for Wellington, and, braving the hail of musketry, he went to watch the battle between Reynier's brave men and Major General Picton's British infantry division.

On this fighting ground, with some of the eleven battalions in Reynier's first division on top of the ridge, Picton had only eight battalions himself. But his troops included the hard-fighting 88th, the Connaught Rangers, the 44th and the 74th as well as some well-trained Portuguese regiments. Picton's men formed firing lines, pouring musketry into the French mass. Wellington himself brought up a pair of guns to add to the shower of metal. 'All was confusion and uproar, smoke, fire and bullets,' wrote one young officer of the 88th, 'French officers and soldiers, drummers and drums, knocked down in every direction.' Under this punishment, the French battalions lost all cohesion, and men started trying to save themselves, running back down the steep hill. A well-timed charge by the 88th and the 45th decided the matter. Wellington and his staff had been under intense fire at times during this episode, but his personal intervention had helped turn the tide.

Wellington went from point to point, often bypassing the usual chain of command – the division and brigade commanders – giving instructions to the commanding officers in person. These commands were usually brief and left no room for confusion. One young subaltern who overheard such directives being given at Bussaco wrote later, 'I was particularly struck with the style of this order, so decided, so manly, and breathing no doubt as to the repulse of any attack; it confirmed confidence.'

As Picton's drama unfolded, Ney's column went in. The lie of the land and clouds of smoke meant he could not clearly see whether Reynier's men had reached their objective, but the fiery-headed Ney was never one to hold back. Here, the French encountered even worse difficulties. Their progress was slowed by swarms of skirmishing green-jacketed riflemen and redcoats from the elite of Wellington's army, the highly trained Light Division. When one determined French brigade commander finally managed to lead a few score stalwarts over the top of the ridge, they came face to face with 2,000 glinting bayonets. The British charged, driving the shattered French battalions down the way they'd come.

Bussaco was an emphatic victory in a way that Wellington's successes the previous year at Talavera and in 1808 at Vimiero had not been. On 27 September 1810, he dealt Massena 4,500 casualties against 1,252 of his own. At Talavera, the cost had been appreciably higher, and after the battle he had lost thousands more troops to sickness – erring in his judgement by keeping them too long in an unhealthy part of Spain. Quite a few officers in the army had remained sceptical about Wellington's abilities at the end of the 1809 campaign. Bussaco convinced many of his skill, with more waverers also falling into line once they saw how Massena's army arrived at the lines of Torres Vedras too weak and demoralised to storm them.

'From the instant when he fixed upon the position of Bussaco, Lord Wellington expressed the firm conviction that he would be attacked there,' his adjutant general and a later historian of the war would write, adding: 'He adhered to that opinion in opposition to the sentiments of every functionary by whom he was surrounded. There was a degree of prescience in this for which it is impossible entirely to account.'

Wellington's conduct of the 1810 campaign in Portugal also changed the way the French thought about him. Men like Massena, Ney and Reynier had shared in many of Napoleon's triumphs and were considered his 'A Team'. Massena, whom the Emperor dubbed the 'spoiled child of victory', had built up a European reputation second only to Napoleon's. Wellington broke it. After Bussaco, French generals became nervous at the prospect of encountering the British Peninsular Army and its skilled leader.

The task given to Ned Pakenham on 22 July 1812 was to prove of the highest importance. It is rare that a locum divisional commander can decide the fate of a nation and seal the reputation of his C-in-C, but that was precisely what would happen. Pakenham was standing in for the foul-mouthed firebrand Picton, who had been wounded at the head of his 3rd Division earlier in the campaign. The orders given to Pakenham that morning had initially brought him down: a hard march from the tail of Wellington's army to its head, overtaking other formations as he went. Now, Wellington had galloped up in person and ordered his brother-in-law simply and directly to manoeuvre into the path of the French army that was marching parallel to their own and attack its leading division.

[133]

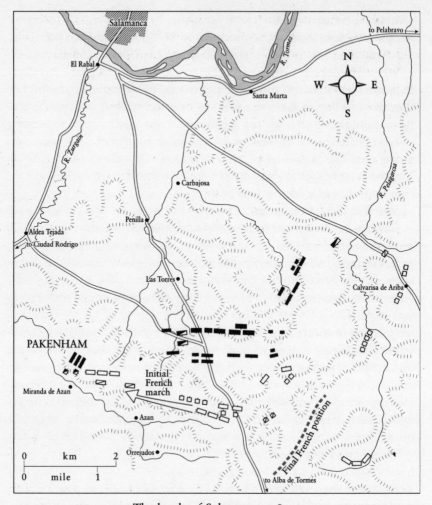

The battle of Salamanca, 1812

On this day, Wellington had managed to hide most of his troops behind Los Arapiles ridge, so the French were unsure of their whereabouts. The Duke had explored this fighting ground some weeks before, so he knew precisely the lie of the land. The troops marching on the 22nd had spent many days in fruitless jockeying for advantage across the hot plains and Castile and Leon. At times the two great phalanxes had marched within sight of each other, just a few hundred yards apart, with the soldiers eyeing the enemy and waiting for an opportunity to exploit any mistake. But now, with the advantages of ground, the British C-in-C had at last spotted his chance. Marshal Marmont's army had become strung out on its line of march, the leading division too far ahead of the following one to be supported quickly.

When Pakenham delivered his attack, it worked magnificently. His regiments moved forward in line, driving back French battalions as they tried to deploy from the march. The commander of the following formation, trying to help, fed his men into the firefight but only added to the confusion. At this point a brigade of heavy cavalry, more than 1,000 men mounted on fine chargers, under Major General John Le Marchant (founder of the Royal Military College) was ordered to canter up the ridge where the French were taking their punishment and exploit Pakenham's success.

Cavalry in this period rarely defeated infantry if the footsloggers formed themselves into a defensive square and remained steady. But, as Le Marchant's horse surmounted the ridge of Los Arapiles they were delighted to see thousands of French falling back, reeling from Pakenham's initial assault, with little semblance of order. The charge was sounded, spurs set to horses, and the fate of eight French battalions sealed in a few frenzied minutes. 'It was a fine sight to see those fellows running, as we held our swords over their heads,' wrote one of Le Marchant's subalterns. An officer of Picton's division saw the consequences of the heavy cavalry's devastating charge: 'Hundreds of men frightfully disfigured, black with dust and worn out with fatigue and covered with sabre cuts and blood threw themselves among us for safety.'

Wellington's design, ably executed by Le Marchant (who fell in his hour of glory) and Pakenham, saw the crushing of two French divisions in less than an hour. It was a blow from which this French army could not recover, for the British continued their simultaneous advance along the front and left flank of the enemy battle line – a terrible combination known to military theorists of the time as an oblique attack. The Emperor's army attempted a spirited counter-attack, but it took little more than two hours for them to be transformed from a self-confident and disciplined force into a broken horde.

It was only at the end of the day, when preparations to prevent the escape of Marmont's force were bungled, that the British triumph was marred in any sense. Not for the first time, Wellington was unable to organise a vigorous cavalry pursuit of a beaten enemy, something that might have yielded many thousands more prisoners.

The Battle of Salamanca proved the high point, nevertheless, of an extraordinarily conceived campaign. As 1812 progressed, Wellington had successively stormed two major French-held fortresses on the Spanish/Portuguese border, opening the way for an invasion of Spain, then set in train a series of complex diversions to tie down possible reinforcements for Marmont's army before striking at that force itself. All the time during this process, Wellington had been reading his enemy's most confidential dispatches, following a code-breaking coup by Major George Scovell, one of his staff. The general's grasp of the need for good intelligence, his steps taken to procure it, and his use of the resulting reports all add to his reputation.

General Foy, a divisional commander in Marmont's army defeated at Salamanca, subsequently penned one of the most glowing tributes to Wellington's handling of that battle. 'At Salamanca [Wellington] showed himself to be a considerable manoeuvrer,' wrote Foy. 'He kept his dispositions hidden almost all day; he waited for our movements before revealing his own; he revealed little; he fought in an oblique order; it was a battle in the style of Frederick [the Great].'

Salamanca also marked a turning point of opinion in Britain. It was only after this victory, for example, that the deeds of the Peninsular Army featured prominently in the work of caricaturists and those flogging commemorative mementoes. Salamanca convinced people at home that the army's four years of campaigning in the peninsula were achieving something at last. Madrid was liberated following the battle, only to be abandoned (a little humiliatingly) when the British army pulled back to the Portuguese border at the end of the campaigning season. Nevertheless, the combined effect of the Battle of Salamanca and the taking of the capital was to sound the death knell of the French enterprise in Spain.

Throughout the winter of 1812/13, Wellington tried to go hunting every few days. His headquarters had lodged in Frenada, a small village on the Portuguese/Spanish frontier, an area of upland which reminded many of the moors at home. Eschewing the delights of Lisbon for his mountain retreat, Wellington had a pack of hounds sent out and found no better relief from the pressures of planning his next campaign than galloping through the ferns, chasing the fox on icy, crisp mornings. The lull in military operations gave many staff officers the chance to set out with a fishing rod or fowling piece and bag something for supper back in the smoky Frenada hovel where they had been billeted. An invitation to go fox hunting with His Lordship was a different matter, though. It divided people.

Wellington was certainly open to advancing men from poorer backgrounds, such as Colin Campbell (his acting Brigade Major at Assaye) and George Scovell (whose codebreaking work was now providing him with the French defensive plan for the 1813 campaign). However, those who had clawed their way up the army by sheer ability while depending on their pay and allowances simply could not afford the fine horses that their general and his golden-haired acolytes rode to hounds. An aristocratic aide de camp might have a hunter that cost one year's pay for a captain. The loss or injury of such an animal might vex him, but it would hardly be ruinous, as it would be to a staff captain, living on his pay, who would then be obliged to borrow money to buy a new mount.

The general's regular hunting companions, his ADCs, were 'nearly all young men of the great political families', points out one historian. Perusing the list, one sees sons or nephews of several cabinet ministers. By doing this, Wellington displayed his shrewd political instinct, since, knowing the Ministry's fragile commitment to the Iberian War, he seems to have bound quite a few of its leading players to the cause by taking their sons on campaign. That said, there was something missing in his personality, an avoidance of equals, an ability to relax only in the presence of youthful versions of himself too callow to offer a serious difference of opinion. Wellington created his own world, his military family, whose company he seemed to prefer to that of his own wife and sons. No wonder that one Peninsular veteran later wrote that the British soldier had fought 'under the cold shade of aristocracy'.

Wellington's hunting parties therefore revealed a sense of fun, a desire to keep fit and a complete indifference to the iniquities of the class system within the staff. Certainly, the general regarded many of those around him as incompetent or dullards, and he had perfected a system in which he took almost every decision of consequence. 'I am obliged to be everywhere, and if absent from any operation, something goes wrong,' he had written home in 1811, after a bad mistake by a subordinate.

This 'obligation' led him to micro-manage the work of many of his staff officers and divisional commanders. He moulded those around him into a tightly constrained executive body, sending home or humiliating those who got in the way. When taxed by ministers about who might possibly take over if he fell in battle, Wellington replied waspishly that a number two would be 'a person without defined duties, excepting to give flying opinions, from which he may depart at pleasure, must be a nuisance in moments of decision; and whether I have a second in command or not, I am determined always to act according to the dictates of my own judgement'.

Some of those around Wellington shared his disdain for the amateurishness of the officer corps. One keen young major wrote home approvingly of his general's control-freakery, 'It is a hard task for a man to teach at once soldiers, officers, commissaries, staff, generals and last of all himself. This, however, he has done.' The task of forging his army was made all the harder by Britain's lack of preparation for Continental warfare. The army had for too long operated as a glorified marine corps, unable to sustain inland operations. Wellington had to provide the missing capabilities, developing his own supply train, siege artillery and intelligence-gathering system.

Much as many a staff officer's or general's letters home leave little doubt that Wellington must have been an extremely difficult man to work for, his command methods were quite appropriate given the state of the Georgian army. The organisation was full of gentleman amateurs who thought a little 'amusement' fighting the French for one campaign would be best followed by some parties in London during the social season. This attitude, and the comings and goings it produced, often maddened Wellington. Evidently, he was justified in trying to insist that those with responsible positions in the army must show commitment and attention to detail. Like Marlborough before and Montgomery afterwards, it took years of continuous campaigning for Wellington to find the right individuals and perfect procedures required to turn his army into a formidable machine.

His failing, and here we return to the Frenada fox-hunting parties, was to superimpose quite explicitly his notions of class and property on those of ability. He expected the army's leaders to be able *and* landed. The facts that much of the aristocracy still disdained military service and that the expansion of the army to meet the Napoleonic threat required its leadership to embrace a far wider proportion of society do not seem to have altered Wellington's prejudices in this matter. The Duke's defenders might argue that he simply reflected the attitudes of his age, but in fact Wellington was a Tory of a very particular hue whose views on social order, punishment and army promotion were reactionary even by the standards of many of his peers.

It was a measure of Wellington's intolerance for disorder that marauding or theft by soldiers in his army prompted such intemperate outbursts from a man otherwise known for his sang-froid. The 1812 campaign ended with a general order castigating his soldiers for poor discipline during their retreat to the Portuguese border. Many of the men who had stormed two fortresses and won the Battle of Salamanca during the preceding months considered this to be outrageously unjust, and never quite forgave their general for it. 'We have in the service the scum of the earth as common soldiers,' Wellington wrote home a few months later, in another fit of rage that is still quoted against him. 'Of late years we have been doing everything in our power, both by law and by publications, to relax the discipline by which alone such men can be kept in order . . . it really is a disgrace to have any thing to say to such men as some of our soldiers are.'

During 1813 and 1814, Wellington led his 'scum' across Spain and into southern France. His army mounted a ruthless and impressive offensive that took by surprise many of those accustomed to four relatively sedentary campaigns near the Portuguese border. The crushing of several divisions and capture of 151 cannon at Vitoria in June 1813 marked one of the most decisive defeats of a French army anywhere in this epoch. All of this made Wellington into a major European military figure.

Late in 1812, the Spanish had at last put aside their pride and granted the Duke full powers to command their armies. He was festooned with honours and baubles by the time Napoleon abdicated in 1814. But, of course, Wellington's reputation lacked one thing: he had never fought the Emperor in person. By the time Wellington had become a diplomat, ready to attend the Congress of Vienna, he had presumably accepted that he would never have the honour of beating 'Boney' in battle.

The fall of La Haye Sainte a little after 6 p.m. on 18 June 1815 must have been one of the worst moments of Wellington's life. The defenders of the fortified farm, gallant Hanoverian light infantry, had withstood several determined French assaults but finally had to abandon their position when their ammunition ran out and the burning of the buildings around them made it impossible to stay. Wellington's position on the Mont Saint Jean ridge, south of Brussels, was anchored on two strong-

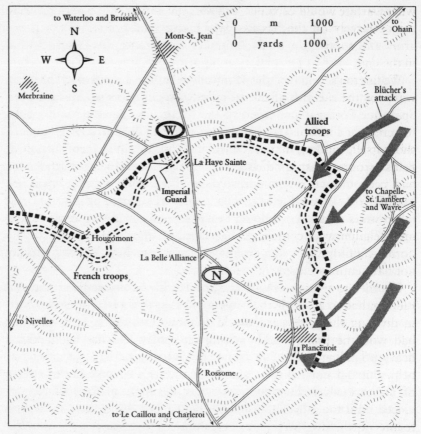

The battle of Waterloo, 1815: situation at 6 p.m.

points – La Haye Sainte on the left and Hougomont on the right. The loss of one of these was therefore a heavy blow, and portended a last, all-out attack by the Emperor. 'The danger was imminent; and at no other period of the action was the result so precarious as at this moment,' one British staff officer close to La Haye Sainte recorded.

Although Napoleon had made his name with agile, creative grand tactics in Italy in 1796–7 and 1800, his later campaigns had been characterised by grim slugging matches. From Wagram (1809) to Borodino (1812) and Leipzig (1813) he had fought with hundreds of guns, mowing down lines of troops. Armies became so big that the battles could not be settled on one field over one day; they spilled over into a series of engagements. There were intimations here of what warfare would become, with the final struggles of 1813–14 being waged largely on the basis of which side could mobilise the larger army and survive the greater number of reverses in order to prevail in the end.

Wellington's years in the Peninsula left him unprepared in many ways for the realities of the Hundred Days campaign. The battles in Spain and Portugal had been intimate affairs; smaller, with more scope for creative command and for the quality of Britain's little army to show itself. Finding himself at the head of an allied force (of which British troops constituted only about one-third) in Belgium, the Duke had been thrown off balance by the speed with which Napoleon's campaign developed. The excellent intelligence system in Iberia had taken years to develop, whereas early reports of the Emperor's march into Belgium were confusing. The speed of that march, facilitated by northern Europe's excellent roads, was also something Wellington may not have entirely expected.

In order to win, the Duke and the Prussians, under Field Marshal Blücher, had to combine their forces effectively; if Napoleon succeeded in dividing them, disaster would follow. On 16 June, the Emperor had won the first round. Fighting separately, Blücher had taken a heavy pounding at the Battle of Ligny. Wellington had promised him help, but did not deliver, instead fighting the least successful battle of his career several miles away at Quatre Bras. The Duke, convinced until too late that Napoleon was marching by a route further to the north, was forced to feed divisions piecemeal into the fight against his old adversary, Marshal Ney. The result was an inconclusive battle in which some of the best units of the British Army (such as two battalions of Guards and the Black Watch Highlanders) got themselves badly mauled by French cavalry. But, as at Leipzig, a single day's action was not decisive, and, luckily for the allies, Napoleon's own attempts to combine forces on the 16th proved almost as poor as their own.

Waterloo thus offered Wellington a chance to win back a campaign that had got off to a bad start. By the time La Haye Sainte fell, the Duke's army had already been under heavy attack for hours. They had been pounded by a 'Grand Battery' of eighty-two cannon, something unheard of in the Peninsula. They had also faced a great tide of French cavalry, sweeping across the battlefield, many of them the armoured cuirassiers, another unwelcome novelty for British soldiers. The redcoats (both British and Hanoverian troops wore them) and their Belgian allies had withstood this initial punishment.

Much of Wellington's experience in Iberia still held good, though. He concealed many troops behind the ridgeline to protect them from the worst of the cannon fire. That and steady discipline had saved the day when many regiments were forced to form square, seeing off the cuirassiers. But as the hours wore on and his casualties mounted, Wellington must have found himself wondering whether Blücher was going to appear, as he'd promised, or whether the Prussians might hold back, repaying the British for Ligny.

As La Haye Sainte fell, Wellington knew that the Prussians were present in force to his left. They had begun to arrive at about 4 p.m. and a fierce battle had developed for control of a village called Plancenoit. Napoleon had anticipated this threat to his flank earlier in the day, deploying an entire corps in Blücher's path, but as the fighting in Plancenoit intensified, more of the French reserves had been drawn into the struggle. Both sides had therefore reached a point where they were desperate for a breakthrough. It was the French who glimpsed a real opening, right in the centre of Wellington's line.

The Duke's response at this critical moment, as so often, was to head to the threatened sector to supervise its defence in person. The French, capitalising on their success, brought an artillery battery close to the burning farm, near enough to the British general's staff to catch them with a discharge of grapeshot. Not for the first time that day, Wellington came within inches of death: his quartermaster general received his mortal wound at this moment, and several other men were cut down close to their chief.

Through the murk and heavy pall of smoke, the defenders of the Mont Saint Jean ridge then saw something they must have dreaded: nine battalions of the Imperial Guard were making their way up the sloping front of the ridge between Hougomont and La Haye Sainte, drums beating and officers to the fore. The British had some Foot Guards, riflemen of the 2nd/95th and two battalions of light infantry (the 52nd and the 71st) standing in their path. Just to the left of them, the broken remnants of Picton's division had been grouped into another two battalions. The French trudged up the hill, barely flinching as the allied cannon found their mark in the packed columns. Wellington appeared once again. He had already checked the flight of some demoralised Brunswick battalions, brought up a hussar brigade (to act as a reserve) and warned a lowly artillery battery commander to expect the French at any moment, when he reached the Guards. He told them to lie down in a cornfield and await his order.

The French attack columns had been visible when they set off, but they were shielded for agonising minutes by dead ground at the front of the Mont Saint Jean ridge. Then the tops of their hats appeared just a couple of hundred yards in front of the British line. Marching through the hail of fire that felled some of their most distinguished officers, the leading Imperial Guard battalions were heading for what seemed to be a gap in the British centre. They must have believed themselves about to clinch an epic victory.

Judging his moment to perfection, Wellington waited until the leading French were less than 100 yards away before shouting, 'Up Guards! Make Ready!' The redcoats stood, cocked their weapons, levelled them and let fly a hideous, crashing volley. Scores of Imperial Guardsmen dropped to the ground, the battalions swaying collectively from this terrible shock. The British commander and those he had trained during the Peninsular years well understood the value of the short-range volley, followed by a cheer and a bayonet charge. 'Now's the time, my boys!' shouted one of the British Guards officers. At the same moment, the CO of the 52nd Light Infantry (one of the few crack Peninsular regiments on the field of Waterloo) manoeuvred his men into position before ordering a charge into the flank of the wavering French column. In a few moments, Napoleon's last reserve was swept away. The dread cry, '*La Garde recule!*' went up among horrified French spectators: the Imperial Guard had broken and was fleeing.

Of the remaining events of 18 June 1815, little need be said. The British army and its commander, not for the first time, were too exhausted to pursue. That task was taken up with alacrity by the Prussians.

At about 9 p.m., Wellington sat down to take supper with Lieutenant Colonel George Scovell, one of the few surviving members of his staff. 'This is too bad, thus to lose our friends,' said the Duke. 'I trust it will be the last action any of us see.'

After Waterloo, Field Marshal Wellington resumed his role as statesman at the Congress of Vienna. His actions and ambitions became more overtly political. He had set himself on a trajectory which was to take him in 1828 to the office of Prime Minister, a unique distinction for a British soldier.

Because of his choice of career, Wellington's achievements in the Peninsula and at Waterloo became the subject of a debate that was coloured from the beginning by party prejudice. One of the areas that this focused on was the Prussian intervention on 18 June 1815.

In his Waterloo dispatch, the Duke noted, 'I should not do justice to my own feelings, or to Marshal Blücher and the Prussian army, if I did not attribute the successful result of this arduous day to the cordial and timely assistance I received from them.' Later, he noted that there was glory enough for British *and* Prussians in the victory. This grasped the essential truth of the Hundred Days campaign: that victory had been possible only because of close cooperation between himself and Blücher. Nevertheless, from an early stage political partisans sought to 'prove' either that the staunch redcoats had won their great victory without Blücher's tardy assistance or that Wellington was a fraud who had been saved by the Prussians. It is easy to forget, given some of the more ludicrous Victorian panegyrics to the Duke and his army, that there were MPs (mainly Radicals and Whigs) who began questioning his record almost from the moment the guns fell silent. One caricature published in 1825, for example, shows a statue of Wellington toppled from its pedestal and broken by an archetypal member of the London mob, who exults, 'His <u>Honour's</u> all a <u>Joke</u> my boys, and <u>Waterloo's</u> all <u>Smoke</u> my boys.'

Wellington's problem was that he was delighted for others to call him the 'Victor of Waterloo' but considered it vulgar to trumpet his achievements openly, as he pursued the prime ministership. He even tried to dissuade one writer who was contemplating a history of Waterloo, wisely telling him, 'The history of a battle is not unlike the history of a ball.' The Duke was concerned that each participant would exaggerate his own heroics or gloss over failings. Throughout the remainder of his life he refused to write memoirs. This decision can be viewed as one of high principle, but equally it ignored the fact that a vast public demand existed for accounts of the Duke's career, and it was filled by various 'friends' who often just muddied the waters or made claims that Wellington himself would have shied away from.

As the years passed, Wellington evidently grew increasingly irritated by the various books devoted to his campaigns. His initial stance – for example, in sharing the glory with Prussian allies – fell by the wayside and he used a variety of proxies to defend his conduct and hit back at critics.

The years following the Napoleonic Wars added little to his reputation. Reformers who had hoped to eliminate flogging or the purchasing of commissions from the army during that conflict found themselves thwarted after it by a complacent clique of generals who assumed that victory validated their every prejudice. Neither the Duke of York nor Wellington himself were able to maintain any momentum for further reform during the 1820s and 1830s, so it became a time of stagnation.

As for his periods as Prime Minister (1828 to 1830, and briefly during 1834), they are notable for only one achievement: the abolition of discriminatory laws against Catholics. This happened under the threat of civil war in Ireland. It is ironic to observe that years before, during the early 1800s, Arthur Wellesley's Tory associates defined themselves by their refusal to grant more freedom to Irish Catholics. Even in 1828, indeed, many dyed-in-the-wool Tories resented Wellington's change of heart.

However, if the record as Prime Minister left behind little of note, we must never forget the way the Duke deployed political skill in support of his military campaigns. William Napier, a veteran of the Peninsula who wrote one of the first great histories of the war, stressed the political constraints that operated on Wellington: 'He modified and reconciled the great principles of [the military] art with the peculiar difficulties which attend generals controlled by politicians who, depending on private intrigue, prefer parliamentary to national interests.' Napier understood well that Wellington's conservative strategies, particularly during 1808–11, resulted from a fear that 'one disaster [would] be his ruin at home'.

It is obvious from the stories of Marlborough, William Howe and the Duke of York how difficult it was for the commander of a British field army to remain above the party fray. Generals were inevitably seen as constituent parts of the government of the day or as instruments of its war policy, and they were therefore considered fair game in the Palace of Westminster. Any major defeat in Iberia, particularly during 1808–11, would, as Napier surmised, have resulted in the recall of the army, or at least of its commander.

If Wellington was sometimes guilty of spin in his official dispatches, it resulted from his desire to prevent the war's opponents from

bringing about withdrawal. His correspondence affords many fascinating examples of the techniques he used to persuade and cajole those
with any influence over war policy. Late in 1811, hearing rumours that
the Peninsular Army might be withdrawn and sent elsewhere on some
whim in London, the Duke wrote a letter to the Home Secretary. This
text is a masterclass in how a wily soldier might educate an intelligent
but ignorant minister in the military facts of life. It concludes:

Our ministers may depend upon it that they cannot establish anywhere such
a system as they have here; they cannot keep anywhere in check so large a proportion of Bounaparte's army, with such small comparative British means; that
they cannot anywhere be the principals, and carry on the war upon their own
responsibility, at so cheap a rate of men and means as they can here.

The Duke also deployed his skills on those outside the cabinet – an
important tactic for avoiding Marlborough's fate of falling because
he was too closely associated with one faction. He wrote to one MP
early in 1813, 'As I have long ceased to think of home politics, it cannot be said that I am of a party different to that to which any other
person belongs. I serve the country to the best of my ability abroad,
leaving the government at home to be contended for by the parties
as they may think proper.' This protestation might seem blatantly
insincere, coming as it did from someone who was actually a minister
before the Peninsular War and returned to the government benches
after Waterloo, but – give the Duke credit – he was soothing the MP
with words the latter wanted to hear, and cleverly cloaking his political ambitions until the time was right. Those who knew him intimately
were not deceived, however. One of the Duke's lady friends telling him
that claims he was 'no politician' while in positions of high command
were 'ridiculous nonsense'.

Wellington's political sensibilities told him he could not afford to
take heavy losses – a 'casualty-aversion' that will be very familiar
to the modern democratic soldier. His enemy, the French Imperial
Army, on the other hand, was an organisation in which life was held
very cheap and the orders were given by somebody who monopolised
military and political power to an astounding degree. Add to this
the British Army's lack of experience (since Marlborough's day) at
sustaining a Continental campaign for several years and it will be
apparent that getting an army to the battlefield in good order was itself
a triumph for the Duke.

Skills at parliamentary and army management were thus essential for his military campaigns, but it is to those events of course where we must look to Wellington's legacy on history. The Peninsula is sometimes derided as a sideshow by those who wish to give the Russians all the credit for breaking Napoleon. But this, like the Prussians at Waterloo debate, is a pointless argument since it overlooks the fact that a coalition, forcing the French to fight on two fronts, was the key to the destruction of Napoleon. If 35 per cent of the Grande Armée had deserted *before* the Emperor reached Moscow in 1812, it was in large measure due to the fact that the quality of his regiments had fallen badly because of the long war in Spain. The heavy French commitment to Iberia also meant that whole divisions of the army that marched into Russia were made up of inferior conscripts from reluctant allies. The Iberian conflict tied down as many as 300,000 French troops for years; the number who died there is estimated at almost the same figure. This Spanish front proved to be a seven-year drain on Napoleon's strength – the proverbial ulcer; it ground down his army's powers more comprehensively than spectacular but brief episodes like the Austrian campaign on the Danube in 1809.

There is a vocal group that seeks to deny Wellington credit even for the Iberian campaign, praising instead the Spanish guerrillas. Once again, this is a pointless diversion, coming generally from those who have a political axe to grind and find themselves unable to give the English or one of their most distinguished generals credit for anything.

From the outset, the British government saw its intervention as a move in support of Spanish resistance. Huge shipments of British weapons and gold kept the guerrillas going. Spanish field armies, by contrast, were repeatedly defeated and shown incapable of facing French ones. A study of their regimental casualty records also reveals that French losses in areas of heavy guerrilla activity were trivial compared to those in the units that faced the redcoats at Bussaco or Salamanca. The guerrillas were capable of increasing the cost of occupation and did so without mercy, but they couldn't liberate their people. In the end, the Spanish government recognised Wellington's gifts and made him C-in-C of their own armies.

Wellington, Canning and some other ministers understood that one of the principal advantages of fighting in Iberia was that it would allow a British general to add substantial forces of Portuguese and Spanish auxiliaries to the small British field army. That was how the intervention was sold to the cabinet in 1809, and that was how things turned out.

Having husbanded his resources carefully during the early years of the Peninsular Wars, Wellington managed crushing defeats of French armies at Salamanca and Vitoria, invaded France before the other coalition powers in 1814 and finally gave Napoleon his death blow at Waterloo. Many proud Spaniards still resent the fact that they were pawns in the British war against France. Others complain that the 'Germans' were not given sufficient credit for 1815, but – too bad – it was war, and the Duke's depended upon using allies. They were paid to do what they were told.

When the Peninsular campaign and its subsequent fighting in southern France ended in the spring of 1814, Wellington came home after more than five years away. His country moved swiftly to heap honours upon him.

The atmosphere in the House of Lords on 27 June 1814 was one of excitement and self-congratulation. Members packed the benches, straining to catch sight of the Duke of Wellington, who stood close to the Woolsack having just taken his oath. During his long absence from the Palace of Westminster he had been campaigning overseas, rising through the steps of the peerage to a ducal title and through those of the army to field marshal. There was some ceremonial catching up to do, as he made the necessary declarations expected of those receiving such lofty honours.

Wellington stood with his customarily erect bearing as the oath-taking finished and the Lord Chancellor rose to give him the House's thanks. The field marshal looked on, resplendent in his red coat with epaulettes and aiguillettes of thick gold, the jewels of his insignia of the Garter glistening. Recounting Wellington's victories, the Lord Chancellor lauded the Duke for his role in defeating Napoleon. Wellington, he said, had inspired the nations of Europe, 'rescuing them from tyranny, and restoring them to independence, by which there has been ultimately established among all the nations of Europe, that balance of power, which, giving sufficient strength to every nation, provides that no nation shall be too strong'.

Marlborough's 1704 Danube campaign marked the emergence of this type of British interventionism, but Wellington's victories gained his nation a pre-eminent position at the Congress of Vienna in

1814–15 which would dictate the terms of Europe's settlement for an entire century. It is true that this diplomatic work was temporarily interrupted in 1815 by Napoleon's return from exile and Hundred Days campaign culminating in his defeat at Waterloo.

In June 1814, shortly after the Emperor's first abdication, however, their Lordships were quite right to be thanking Wellington. For, notwithstanding Napoleon's brief subsequent campaign, it was during the early summer of 1814 that allied invasions of France (led by the British in the south, advancing across the Pyrenees after their long campaigns in the Iberian peninsula) broke the Emperor's spell over his countrymen. The 1815 events were no more than a bad aftershock, following a series of tremors that had rocked the Continent for decades. Once the Congress of Vienna resumed its business after Waterloo, Britain found itself playing a bigger role in defining Europe's future than it has before or since.

Replying to the Lord Chancellor's oration, Wellington expressed himself, 'entirely overcome by the honours which have been conferred upon me'. He continued, 'In truth, my Lords, when I reflect upon the advantages which I enjoyed in the confidence reposed in me, and the support afforded by the government and by HRH the Commander-in-Chief . . . I am apprehensive that I shall not be found so deserving of your favour as I wish.' It is only fair to note that Wellington wanted to acknowledge the Duke of York's contribution to bolstering Britain's status as a European power. The great work of defeating Napoleon was, as far as British generals went, the work of Wellington first and York second, with the Commander-in-Chief ranking ahead of many more successful battlefield commanders.

The military mind of Wellington was critical in turning the Napoleonic Wars from a struggle for national survival into a triumphant episode. He helped define the strategy and carried it out brilliantly. His victories, along with those of Nelson, assumed a place at the centre of national mythology. The British Army at last became something respected by society at large, and in the process of winning these victories, British concepts of balance of power were used to define the shape of modern Europe.

Charles George Gordon

1833–1885

We trusted him to the utmost.
WILLIAM GLADSTONE

"MIRAGE."

GENERAL GORDON. . . . . . "*WHAT* IS IT THAT I SEEM TO SEE
ACROSS THE SAND WASTE?· IS IT THE QUICK GLEAM
OF ENGLISH STEEL, OR BUT A DESERT-DREAM?
HELP—OR, THAT LAST ILLUSION OF DISTRESS,
THE MOCKING *MIRAGE* OF THE WILDERNESS?"

At dawn the Taiping lookouts examined the great Imperial flotilla on the canal to their west. Their post, Quinsan, crowned a hill that rose out of the flatlands of Kiangsu Province, dominating the canals, lakes, paddies and farmsteads that stretched away in all directions.

That morning of 30 May 1863, the Taiping rebels registered the usual Imperial gunboats, little more than junks adorned with flags and a few scrofulous crewmen, but they saw something else, too. Ploughing down one of the canals to their south, towards their besiegers' little fleet, was a paddle steamer, the *Hyson*. This thrusting embodiment of progress was greeted with alarm. It was a gunboat, mounting a real killing machine, a 32-pounder cannon that could smash down their fortifications. But the most dangerous thing about the *Hyson* was invisible from Quinsan's battlements. It was not the powerful gun or the steam boilers, driving the boat along in contempt of the wind, but the small, busy man on its bridge.

Charles Gordon, a thirty-year-old major in the Royal Engineers, had been given a general's commission in the Imperial forces. He surveyed the wooden stockades and defensive lines around Quinsan with an expert eye. Wellington's officers may have had an embarrassing lack of professional education, but Charles Gordon had sat through a bellyful of it: three years at the Royal Military Academy in Woolwich, followed by two more learning the sapper's art. He had examined the way the Manchu Emperor's men were trying to prosecute their siege against the rebels and he had not been impressed. The British officer felt he could bring about dramatic change. When he had briefed the Imperial general on his plans the night before, the Chinese officer was quite put out. 'General Ching was as sulky as a bear', wrote

Gordon, 'when he was informed that I thought it advisable to take on these stockades.'

In seeking to crush the rebels, the Emperor intended to make full use of modern weaponry and foreign expertise. But Gordon noticed that the European engineers often brought in to direct batteries in siege operations could open up breaches in a city's walls, but were power-less to conclude the siege by storming them. The poorly led Imperial footsloggers simple wouldn't do it. It was for this reason that he brought up 350 stormers – the 4th Regiment of what the Chinese called the 'Ever Victorious Army'. This was a mercenary operation, funded by the merchants of Shanghai, in which white officers (mostly British and American) led Chinese rank and file. Though small in relation to the forces overall, the 4th Regiment would be needed to spearhead any assault, and Gordon knew that he must be prepared to lead by personal example. These men were moved forward in some of the eighty vessels under Gordon's command.

At about noon the gunboats reached a defensive line of stakes that the Taipings had used to block the canal. Under a hail of fire, Imperial troops chopped their way through the obstacle. As the *Hyson* pushed through the splintered wood, thousands of rebel soldiers occupying positions down by the waterways knew they had been outflanked; they broke and ran. Chinese generals were willing to take and inflict huge casualties in battle, but Gordon eschewed such brutality, considering it counter-productive. 'The great thing . . . is to cut off their retreat,' he wrote, explaining why he sought to get around rebel positions, 'and the chances are they will go without trouble; but attack them in front, and leave their rear open, and they will fight most desperately.'

Within minutes of breaking through the palisades, Gordon's flotilla had sailed into a larger waterway, the main canal linking Quinsan with another Taiping stronghold twenty-two miles to its west, Soochow. The horde of fleeing Taipings split in two directions: some to the nearby safety of Quinsan's walls; others, fearing the city doomed, towards Soochow. Gordon divided his forces, sending the 4th Regiment to pursue towards Quinsan and steering the *Hyson* west, down the main channel towards Soochow.

That night, the *Hyson* steamed up and down the canal, harrying swarms of panicked Taipings, frightening them with the blast of its steam whistle and the killing power of 32-pound ordnance. At times, Gordon feared his men would be overwhelmed by sheer numbers, but

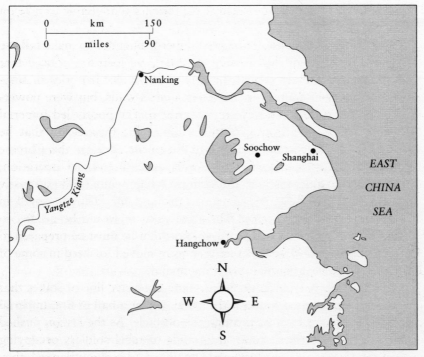

East China, 1863

as it became clear to everyone that the Taiping defences had gone to pieces, local peasants emerged and began to take bloody retribution on the soldiers who had terrorised them. Many of the rebels were beaten to death with farm implements while others drowned in the canals and lakes; something in the order of 4,000 perished.

The following day, Gordon's men took Quinsan. He commented, 'The rebels did not know its importance until they lost it.' There was a touch of sapper arrogance, but also something special about his tactical eye and the inspirational force of his command. In many of the fights in which he led the Ever Victorious Army, Gordon went forward on foot, armed only with the swagger stick (which his men dubbed a magic wand); he seemed to display a contempt for danger and an indefatigable will to succeed. One young British officer who took leave from the 99th Foot in order to join this private army sketched the following pen portrait of its commander: 'a light-built, wiry, middle-sized man, of about thirty two [*sic*] years of age, in the undress uniform of the Royal Engineers. The countenance bore a pleasant frank appearance, eyes light blue with a fearless look in them, hair crisp and inclined to curl, conversation short and decided.'

Through the summer and autumn of 1863, Gordon fought a series of battles to take Soochow's outlying defensive forts and cut it off from its sources of supply. During this long and difficult process, he stemmed incipient mutiny in the Ever Victorious Army. One of its former commanders tried to lead it over to the Taipings, and on one occasion, at least, Gordon ordered the summary execution of one of his soldiers to stem the subversion. He had no illusions about the loyalties of his mercenary band – foreigners and Chinese within it sought plunder and riches and didn't mind serving whoever might give it to them.

The Emperor's war against the rebels (who were motivated by a distinctively Chinese messianic interpretation of Christianity) was an unspeakably brutal affair – claiming in excess of 20 million lives during thirteen years of fighting. Since the rival armies stripped the countryside, many peasants in the contested provinces were stalked by starvation. Cruising back and forth along the many waterways of the Shanghai hinterland, Gordon became oppressed by the suffering he witnessed. 'The horrible furtive looks of the wretched inhabitants hovering around one's boats haunts me,' he wrote, 'and the knowledge of their want of nourishment would sicken anyone; they are like wolves. The dead lie where they fall, and are, in some cases, trodden quite flat by passers by.' Some would later claim that he staunched these feelings with drink, but his principal palliative would become his Bible, for the young Gordon was developing into an intensely religious man.

By early December, with the fall of Soochow imminent, Gordon opened negotiations with the rebel commanders, hoping to avoid an all-out assault. Under this correspondence, he promised them that their lives would be spared if they surrendered the city.

On the morning of 5 December, Gordon and his staff walked into Soochow and met the enemy commanders. As a precaution against pillaging, he ordered the Ever Victorious Army a little further away from the prize. The only men who followed him into the city were therefore Chinese Imperial troops under the provincial governor. Soochow was an important prize, but the war was hardly over. Later, while Gordon busied himself with preparations for his next battle, the governor's soldiers executed the Taiping leaders. Gordon flew into a blind rage. Some accounts suggest he prised a revolver from one of his staff and set off with the intention of shooting the governor. Certainly, several of the letters in which he fulminated survive. In the first place, Gordon considered the executions militarily stupid, noting, 'if faith had been kept, there would have been no more fighting as every town would have given in'. But infuriating him even more was the knowledge that men whose safety he had guaranteed face to face had been so perfidiously killed. Gordon respected the Taiping commanders, he thought them better, man for man, than the Imperial ones, and now he had been made complicit in a massacre.

On 1 January 1864 word reached Gordon, telling him to prepare for the arrival of an Imperial messenger. He ran from his house, down to Soochow's west gate, where he found a procession of flunkeys decked out in fine silks. Several of the servants held open treasure boxes, containing 10,000 silver coins; others carried special banners, gifts from Imperial generals. At the head of the party, a distinguished mandarin known to Gordon brandished a decree. Gordon invited this man into his quarters, but he sent away those bearing gifts. A translator read out the message from the Emperor, which was inscribed with suitably fine calligraphy on yellow silk. It recorded joy and satisfaction at the conquest of Soochow, and bestowed handsome rewards. The British officer took a pen and wrote on the back: 'Major Gordon receives the approbation of His Majesty the Emperor with every gratification, but regrets most sincerely that owing to the circumstances which occurred since the capture of Soochow, he is unable to receive any mark of His Majesty the Emperor's recognition.'

Effectively, Gordon's mission in China was at an end. He did give advice at the siege of Nanking (the bloody denouement of the revolt, in which 100,000 soldiers were killed) but withdrew the Ever Victorious Army from the campaign and, still fearing it might change sides, disbanded it in June 1864. A young Scot who had been sent out to run the Shanghai Customs and who met Gordon many times during these months noted, 'he shows the Chinese that even an able and reliable man, such as he is, is unmanageable'.

Although the authorities in Beijing may have resented Gordon's last actions as commander of the Ever Victorious Army, they felt that they must show gratitude for his leadership in thirty-three successful battles and his invaluable advice in prosecuting sieges. Gordon did not want money – as he had dramatically proved in Soochow – so instead he squeezed a supreme symbolic distinction out of them: admission to the

Emperor's ceremonial bodyguard. This post, limited to forty men, was known as the Yellow Jacket, after the garment of Imperial silk that its holders were entitled to wear. Along with this singular honour came promotion to *ti-tu*, the Chinese rank equivalent to field marshal – heady stuff for a thirty-one-year-old who was still only a major in the British Army.

Before Gordon left Shanghai, he also received the grateful thanks of the trading houses who had hired the Ever Victorious Army in the first place. Once again he eschewed financial rewards. 'I know I shall leave China as poor as I entered it,' he wrote a few weeks before his departure from China, 'but with the knowledge that, through my weak instrumentality, upwards of eighty to one hundred thousand lives have been spared. I want no further satisfaction than this.'

To those looking at Gordon's actions now, the thanks of companies trading in opium or of a government that killed millions in its suppression of rebellion might seem like the most poisonous endorsements. But at the time people saw a brave man who acted with humanity in an otherwise ghastly conflict, standing out from the other mercenaries, adventurers and cut-throats in wanting almost nothing for himself. *The Times* lionised him in August 1864: 'the part of the soldier of fortune is in these days very difficult to play with honour . . . but if ever the actions of a soldier fighting in a foreign service ought to be viewed with indulgence, and even with admiration, this exceptional tribute is due to Colonel Gordon'. The newspaper paeans were followed by a book extolling the deeds of the Ever Victorious Army. The man who returned home to the garrison duties of Commanding Royal Engineer at Gravesend had become an exotic celebrity, known thereafter to many Britons as 'Chinese Gordon'.

He was to serve for six years in this dull posting in eastern England. One of the few compensations for Gordon, who was often nervous and diffident with strangers, was that his noteriety faded somewhat during this time. He did have a circle of army and family friends, so it would be wrong to cast him as a dysfunctional loner. However, Gordon did not marry; nor was he romantically linked with any woman or, for that matter, man. He seems to have been 'asexual', finding physical intimacy impossibly difficult.

To his family, Gordon shrugged off suggestions that he should marry by asserting that his life as a soldier and desire to serve again overseas effectively made him a dead man, unable to bring anything but heartache to a wife. He devoted much of his spare time in Gravesend to charitable work, trying to do something for the boys he found begging on the street. It is possible that he had sexual feelings for these urchins, but there is no evidence that he ever acted upon them. We can only speculate that his increasing religious devotion may have been an outward manifestation of an internal struggle against sexual temptation.

The Britain that this sometimes tortured Gordon would have observed while superintending the Thames Estuary defences was a place of dizzying change. Reform Acts were extending the franchise: the one in 1867, for example, doubled the electorate to over 2 million. This gave votes to urban artisans or householders, while a further Act in 1884 brought men in the countryside up to a sort of parity and took the electorate to over 5 million. There were millions of proud John Bulls among the newly enfranchised who cared a great deal for the rights of Britons and the prerogatives of empire and very little for foreigners. The implications for policy, particularly overseas, were profound.

These changes brought good and bad to those in uniform. On the positive side, soldiers could reflect that their army had become a source of national pride – the public contempt of the 1790s, as noted by Napier, had been replaced by celebration of the redcoats' derring-do at Quebec, Assaye and Waterloo. Within the army itself, though, there was a looming anxiety that it was desperately in need of reform. The officers worried about some reverse damaging public esteem. The Crimean campaign (1854–5; Gordon was a veteran of it) had already shown the risks of stagnation and inefficiency. At Horse Guards they struggled to keep pace with technological change, industry's thirst for manpower (at the expense of the army) and constant demands for policing operations in far-flung corners of the world.

Firepower was being revolutionised: new rifles like the Martini-Henry had an effective range an order of magnitude greater than the Brown Bess musket; the artillery was switching to breech-loading, rifled cannon that marked a similar change; and early machine-guns were appearing. The time it took a man to run 500 yards was constant, but the dramatic advance in firepower increased manyfold a defender's chance of felling his attacker before he could close. Initially, Zulus or Afghans learned the ghastly lesson of what this meant, but in time the British soldier would also get his grim education. Railways, steamships and the telegraph were bringing about similar changes in strategic movement and the ability of nations to mobilise. America's civil war had shown the devastating scale of conflict between industrial powers.

Ministers and generals tried to keep what was good about the Wellingtonian army and scrap what was bad. The purchase of officers' commissions was ended (1871), as was flogging in peacetime (1881); the famous red coat was ditched in favour of khaki (from around 1883). During the latter part of the nineteenth century, though, change itself became increasingly controversial within the army, with the result that many came to regard it as a bastion of conservatism in all things.

As the franchise widened and successive Reform Acts changed the character of elections, the old system of landowners getting their sons elected to the Commons began to decline. Since this class still sent many of its offspring into the army, the net effect was to reduce military representation at Westminster. Something more profound was afoot too: people expected greater professional commitment from both their military and their MPs, making it harder for anyone to combine the two occupations. 'How can a man serve the Crown and the People at the same time?' asked the Speaker of the Commons during a debate in 1880. 'These days faithful service of the Crown and People is almost impossible.'

The army's declining presence at Westminster was but one facet of the great social change that produced an all-powerful House of Commons and, through it, demands for tougher civilian scrutiny of the military. The year in which Gordon was finally to escape his posting at Gravesend was also the one in which the (civilian) War Office and (military) Horse Guards merged as one of the post-Crimean War measures designed to give politicians greater control over the army's finances and administration.

Divisive debates about reform and civilian supervision triggered bitter battles between generals. Some blamed the Commander-in-Chief (the Duke of Cambridge) for failing to seize the initiative in matters of reform, calling him an 'utter reactionary'. Others cast the net far more widely, believing that the officer corps carried the ethos of the gentleman amateur to ridiculous extremes. Those who saw in the victories of the previous century proof positive that it was a man's character that qualified him for command often promoted the dim, eccentric and plain loopy to the top of the organisation.

The 1870s and 1880s therefore saw Britain as a nervous superpower, with endless committees, books and newspaper columns discussing diverse threats to its dominance. In the atmosphere of burgeoning technology as well as democratic change, the army often looked to its most educated soldiers – the gunner and sapper officers who graduated from Woolwich – to make sense of these challenges. Gordon, with his Chinese experience, was thus eminently employable. Almost as soon as he had arrived in Gravesend he had feared boredom and expressed a desire for more foreign service. As his years there came to an end, he found himself utterly sick of the social round and public posing that made up so much of life on home service. In 1871 he finally left the garrison, embarking on foreign adventures that would take up most of his remaining years.

The figure who appeared through Darfur's shimmering desert heat haze bore little similarity to the colonel commanding at Gravesend. Mounted on a strapping charger, the forty-four-year-old Gordon wore the dark blue dress tunic of an Egyptian *pasha*, or general. The lapels, cuffs and collar were embroidered with florid gold. On top of his head was the red *tarboush*, or fez, that distinguished a man of substance in the Ottoman culture. His hair was a little greyer and receding; he was a little heavier too, and sunburned; but his blue eyes still burnt with brilliant energy. The Gordon who thus rode out on 2 September 1877, as if dressed for an official do in Cairo, was traversing a province in open revolt, heading for the camp of an apparently implacable opponent. He had with him only a few *bashi-bazouks* of the nearby garrison as an escort, and knew that these troops manned their posts in Dara (the local caravan stop) in fear and trepidation, daily expecting to be massacred by the hundreds of rebels who lurked near by.

Gordon reasoned that the best way to confront his enemies – a ruthless band of Darfuri slave traders and malcontents – was to behave with the dignity and confidence of a man backed by some huge power. It was vital not to show fear, and this was something Gordon always managed, not because he was good at hiding it but, many accounts and his own writings suggest, because he was so completely trusting in divine providence that he almost never felt it.

Nearing the rebel encampment, Gordon was met by Suleiman, leader of the rebel band. The twenty-two-year-old Arab was the son of a man called Zubair, Sudan's most notorious slave trader. They knew that Gordon was not good for business. Writing home to his sister, Gordon *pasha* described what happened next: 'I . . . rode through the robber bands, there were about 3,000 of them, boys and men. I rode to the tent in the camp, the whole of these chiefs were dumbfounded at my coming among them.' Once seated inside, the lone general delivered a peremptory summons: Suleiman was to come to Dara to discuss how an end might be brought to the state of rebellion.

During that second meeting in Dara, Gordon told the young chieftain that he would 'disarm them and break them', if they did not accept the government's authority. These were tense moments, for the Darfuris had entered the meeting armed, which was a breach of desert courtesy, as well as being in marked contrast to Gordon's own courageous behaviour. There was the promise of carrot as well as stick, though. If Suleiman and his cohorts disbanded their raiding party (which roamed the country abducting youngsters, spiriting them away to be sold as slaves), administrative posts would be found for them. There was an uneasy stalemate for days, until one of Suleiman's lieutenants broke ranks and pledged loyalty to the authorities. Suleiman himself grudgingly followed suit, to be sent to a minor job in another province. Word of Gordon's icy determination and extraordinary bravery travelled through Sudan.

Gordon had been Governor General since early 1877. Prior to that, he had been posted to the governorship of Equatoria, the southern province of Sudan where the people were mostly black tribesmen who worshipped the spirits of the rain forest but were being busily converted by Christian missionaries. These Africans had naturally supported Gordon's attempts to bring greater order to their region because they were the principal victims of the Arab slave traders. With his promotion to the governor generalship Gordon was given a far wider canvas for his attempts to suppress this traffic. The only forces available to him to impose his will, first in Equatoria and then across the whole of Sudan, were poorly trained native troops (from either Sudan or Egypt) belonging to the Egyptian Army.

Gordon's trappings of power were those of the Ottoman Empire, but for decades a succession of khedives (dictators in Cairo) had run their own show, directing matters in both Egypt and Sudan. From time to time, new *pashas* were sent out by order of Istanbul – Turkish, Circassian or Balkan generals who gripped some province or other, extorted money from the locals, passed some of it up the chain of command and pocketed the rest. Their interests were in preserving a measure of administrative stability and in kickbacks, or *baksheesh*. In theory, the European officers who came to serve as *pashas* were there to give the Khedive exactly what they had given the Manchu Emperor in China: some foreign drive and know-how in return for rank and cash. In practice, though, other European agendas were playing themselves out in Egypt and its Sudanese dependency.

The khedives' system was bankrupt in virtually every sense. Paying the army or trying to modernise by railway or port construction meant these rulers were increasingly indebted to European lenders. The Suez Canal, in particular, proved enormously costly. The scramble for Africa was at its frenzied peak – the European powers competed to carve up unclaimed regions of the 'dark continent'. In London, Paris or Rome they greedily eyed the 'sick man' of the Ottoman system, awaiting its collapse, but ready in the meantime to use credit as a point of leverage.

To the British government, slavery was important. The Anti-Slavery Society had emerged as an early, powerful, lobby group. Newspaper readers in Bolton or Beaminster had become enraged by stories about chained black children, cruelly abducted, being sold into the slave markets, and they applauded enthusiastically reports of the Royal Navy boarding the traffickers' boats and liberating their human cargo. The Reform Acts gave many of these angry Britons electoral power.

On interviewing Gordon, en route to Equatoria in 1874, Khedive Ismail had remarked, 'What an extraordinary Englishman! He doesn't want money.' Given his Christian devotion, it should be no surprise that this incorruptible officer was more interested in suppressing the slave trade, even if he sometimes found the pronouncements of the Anti-Slavery Society irksome and naïve. But Gordon wanted something else, too. Asked later about his years as Governor General, he said, 'I taught the natives they had a right to exist.' It was the oppressive nature of the system of power itself that increasingly he sought to reform.

The years of his governorship were times of ceaseless travel, with the British officer often riding his camel for days across the desert, outstripping his escort to reach some remote outpost or near-mutinous garrison. In each place he tried to reconcile the Sudanese to the authority of Khartoum, to new ideas of how the country should be run, and to instil better discipline in the 40,000 or so troops who garrisoned the country.

Accounts of his comings and goings from the Governor's Palace on the banks of the Nile in Khartoum give a good idea of his popularity. 'Government officials, consular agents and native people awaited him in large numbers,' wrote one observer who watched Gordon disembark from a river steamer. '[They] celebrated H.E.'s arrival with an indescribable uproar.'

There can be no doubt that this acclaim (a public acknowledgement of his energy, bravery and honesty) seduced the solitary warrior. However, when it came to bringing about substantial change in the mid-1870s, he faced enormous difficulties. For example, Gordon helped draft the Anglo-Egyptian Slave Convention of 1877, which sought to outlaw the trade in twelve years. But he soon found resistance to it at every level, from the *bashi-bazouk* irregulars, who were supposed to patrol the borders (but took bribes to allow the slavers' caravans to pass), to the *pashas* themselves, who refused to enforce the new laws. By the time he left, early in 1880, he had been forced to accept that progress against slavery had been slight.

In struggling to bring about change, Gordon tried to use foreigners but faced the usual colonial dilemmas: the Europeans who were available were often inept or corrupt misfits; the *pashas* subverted change; tribal and religious differences simmered under the veneer of nationhood.

Licurgo Santoni, an Italian brought in to reorganise the Sudanese post office, left this lucid assessment of Gordon's rule:

as his exertions were not supported by his subordinates his efforts remained fruitless. This man's activity with the scientific knowledge which he possesses is doubtless able to achieve much, but unfortunately no one backs him up and his orders are badly carried out or altered in such a way as to render them without effect. All the Europeans, with some rare exceptions, whom he has honoured with his confidence, have cheated him.

By the time his three years as Governor General were over, a thwarted Gordon was physically and mentally spent. One of those who saw him travelling back through Egypt declared Gordon 'rather off his head'. The outgoing Governor General had been trying to send telegrams full of biblical quotations to various departments in London. On 8 January 1880 he boarded a steamer at Alexandria and headed for home.

If Gordon's life was a voyage, his 1877–80 term in Sudan marked a halfway point between him doing what he did best – leading soldiers in battle – and its final chapters when his political ineptitude would produce an epic tragedy. Episodes like his lone ride at Dara could still inspire, but his piecemeal attempts to reform an entire system of power showed that he had strayed too far from the practical certainties of siege warfare, his grasp of which had been so impressive in China. Rank and reputation had carried Gordon into the world of political management, where his sense of destiny, biblical inspiration and personal idiosyncrasies all counted against him.

William Stead, editor of the *Pall Mall Gazette*, moved with commendable journalistic vigour one murky January morning in 1884. He took the train to Southampton, making his way to Rockstone Place, the home of Augusta Gordon, the general's sister. During the years since leaving Alexandria her brother had criss-crossed the globe: passing through Africa, India, China and finally Palestine, where he allowed himself almost one year's 'career break' exploring biblical sites and his own spirituality. Stead, an active thirty-four-year-old, knew that it was rare to catch Chinese Gordon in England, so, ignoring the general's telegram telling him not to come, he made his way to the front door of a modest house in Southampton.

The editor had an agenda. In the first place, he wanted Charley Gordon's views on the revolt in Sudan. Since August 1881 Mohammed Ibn Ahmed al-Sayyid Abdullah had led a popular army, snuffing out garrisons of the Egyptian Army. This subversive had proclaimed himself the Mahdi – messenger of the Prophet Mohammed. The revolt had thus assumed a religious hue, gathering pace and supporters, until in November 1883 it inflicted a stunning blow against the *pashas*. A column of 8,000 Egyptian Army troops led by William Hicks (a veteran British officer serving as a *pasha*) had been wiped out by the Mahdists in western Sudan. By this victory the rebels obtained Krupps field guns and hundreds of modern Remington rifles. The symbolic importance of defeating such a large column and killing a British general was even greater, of course. The British public received these reports with apprehension, but it is worth recording that there were few calls to avenge the death of Hicks, for he was no military celebrity.

The Mahdi's rebellion gained hundreds of thousands of adherents in the western provinces of Darfur and Kordofan, as well as in the east, where a charismatic leader called Osman Digna mobilised the Haddendowa tribes – the men later dubbed 'fuzzy-wuzzies' by British soldiers. Government forces had, by the end of 1883, been hemmed into narrow corridors: along Sudan's Red Sea coast, where their posts were besieged by Digna's warriors, and the Nile valley, which bisected the country broadly north to south and included the capital Khartoum. So intimidated were the Sudanese, Egyptian and Turkish members of these garrisons that their survival relied upon waterborne firepower – from river steamers along the Nile, the Royal Navy and Egyptian gunboats at sea – keeping the rebels at bay.

There were influential people in London who considered it Britain's duty to crush the revolt, so Stead did not just go to Southampton to seek Gordon's opinions as a Sudan expert. The terms of engagement in Egypt and Sudan had shifted dramatically since Gordon's previous service there. British forces had intervened in Egypt in 1882, putting down a revolt by a nationalist army officer, in the process sucking that nominally Ottoman possession into the Imperial orbit. Having troops in Egypt, being a principal creditor and installing a new khedive, Britain thus owned a big stake in the country and its Sudanese dependency to the south. Even so, if there were army officers who saw the Mahdist revolt as a threat to Britain's hegemony in Egypt, this was certainly not the Prime Minister's view.

William Gladstone, already a septuagenarian titan of the political scene, had set his face against intervention in Egypt. Having been outmanoeuvred by the War Office in 1882, he was quite sure that he did not intend to send British troops into Sudan as well. 'Gladstone was ducking and weaving to try and preserve the standards of mid-Victorian restraint in the much more imperialist climate of the 1880s,' according to his recent biographer Roy Jenkins. The Prime Minister came to the view that the Sudanese rising was a spontaneous movement that had more in common with his own views of progress than with the plans of those who would reconquer the country. Britain had no place in Sudan, he believed, except to assist in the complete withdrawal of the Egyptian Army from that country.

The journalist who was led into the parlour at Rockstone Place knew that some important people wanted Gordon to suppress the Mahdists. But it wasn't just Mr Gladstone who had other ideas. Major General Gordon was about to take up a position in the Belgian service, running the Congo. As their conversation began, Gordon spread a map of the Belgian colony on the floor and spoke volubly about his plans. Stead tried to change the subject to Sudan. The general parried him; he didn't want to talk about it. Tea arrived. The journalist persisted; he wanted to hear Gordon's views about the Mahdist revolt. Captain John Brocklehurst, a friend of Gordon's who was also in the parlour, must have wondered whether Stead was about to offend the general with all this prodding. But then Gordon cracked, and once he had started, he poured forth excitedly on the subject for the next two hours.

Stead raced back to London with his scoop, which was published in the *Pall Mall Gazette* on 9 January. He had taken no notes during Gordon's long tirade, but the general never disputed the lengthy passages of direct quotation produced in the paper. Captain Brocklehurst, indeed, even commented that Mr Stead had remembered his friend's pronouncements with remarkable accuracy. 'A population which had begun to appreciate something like decent government', said Gordon, reflecting on his earlier period in Khartoum, 'was flung back to suffer the worst excesses of Turkish rule.' He saw the revolt in very self-centred terms, arguing it was the natural reaction of a people whom he had taught they had a right to exist. He dismissed the Islamic dimension, saying, 'I am convinced that it is an entire mistake to regard the Mahdi as in any sense a religious leader: he personifies popular discontent.'

As for what Britain should do about it all, Gordon articulated views that were identical to those of certain Imperialist ultras at the War Office and diametrically opposed to the Prime Minister's thinking. The mighty Nile linked events in Sudan inextricably to those in Egypt. Gordon was in favour of vigorous intervention to crush the revolt. 'The danger', he said, expounding a domino theory, 'arises from the influence which the spectacle of a conquering Mahometan Power established close to your frontiers will exercise upon the population which you govern. In all the cities of Egypt it will be felt that what the Mahdi has done they may do; and, as he has driven out the intruder, they may do the same.' Gordon ridiculed the idea that Britain might draw a new defensive line on Egypt's desert border with Sudan – precisely the strategy the Prime Minister was advocating.

The *Pall Mall Gazette* accompanied its interview with a leading article headlined 'Chinese Gordon for the Sudan'. The message, obviously enough, was that only one man had the skill and moral qualities required to stabilise the disastrous situation in Sudan. With this leader, William Stead's real motive in going to Southampton revealed itself at last. As to who tipped him off that the general would be staying there for just a couple of nights, we can only speculate.

Gordon himself then set off on a progress through England, visiting friends, while the shock waves caused by his interview and the paper's direct advocacy reverberated around Whitehall. It was not the first time that Gordon's name had been mentioned in connection with Sudan, but until that moment those opposed to such an appointment had easily batted it away. The chief doubter was Sir Evelyn Baring, a fellow graduate of the Royal Military Academy at Woolwich (albeit a gunner) who had risen to the powerful civilian position of British Agent in Cairo. Baring remembered difficult encounters with Gordon during his previous posting to Khartoum – indeed, the British Agent's support for Ismail's replacement as Khedive was one of the principal reasons why Gordon had quit the governor generalship. Privately, Baring considered Gordon to be unstable, and entirely unsuitable for the job, but in official correspondence he confined himself to political considerations, such as the undesirability of sending a staunch Christian to quell a Muslim rebellion.

However, neither Baring nor Gladstone had any idea what they were up against. The *Pall Mall Gazette* articles, in short, began a new chapter in international politics: powerful men using media manipulation of public opinion to trigger war. It is often suggested that the campaign by William Randolph Hearst's papers that led to the US invasion of Cuba in 1896 was the world's first episode of this kind, but the British press deserves these dubious laurels for its actions a full twelve years earlier. The day after Gordon's interview was published, the Foreign Secretary sent a telegram to Cairo, asking Baring to consent to the general's appointment. Once again, Baring refused.

On 14 January, a further blow was struck by those lobbying for Gordon's appointment. A letter from him to another general with an interest in Sudan policy was passed to *The Times*. It contained more forceful statements in a similar vein to those reported five days earlier. The paper published it and there was an instant clamour in gentlemen's clubs and even in fashionable salons: 'Chinese Gordon for the Sudan'.

Who, though, were the powerful men who sought to outwit Baring, subvert the Prime Minister's policy and intervene in Sudan? Their most strident voice in the War Office was undoubtedly General Lord Garnet Wolseley, the Adjutant General. It was he who summoned Gordon up to London to talk about Sudan. Minutes of his 15 January meeting with Gordon at the War Office do not survive, but it was apparent that he suggested 'Chinese' forget about his Congo plans and head to Sudan instead. At this point, Wolseley relayed the cabinet's message that the purpose of the mission was to withdraw the Egyptian Army's remaining garrisons, although within a matter of weeks the Adjutant General would reveal quite different ideas. For Wolseley was a committed expansionist. His command of the 1882 British expedition to Egypt had set the seal on an impressive record of colonial soldiering in Canada and West Africa. Small, active and choleric, he was purportedly the 'very model of a modern major general' celebrated by Gilbert and Sullivan. There is no clear evidence that Wolseley had sent Stead to Southampton and orchestrated the subsequent press campaign, but we may suspect it. He shown himself ready to use the newspapers during many battles over army reform and in his campaign to oust the Duke of Cambridge, whom he despised, as C-in-C.

General Wolseley wrote that 'the press has become a power which a man should try to manage for himself'. In pursuing his goals, it is clear that the Adjutant General was ready to woo journalists, politicians and even the Queen. Initially, this meant forming close ties with Gladstone's Liberals, but the Egypt and Sudan issues eventually destroyed this relationship. Embittered by his failure to manipulate these debates more effectively, Wolseley developed a contempt for most politicians and sought to limit their influence over the army and even over strategic policy more generally.

Around the same time that Gordon left Wolseley's office, the Foreign Secretary, doubtless having read *The Times*, was sending a telegram to Egypt, again urging Baring to accept the appointment and assuring the British Agent that 'his mission [was] to report to Her Majesty's Government on the military situation, and to return without any further engagement'. It proved to be third time lucky. Baring replied on the 16th, putting a brave face on his acquiescence: 'I would rather have him than anyone else, provided there is a perfectly clear understanding with him as to what his position is to be and what line of policy he is to carry out.'

On 18 January, Wolseley took Gordon to meet four members of the cabinet for an official interview to ratify his appointment. As the two generals entered, they were greeted by those representing the War Office, Admiralty, Foreign Office and, since ministers were scarce in London that day, the Local Government Board. Gladstone and some other cabinet members who worried about extending colonial entanglements were not there. The conversation was brief, being led by Lord Hartington, an old-school Whig aristocrat who was Secretary of War. Did Gordon understand his instructions? When could he leave? 'Tonight,' came the reply.

Just a few hours later, Gordon was packed off on a train from Charing Cross before anyone could change their mind. The Foreign Secretary bought the ticket to Cairo; the Duke of Cambridge held open the carriage door (having hot-footed it from shooting 178 birds in Richmond Park); Lord Hartington and General Wolseley said good-bye. They handed Gordon a bagful of cash that had been collected on a swift trawl of London clubs and bade him God-speed. Chinese Gordon was off on another adventure.

The wiser political heads present at that fateful meeting felt uneasy afterwards. They knew that they had been pushed by a press and army campaign into sending a man who was publicly at odds with the policy of their own government. 'We were proud of ourselves yesterday,' wrote the Foreign Secretary to Lord Hartington the next day, before asking pointedly: 'Are you sure we didn't commit a gigantic folly?'

Less than three weeks after Gordon's departure, Valentine Baker found himself at the head of a motley force of native troops marching out of Trinkatat, a port on Sudan's Red Sea coast. He had about 2,500 men, most of them Egyptian gendarmes who were little more than a pressed rabble. They had joined the police in order to avoid serving in the army in Sudan only to be shipped there in order to prop up the *pasha's* crumbling power. Baker was an archetypal Victorian cad: a skilled cavalry officer, he was cashiered after indecently assaulting a woman on a train. Since the British Army would no longer have him, he ended up in the service of the Khedive. Baker's brigade was striking out towards an inland garrison besieged by Osman Digna's men. It did not get very far.

The Haddendowa were experts at concealment, lying in rocky clefts or behind thorn bushes, thousands of them remained invisible to Baker's column as it marched right into their midst. When the signal was given, they sprang up. Men clad only in loincloths, armed with short spears or swords and carrying flimsy hide shields, charged the Egyptian infantry. In seconds they were among them, launching themselves into scattered rifle fire as panic gripped Baker's levies. In this

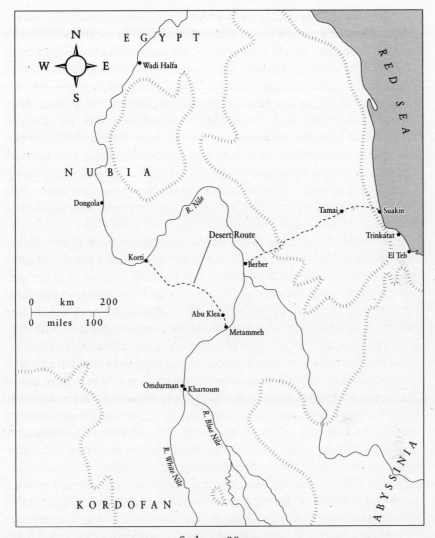

Sudan, 1884–5

situation no quarter was given. The Haddendowa hacked and stabbed the screaming northerners as they begged for mercy. Baker and a small bodyguard of horse cut their way through the mêlée and were pursued by enemy cavalry for five miles before making good their escape. It was another massacre: more than 2,300 of Baker's men lay dead.

Although Gordon hadn't even reached Khartoum yet, Baker's defeat caused the ultras in London to declare their real aims. General

Wolseley started advocating the British annexation of Sudan. Queen Victoria, who emerged as a powerful supporter of the London-based Imperialist faction, wrote anxiously to her private secretary, 'It is *our prestige*, the British name, wh. is humiliated, our *safety* in India and *every* where in the Colonies wh. is being imperilled. It *really* is too *dreadful*.' Although Gladstone dismissed the Queen's views on strategy as 'quite worthless', he nevertheless consented to the landing of marines and urgent dispatch of a British Army brigade to eastern Sudan to prop up what remained of government power there. Direct intervention had begun.

Gordon's reaction to the worsening situation was hardly what one might expect from a good Christian. Calling the rebels 'a feeble lot of stinking Dervishes', he urged the government to 'smash up the Mahdi'. It was this outspoken advocacy, replayed through the newspapers, that made Gordon more responsible for what happened than the secret whisperings of Viscount Wolseley.

As he progressed towards the Sudanese capital, Gordon accompanied bellicose messages home with some disastrous public acts. Shortly after entering the country, he made a proclamation that his earlier anti-slavery policies would no longer be enforced. This caused bewilderment in Britain. For many people, Gordon's credentials as a fighter against human trafficking were among his most impressive qualities. Travelling south by Nile steamer, news of further bizarre initiatives by the general reached Cairo almost daily. He sent an offer of reconciliation to the Mahdi, and enclosed the ceremonial garb of a provincial governor. It was the height of naïvety to think the leader of this popular revolution might subordinate himself to a non-believer. When Gordon eventually received a reply, it was in the form of an invitation to accept Islam and came with a *jibbeh*, a tunic that symbolised the Mahdist revolt.

The Governor General's most stupid mistake, though, came on 12 February 1884. Addressing a group of tribal leaders in Berber, about 150 miles downstream from the capital, he revealed his secret orders from the Khedive: that he had come to Sudan in order to evacuate the Egyptian Army. In his *Pall Mall Gazette* interview of the previous month, Gordon himself had discussed the dangers of announcing a withdrawal, noting, 'The moment it is known that we have given up the game, every man will go over to the Mahdi.' He was right in this particular anyhow, for, in the weeks that followed the Berber meeting, all of the tribal leaders who had been present joined the revolt.

This was to prove particularly disastrous to his own mission, because these men would help the Mahdi to cut the route from Khartoum north to Cairo. Gordon later conceded his mistake at Berber in his own journal.

On 18 February, he at last reached Khartoum and for a couple of weeks attempted to carry out the gist of his original mission, which was to form a government from leading Sudanese families prior to beginning the withdrawal. But the Mahdists were gathering strength by the day, so nobody of real stature would cooperate; increasingly, Gordon seems to have been preparing for a siege of the city.

Back in London, General Wolseley, detecting the consternation in Whitehall at Gordon's pronouncements during the trip down, was worried that his man might prove a loose cannon, obstructing rather than furthering his plans to take over Sudan. He sent Gordon a damage-limitation message which encouraged him to keep his civilian masters in the dark: 'My private advice. Do not answer telegrams about your doings.'

The Governor General, however, had no intention of being silenced by Wolseley or anyone else. Soon after arriving, he met Frank Power, an Irishman in his mid-twenties who combined the posts of British Consul and correspondent for *The Times*. Power fell under Gordon's spell at once, having realised that Gordon shared none of the anti-Catholic prejudice of the British ruling class, and enthused, 'He is indeed I believe the greatest man of this century.' With Power on side, Gordon once again had a direct channel for rousing public opinion back in Britain. In the weeks that followed, the Irishman's dispatches switched the story from the tangled detail of Gordon's political errors and back to the simple narrative of the lone British hero standing firm against hordes of murderous fanatics.

During the latter part of February and the following month, the mission sank into crisis. On 13 March, British units advancing from the Red Sea coast fought Osman Digna's warriors at Tamai. They were on their way to relieve an Egyptian garrison, but their move was also a possible first stage towards a push deeper inland to Berber, aimed at taking the pressure off Gordon or even relieving him. The army got a nasty shock at Tamai, for at one point one side of a British square (the Black Watch, no less) had opened its formation, only to be rushed, seemingly from out of the ground, by fearless Haddendowa – a critical situation many soldiers saw as the prelude to a massacre. The Highlanders fought back well (their generals later even declared a victory), but 106 British officers and men were killed. The enemy had rushed into the fire of Martini-Henrys and machine-guns manned by naval parties. Surveying the field afterwards, British soldiers saw hundreds of fuzzy-wuzzies with great chunks blown out of them by the slugs from their weapons. Even these critically injured Haddendowa had still tried to stab their enemies, with one British observer noting grimly, 'We killed nearly all the wounded, as it wasn't safe to leave them.'

The British returned to the port of Suakin, where they shut themselves in and awaited further guidance from London. One war correspondent who had been at Tamai wrote: 'There is more grumbling than I have ever known among soldiers and officers about the whole business. They are constantly asking, "Why are we here? Why are we killing such brave fellows? Surely not for the sake of the wretched Egyptians." It is impossible to magnify the intensity of the feeling thus indicated.'

Encumbered by poor morale and a grim sense of the strength of their enemy, the brigade commander decided to abandon attempts to force his way through to Berber. He later blamed government orders for this, and it is true that Whitehall was anxious about this brigade being sucked deep into the country. Equally, to have pressed ahead to Berber in the face of the resistance displayed at Tamai would have been an act as rash as 'Gentleman Johnny' Burgoyne's disastrous 1777 advance to Saratoga. Those in London who favoured taking over Sudan had underestimated their enemy and expected too much of British soldiers.

The battles in the east and the abandonment of any thrust towards Berber were interpreted by the Sudanese as a defeat for the British (even though the cost was thousands of Haddendowa dead). As news of these events reached the Nile town where Gordon had made his ill-fated remarks in February, the tribes north of Khartoum formally declared their support of the Mahdi. Gordon resolved to fortify Khartoum and hold out there. He began using his official dispatches to support his personal policy, later writing on the cover of one, 'No secret as far as I am concerned.' As in Marlborough's or Wellington's day, letters written on public business were public property and could be published without restriction. There was still no culture of official secrecy at this time (the first stirrings in this regard came in Whitehall during the 1880s), and there had been a dramatic expansion of voters and the newspapers that they consumed since Waterloo. So the press made the most of it as the debate in Britain turned away from any notion of withdrawal and towards the issue of what on earth the government could do to save Gordon.

During the final days of March tens of thousands of Mahdist troops surrounded Khartoum. Initially, it was more of a blockade than a siege, but gradually that was precisely what it became. This crisis gave great drama to Frank Power's articles in *The Times*. Late in March he wrote: 'We are daily expecting British troops. We cannot bring ourselves to believe that we are to be abandoned.' Within weeks the telegraph lines were cut and messages from this correspondent and the general he admired so much had to be smuggled out by messenger.

The clamour for a rescue mission posed a dilemma for the cabinet. A few members thought Gordon's insubordination meant he deserved everything he got. However, the government could not ignore the political realities. The India Secretary, one of those doubters absent from the 18 January meeting that had appointed Gordon, summed it up eloquently: 'The London newspapers and the Tories clamour for an expedition to Khartoum, the former from ignorance, the latter because it is the best mode of embarrassing us . . . Of course it is not an impossible undertaking, but it is melancholy to think of the waste of lives and treasure which it must involve.'

As Prime Minister, Gladstone listened to this debate with growing annoyance. He could see that he was being outmanoeuvred by those bent on an interventionist policy that ran counter to everything he believed. At the end of February, he wrote to the Queen that he would try to help the general but noted difficulties had been created by 'the number and rapidity of his various declarations, in some instances from their want of consistency, and from his too free communications with persons who act as correspondents of the public journals'.

Gladstone was experiencing the power of the press to mobilise a highly nationalistic people, and it drove him to distraction. One contemporary who was accompanying the Prime Minister on a trip to the provinces recorded what happened when he saw the latest dispatches from Khartoum in that morning's paper: 'As he read, his face hardened and whitened, the eyes burned as I had seen them once or twice in the House of Commons when he was angered – burned with a deep fire, as if they could have consumed the sheet on which Gordon's message was printed . . . Then he rose without a word, and was seen no more that morning.'

Gordon's telegrams, in the last few days before the lines were cut, became strident indictments of government policy and were evidently intended for publication. In one he fulminated to Sir Evelyn Baring in Cairo: 'You state your intention of not sending any relief force up here to Berber . . . I shall hold on here as long as I can, and if I can suppress the rebellion I shall do so. If I cannot, I shall retire to the Equator [i.e., south of Khartoum] and leave you with the indelible disgrace of abandoning the garrisons.'

In London General Wolseley took the cue to lobby harder for a major military expedition. Secretary of War Hartington was still sitting on the fence, trying to reconcile different cabinet views on the best way out of the imbroglio, but he was receiving increasingly shrill messages from his generals. In one of his mid-April memoranda, Wolseley threatened his minister thus: 'The English people will force you to do this, whether you like it or not.'

The pressures on the government built to such a point that in early May there were public meetings in which thousands declared their support for Gordon. Gladstone's ministry narrowly beat a House of Commons motion of censure. Although the Prime Minister still loathed the idea of sending thousands of troops to rescue Gordon from a mess largely of his own making, he had been pushed a little further towards such a step. But since the word from Khartoum was that supplies would last almost until the end of 1884, Gladstone saw no need for hurry.

At 10 a.m. on 17 January 1885, the Desert Column of the Gordon relief force set out, marching towards some wells to their front. It was already baking hot, and many men's tunics were soaked with sweat. As they went, Dervishes capered about them, taking pot-shots and generally keeping everyone on their mettle. Enemy war drums beat out a repetitive rhythm; it had been pounding throughout the preceding night. The British were advancing in a square, the best formation to adopt when fearing attack from a much larger but poorly armed enemy.

Nearing the top of a small rise, soldiers began to see Mahdist banners popping into view on the plateau ahead. By the time they could make out the men who held them, it was apparent to British officers leading this force of around 1,100 that the enemy outnumbered them by ten to one.

The British halted their square about 200 yards from their enemy, which is when the attack began. Mahdist commanders, accompanied by standard-bearers, led their masses forward in great columns. The British soldiers (Guards, cavalry, marines and Royal Sussexes, formed into two regiments that marched by camel but fought on foot) fired away for all they were worth. Their hail of bullets soon carved lanes in the Mahdist ranks.

In such contests of will against weaponry, the attackers gravitated towards the corners of the square, since the intensity of fire was less there. One great horde, moving to the left-rear angle, seized their moment when a machine-gun placed at that vulnerable point jammed. In moments, some of the Sudanese warriors were inside the square, but they were swiftly bayoneted. The British had survived the initial rush. By some unspoken signal, the Mahdists slackened off. In five minutes of firing, the Martini-Henrys and machine-guns had killed more than 1,000 Sudanese. The square's faces had been forced in by the violence of the attack and many men stood back to back with other defenders. Quite a few of the soldiers had experienced the grim foreboding of knowing that they had only a couple of cartridges left when the firing mercifully stopped.

The British won the Battle of Abu Klea, but, like Tamai, it was at a considerable cost. Eighty-one Desert Column soldiers had been killed, and the survivors were sobered by the intensity of the enemy attacks.

Gladstone had bowed to pressure, the final straw being when Lord Hartington finally committed himself and threatened to resign in late July. In September 1884, the government sent out a relief mission. Its leader was none other than General Wolseley. He had brought his forces slowly up through Egypt before reaching the northern Sudanese town of Korti. There he divided them into a River Column, on board steamers, and a Desert Column, which would cut across the Baruda Desert, a distance of about 130 miles, missing out a great loop of the Nile and bringing them back to that river at Metammeh. There they would be only a couple of days' steamer journey from the capital.

In the four days after Abu Klea, the Desert Column fought another battle and reached Metammeh, but found it too strongly held by the enemy to take. Then, four steamers sent by Gordon arrived there, having escaped Khartoum and run the gauntlet of enemy gun batteries along the river. They carried word of the defenders' desperate plight.

During the months of siege, the population of Khartoum had dwindled from about 35,000 to 14,000, with most Mahdist sympathisers leaving the town and Gordon grateful that he had fewer mouths to feed. As for the garrison, it had started at 9,000 men, but several defeats and desertion had reduced it to around 6,000 by early 1885. Gordon had used his sapper's skill to lay out defences of earth, barbed wire and mines. The Mahdists were poorly equipped to undertake 'regular approaches' but managed to use their captured field guns to good effect.

On 5 January, Omdurman, Gordon's major outpost across the Nile from the city, fell. This was a dread moment for the besieged, because it allowed the Mahdi's cannon to enfilade their defences. The enemy had also built forts along the Nile that made it increasingly difficult for Gordon's little fleet of gunboats to operate. The Mahdi had known about the garrison's desperate straits since September, when a steamer carrying the Governor General's chief of staff and Frank Power, among others, had grounded. The occupants had been killed and vital dispatches seized. For the last weeks of the siege, it became virtually impossible for Gordon to get messages out. In one of his final letters he showed how well he understood the wider stakes, noting, 'I expect Her Majesty's Government are in a precious rage with me for holding out, and so forcing their hands.'

Gordon's journals, which he stopped writing a few weeks before the Battle of Abu Klea, show a man in a state of nervous collapse. They were full of underlining, printed words and fulmination against Baring and others. Quite how he would have responded if the relief force had reached him sooner is unclear, for in his journal he wrote, 'If any emissary or letter comes up here ordering me to come down I WILL NOT OBEY IT, BUT WILL STAY HERE, AND FALL WITH THE TOWN.'

Increasingly, those who saw the chain-smoking, shambling figure in the Governor's Palace thought him bent on self-destruction. 'Better a ball in the brain than to flicker out unheeded,' he confided ominously in his journal. He could, of course, have abandoned the town's defenders at any point and saved himself on one of the steamers. While his decision not to do so might be seen today as idiotic or suicidal, it was regarded by many at the time as highly honourable.

A Lebanese merchant who called on Gordon at this eleventh hour was alarmed when an enemy shell burst near the Governor General's residence. Suggesting that Gordon might dim the lights and sandbag the windows, he drew this response: 'He called up the guard and gave them orders to shoot me if I moved.' Gordon then lit a large lantern, put it in the window to help the Mahdi's gunners and shouted to the merchant: 'Go, tell all the people in Khartoum that Gordon fears nothing, for God has created him without fear.' These rages became more common, and he often took out his frustration by hitting his staff. Deprived of the company of Englishmen, he began talking to a mouse that inhabited his office.

On 26 January, the Mahdi's men stormed the city and Gordon met his maker. Since the moment was not observed by any reliable witness, and the Victorian public's desire for details was so great, a number of writers and artists resorted to invention. A famous painting by G.W. Joy shows a dignified Gordon awaiting the Mahdi's men at the top of a staircase. Another version suggested that at the end he bared his breast to the enemy, inviting oblivion. All that can be said with certainty is that during the final assault on his palace, the Governor General's head was severed.

A European general who was imprisoned in the Mahdi's camp at Omdurman had Gordon's head brought to him, later describing the grisly moment. This trophy was then displayed close to the enemy headquarters, hung from a tree. Two days later, British troops on board steamers reached the outskirts of the city, learned what had happened and turned back.

It has been remarked that the closeness of rescue allowed different partisans to blame whomever they pleased for the fall of Khartoum. The notion that Gordon was just two days from deliverance added to the drama that gripped the British public for a whole year but was a little deceptive. Certainly, it is likely that the Mahdi could have attempted to storm the city at any time after the fall of Omdurman, and would have tried it earlier if his scouts had warned him sooner of the approaching British column.

Very few people in Britain at the time wanted to ask searching questions about why General Wolseley's relief force had taken so many weeks to arrive from Egypt. There were excuses about the level of the Nile, supplies and even problems buying camels. But Wolseley emerges as a man who urged dispatch or predicted easy victories over the Sudanese while he was in London, but turned into a paragon of caution and maker of excuses once in the region. The experiences of the spring push towards Berber and several months later at Abu Klea convinced many officers that the Mahdists had to be tackled with the greatest care if a massacre of British troops were to be avoided.

News of the failure reached London on 5 February. Queen Victoria sent an angry telegram to Gladstone as he travelled through northern England by train. It blamed him for failing Gordon and she deliberately left it uncoded so that its contents would leak. His reply was about as icy as any from a British prime minister to a sovereign: 'Mr Gladstone does not presume to estimate the means of judgement possessed by Your Majesty. He put her in her place, then blamed the generals for what had happened: 'Mr Gladstone is under the impression that Lord Wolseley's force might have been sufficiently advanced to save Khartoum had not a large portion of it been delayed by a circuitous route along the river, upon express application of General Gordon.'

Across Britain, though, people smarted from the humiliation of it all. Saloon-bar wags reversed the familiar acronym for the Prime Minister – GOM, standing for Grand Old Man – to MOG, Murderer of Gordon. Gladstone's political instincts did not fail him in his diagnosis of the situation: he told the cabinet that the public had cared a great deal for Gordon and very little for Sudan.

The 13th March 1885 was marked as a day of national mourning for the 'fallen hero of Khartoum'. There were church services across the country. The Bishop of Chichester caught the mood, with one newspaper reporting his sermon as follows: 'Nations who envied our greatness rejoiced now at our weakness and at our inability to protect our trusted servant. Scorn and reproach were cast upon us, and could we plead that it was undeserved? No; the conscience of the nation felt that a stain rested upon it.' *The Times* picked up on these remarks in its leader of 14 March, suggesting that this mark on British honour would have to be wiped out, a process that would cost many more lives.

Sir Evelyn Baring tried to circulate his own version of events privately. He suggested that in the mood of 'national hysteria' over Gordon's death, public attacks on him would be akin to questioning the sacred tenets of Christianity. It took many years for his criticisms of Gordon's behaviour to be vented in public.

Gladstone licked his wounds, but a note he penned several months after the denouement in Khartoum shows him trying to make sense of this enormous political setback. 'We trusted him to the utmost,' he wrote of the man they had sent to Sudan. 'Gordon, perhaps insensibly to himself, and certainly without our concurrence, altered the character of his mission and worked in a considerable degree against our intentions and instructions.'

As for Wolseley, his hopes of pressing on to Khartoum regardless of Gordon's fate and completing the suppression of Sudan were soon dashed. His expedition was recalled by the government and he did not take it well. Wolseley's prophecies of doom for Egypt if the revolt was not smashed were brushed aside by Gladstone. 'When professional soldiers and sailors warn the people on these serious subjects, professional politicians jump up and pooh-pooh all their warnings,' Wolseley wrote angrily to Queen Victoria, before rounding on the wider nation whose opinions he had tried to shape. 'The foolish public prefer believing the tradesman who has become a politician to the gentleman who wears your Majesty's uniform.' Wolseley might have been thwarted but the story of British intervention in Sudan was far from over.

Gordon is significant because he represented a perversion of the democratic process. Of course, the idea of revenge was supported by millions of Britons after his death, but he, Wolseley and several others managed to subvert government policy, dragging the country into a long and costly war. Gordon stands for what happens when unscrupulous men combine with naïve journalists to shape excitable public opinion. The Gordon relief expedition marked the beginning of a modern context for decisions about war and peace. In this new world mastery of the media and direct appeals to public opinion counted for a great deal. Soldiers would have to learn those skills, but they would also have to be taught to exercise them in support of the government's aims, not against them.

As a young officer involved in the reconquest of Sudan, Winston Churchill initially shared many of his countrymen's assumptions. But as he worked on *The River War*, his book about the events in that country, he began to reconsider Gordon's role. After spending a couple of hours with Baring, he qualified earlier views, writing in a letter: 'Of course there is no doubt that Gordon as a political figure was absolutely hopeless. He was so erratic, capricious, utterly unreliable, his mood changed so often, his temper was abominable, he was frequently drunk, and yet with all that he had a tremendous sense of honour and great abilities.'

Public revisionism began with Lytton Strachey's *Eminent Victorians* in 1918. This passage about the besieged 'hero' gives a flavour:

while he jibed at his superiors, his subordinates learned to dread the explosions of his wrath. There were moments when his passion became utterly ungovernable and the gentler soldier of God, who had spent the day in quoting texts for the edification of his sister, would slap the face of his Arab aide-de-camp in a sudden access of fury, or set upon his Alsatian servant and kick him until he screamed.

In time, many of Britain's military and political leaders came to see what a disaster Gordon had been and how the whole episode represented a case study in the miscarriage of foreign policy. Field Marshal Montgomery, for example, considered Gordon, 'unfit for independent command, mentally unbalanced, [a] fanatic, self-imposed martyr'.

It is true that Gordon could have appealed to Britain only at a very specific moment in history – the Imperial zenith that lasted from about 1870 to 1918. It was a period when an insult to a British agent or businessman might result in a gunboat being sent to wreak revenge, when a jingoistic public cared little about the slaughter of thousands with dark skins. It took the carnage of the First World War and the enfranchisement of women for some common sense to be restored.

This, though, is jumping ahead, for in 1885 Britannia was humiliated and contemplating revenge. One of the intelligence officers who had been sent into Sudan to communicate with Gordon wrote, 'Never was a garrison so nearly rescued, never was a commander so sincerely lamented.' The author was Colonel Herbert Kitchener, and it would be to him that the task of avenging Gordon would fall.

(Horatio) Herbert Kitchener

1850–1916

He is more like a machine than a man.
G. W. STEEVENS, *Daily Mail*

THE SCENE ABOUT KOSHEH that afternoon in September 1896 was dazzling. The sun beat down relentlessly, bleaching the colour out of everything. Here and there the rays of light were reflected by the waters of the great Nile as it flowed past. But to the officers who had gathered on the river bank, the real brilliance was that of British ingenuity, British grit and British war machines.

All eyes were upon the *Zafir*, a 'great white devil' of a gunboat, 140 feet long and 24 feet abeam. Her steam boilers could drive her, via a great stern paddle, up the Nile at 12 m.p.h. When the Queen's enemies were found, they could be dispatched day or night (*Zafir* was fitted with electric searchlights) by a 12-pounder, two 6-pounders and a couple of Maxim machine-guns. Three more salient facts about this juggernaut suffice: she drew just thirty-nine inches of water, allowing her (usually) to cruise over the rocky beds of the Nile's treacherous cataracts; she had been built to order in London in just six weeks; and the construction was in sections to allow *Zafir* to be dismantled and transported by ship and railway to the theatre of war.

The kit of parts had been brought up to Kosheh on flatcars during the preceding weeks, offloaded by steam cranes, and assembled in a purpose-built dock at the riverside. The railway itself, jutting 105 miles into the northern part of Sudan from Wadi Halfa on the Egyptian border, had been in operation only since early August. Those who watched the gunboat being put together knew that two more were on their way, sister ships that would give their commander a vital advantage in a country dominated by the Nile. It was all planned like clockwork.

Science was being applied to this campaign, guided as it was by a Royal Engineer, a British officer of fearsome dedication who held the rank of *sirdar*, or commander, of the Egyptian Army. But as the great six-foot two-inch figure of Herbert Kitchener strode along the quayside, he knew acts of God could discomfit every calculation. Further setbacks simply could not be allowed to happen. Kitchener intended to push south towards Dongola in four days' time.

Days before, at the end of August, following the worst storms for fifty years, a flash flood had carried off a twelve-mile stretch of railway embankment. Kitchener had joined his native railway workers relaying the sleepers and rails, working around the clock. He knew that the long African summer had starved the river, and that soon it would fall to its lowest level of the year, threatening even the *Zafir*'s ability to get up river.

As he boarded the ship with Commander Stanley Colville, the naval officer in charge of the river flotilla, though, Kitchener's troubles were not over. Lines were cast off, fore and aft. The *Zafir*'s bow moved out into the Nile and hundreds of spectators on the banks sent up a cheer. Engineers opened the valves driving the great wheel. But 'The stern paddle had hardly moved twice', according to one account, 'when there was a loud report, like that of a heavy gun, clouds of steam rushed up from the boilers, and the engines stopped.' A key valve had blown. Kitchener turned to the commander: 'By God, Colville, I don't know which of us it's hardest luck on.'

He stepped off the stricken vessel, ordered the guns to be shipped onto others and retired to a different boat's cabin. One of his ADCs found him there, crying. 'What have I done to deserve this?' the forty-six-year-old general, eyes reddened and face drawn with exhaustion, asked a subaltern in his early twenties.

Kitchener's orders in September 1896 were to take Dongola Province, the northern portion of Sudan that bordered Egypt. It was not a full-blown conquest of the country, though many British generals longed to do just that. The motive of avenging Gordon played strongly with many of these men – Kitchener himself having served in 1884 with the Desert Column – but far less with the government of the day.

The Tory administration of Lord Salisbury was in power and in matters of foreign and military policy it adopted a very different tone from Gladstone's. Salisbury was prickly, portly and patrician. He cared little for the popularity of public meetings or indeed the officers' mess and intended to keep an iron grip on his military policy. He had sanctioned the attack on Sudan's northern province in order to take some pressure off his Italian allies to the south-east. They had suffered an epic disaster at Adowa in May, when an Italian brigade was largely wiped out by Abyssinian tribesmen. The British Prime Minister wanted to draw the Dervish armies of the Khalifa (the Mahdi's successor) towards Dongola.

In London and Cairo those in the know understood that Kitchener's 1896 campaign might serve as a preparatory move to taking the whole country, but they were equally convinced that they did not want to commit themselves to such a course for the time being. Salisbury was quite clear that he did not want any further Gordon-style adventurism. So General Lord Wolseley, who had by now become Commander-in-Chief in Whitehall, was excluded as far as possible from the chain of command. As the Dongola expedition was being prepared, the Prime Minister wrote to the Secretary of War, 'My advice will be not to pay too much attention to your military advisers.'

Salisbury's words give some sense of how deep and acrimonious the divisions between political and military leaders had become. At the end of the nineteenth century, unresolved questions about the respective roles of the army, government and sovereign caused considerable friction. Wolseley tried to prevail by making alliances with politicians. He had fallen out with the Liberals over the Gordon relief expedition. Having then aligned himself with the Tories, he was indignant when Salisbury prevented him lobbying publicly and reduced his influence over strategy. 'The men of talk will give way to the men of action,' Wolseley wrote to his wife in 1897, in perhaps his most violent outburst against politicians, 'and all that most contemptible of God's creatures will black the boots of some successful cavalry colonel. A new Cromwell will clear the country of these frothing talkers, and the soldiers will rule.' Wolseley was ready to act against the government of the day on many matters, including, for example, Irish home rule. There can be little wonder, then, that in contemplating military action in the Sudan, the Prime Minister wanted this general involved as little as possible.

Once Kitchener's force began its advance, Salisbury put the venerable British Agent in Cairo, Evelyn Baring (who was by this time styled Lord Cromer), in overall control of operations, thereby bypassing Wolseley.

Cromer was convinced of Kitchener's qualities. He had backed the appointment to *sirdar*, and watched with satisfaction as this driven man, with a team of 108 British officers, had rebuilt the Egyptian Army. As the expeditionary force moved further into northern Sudan, the Prime Minister had worried at one point whether Kitchener might make a dash for Omdurman (capital of the Khalifa, who ruled Sudan as the Mahdi's successor, just across the Nile from Khartoum). Cromer had reassured Downing Street that Kitchener was 'not at all inclined to be rash'. The care and quality of the *sirdar*'s logistic preparations were in marked contrast to Wolseley's 1884–5 relief mission, which Kitchener himself considered to have been hopelessly organised. There were other obvious differences between the two men, too. 'K', as almost all his officers called him, was tall and deliberate in his movements, whereas Gordon had been small and constantly active. They had some traits in common, notably their background as sappers, Christian faith and shared disdain for English society in Cairo, being more comfortable in the desert among the Arabs. If there was one area where Kitchener might be unfavourably compared to Gordon, it was as a leader of men. K rarely made eye contact, possibly because he had a natural squint that had been exaggerated by a wound to the side of his face. His shyness meant he rarely opened up to his brother officers. The prominent brow and the huge moustache that later became his trademarks served to mask the emotions of a naturally closed character and gave him a forbidding mien.

Kitchener came from a respectable but cash-strapped family. His mother died when he was in his teens, and he grew into an introspective young man. During survey work in Palestine, and later working as an intelligence officer for the Egyptian Army, he was able to immerse himself in Arabic language and culture, as well as escaping the irksome routines of the officers' mess. Shortly after joining the Gordon relief force, he wrote, 'I have grown such a solitary bird that I often think I were happier alone.'

Many of those serving with Kitchener in September 1896, as he struggled to overcome setbacks to his plan, found his combination of relentless drive and personal remoteness hard to take. 'He was always inclined to bully his own entourage, as some men are rude to their wives,' noted the same young staff officer who found K crying. 'He was inclined to let off his spleen on those around him. He was often morose and silent for hours together . . . he was even morbidly afraid of showing any feeling or enthusiasm, and he preferred to be misunderstood rather than be suspected of human feeling.'

To Kitchener's superiors, the fact that he achieved impressive results clearly made up for some of these unpleasant personal qualities. 'A good brigadier, very ambitious,' noted his confidential report for 1890, before adding: 'not popular, but has of late greatly improved in tact and manner . . . a fine gallant soldier and good linguist, and very successful in dealing with orientals'.

Using forced marches through the desert, Kitchener drove his men along the Nile and overcame the early setbacks. On 23 September, the town of Dongola was taken. The scene was set for further advances into Sudan, if only the political will and money could be found.

The prospect on the banks of the Nile just under two years after the Zafir's maiden voyage was once again one of feverish anticipation. This time, though, the khaki-clad soldiers were hundreds of miles to the south of Kosheh. Kitchener's invading army had advanced to just a few miles north of the Khalifa's capital, Omdurman. The invaders had brought 8,200 British as well as 17,600 Egyptian Army troops (many battalions being officered by Britons) to the heart of Sudan.

Kitchener's army bivouacked on 1 September 1898 with their backs to the Nile, the bend of the river forming the line into a crescent. It was a deployment that would allow them to focus fire on any enemy that attacked their front. The ends of this curved deployment were secured by gunboats, able to enfilade any lines of Dervishes advancing towards the British.

Despite the enormous firepower at the disposal of this force, some of Kitchener's men worried. Their line, like that of Wellington, was two deep. In places a reserve company supplemented it, with men ready to step into the gaps left by casualties or fetch ammunition boxes. But overall it was not a robust square, rather a fragile deployment of soldiers with their backs to water. Along much of its length the usual zariba of thorn bushes raked together formed an obstacle of sorts, but what if thousands of enemy rushed them? Reports suggested the Khalifa's army might number 50,000 or more. They too had moved on since the battles of 1884–5. There were many more armed with rifles, and the Khalifa's arsenal now contained dozens of cannon. K, though, was confidence itself. When alerted to a possible enemy push that afternoon, he had replied, 'We want nothing better, we have an excellent field of fire and they might as well come today as tomorrow.'

The journey between Kosheh and Omdurman had been an epic struggle. Fighting sandstorms, Dervishes and government accountants,

Kitchener had extended his railway from Wadi Halfa, 360 miles across the Nubian Desert, close to Berber, where the Nile route and the camel trail to the coast met. At times he had reclaimed sleepers from peasants' roofs to save money; at others he had written to friends that the burden of organising it all made him want to die. But he had kept doggedly on, and his arrival at Omdurman was a triumph of organisation and supply.

'Fighting the Dervishes was primarily a matter of transport,' wrote Winston Churchill, who accompanied the expedition as a subaltern in the 21st Lancers and correspondent for the *Morning Post*. 'The Khalifa was conquered on the railway.' Throughout the two-year odyssey, biting off bits of the Sudanese Khalifate, Kitchener had been nourished by the supply train he created and the information provided by his director of intelligence, Major General Rex Wingate. Like K himself, Wingate had spent the best part of a decade in this part of the world. Both men had attained such a fluency in Arabic that they could even adopt the dialects of different tribes.

When the final push on Omdurman began, Wingate sifted reports from dozens of agents, many of whom had been on the books for years. They ranged from itinerant traders to servants of wealthy merchants and members of the small remaining European community. Even the Khalifa's adviser on foreign affairs, a German *pasha* who had adopted Islam, was one of Wingate's spies. Wingate, yet another Woolwich graduate (a gunner), had at times been maddened by Kitchener's methods: 'K irritates me by keeping his movements secret,' Wingate wrote in his journal after one particularly frustrating day. But the two men eventually evolved a relationship of mutual trust and, by the early hours of 2 September 1898, their great common labour was close to fruition.

At around 5 a.m. reports reached the British camp that the Khalifa's army was on the move. Great columns of men were marching out of the Omdurman fortress. A British 5-inch howitzer battery placed on the eastern bank of the Nile opened up, lofting 50-pound lyddite shells into the fortifications, sending billowing clouds of dust into the sky. Great wheeling masses of Dervishes, under hundreds of banners, moved to the south of Jebel Surgham, high ground to the front of the British line. 'It was not alone the reverberation of the tread of horses and men's feet I heard and seemed to feel as well as hear,' wrote Bennet Burleigh, the *Daily Telegraph's* correspondent, 'but a voiced

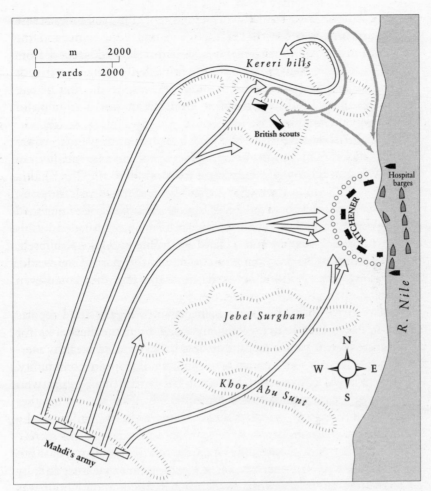

The battle of Omdurman, 1898

continuous shouting and chanting – the Dervish invocation and battle challenge "Allah el Allah Rasool Allah el Mahdi!" they reiterated in voxiferous rising measure, as they swept over the intervening ground.'

British officers had surveyed the land in front of them and knew exactly when to use the different weapons in their arsenal to best effect. At 2,800 yards, Royal Artillery 15-pounders opened up, the shells fused to air burst, showering the white-robed phalanxes with red-hot metal. 'Above the heads of the moving masses shells began to burst, dotting the air with smoke-balls and the ground with bodies,' observed Churchill, who was with a picket of lancers on the jebel in front of the

[191]

British position. Then the Maxims joined in – German machine-guns selected by the War Office for their reliability and range. During the two hours of this engagement, one section of six British Maxims would fire 54,000 rounds. With the enemy still 2,700 yards away, the Grenadier Guards were invited to stand and deliver the first platoon fires with their Lee-Metford rifles. Both Dervishes and whistling bullets were getting too close for comfort, so it was time for Churchill and the other scouts out front to scurry back behind the British zariba. The pickets led their panting horses down to the river for a drink, and young Winston borrowed a biscuit tin to stand on so that he could see over the steep bank to the higher ground beyond the British firing line. It was not a spectacle he would ever forget: 'A ragged line of men were coming on desperately, struggling forward in the face of the pitiless fire – white banners tossing and collapsing; white figures subsiding in dozens to the ground . . . valiant men were struggling on through a hell of whistling metal, exploding shells, and spurting dust – suffering, despairing, dying.'

Thousands of Dervishes were being cut down. The Lee-Metfords fired a hollow-nosed bullet – a ghastly invention that caused a kind of explosion when it struck flesh, intended to blow a limb clean off or gouge a great cavity in a man's trunk. Such bullets were later banned by international convention. Many of the British officers watching this spectacle were uneasy. Even Kitchener's brother Walter, who was serving with the army, wrote, 'One's feelings went over to the enemy, they just struggled on.'

For the most part, the Khalifa's men did not get within 800 yards of the British line. One desperate charge by some cavalry managed to get to 300 yards, but that was the exception.

By 8.30 a.m., the Dervish attack had collapsed and Kitchener ordered a general advance. He was worried that thousands of enemy warriors might race back into Omdurman, forcing him to carry out a protracted siege. The British brigades moved forward in line, wheeling south as they crossed the plain just north of the city. Kitchener, on horseback, went up to Jebel Surgham, and seeing the thousands of dead and wounded Dervishes carpeting the landscape remarked, 'Well, we have given them a damn good dusting.'

The battle was not over yet, though. There were still several columns of the Khalifa's troops manoeuvring about the city. The British troops, advancing in their brittle formations, at times had large groups of

Dervishes on their flanks and to their rear. This fighting was bloody and confused: quite a few wounded enemy warriors were dispatched because they were still resisting as the British and Egyptian Army troops marched through. At one point, Kitchener narrowly avoided being killed by a salvo of bullets from his own men.

During this advance the colonel of the 21st Lancers ordered his regiment (just under 400 mounted men) to charge some Dervishes who threatened the flank of one advancing brigade. Churchill took part in this desperate affair, an action some later compared to the charge of the Light Brigade. The lancers' plan was to charge a group of riflemen, but after they set spurs to their mounts about 1,000 Dervishes appeared from a stream bed in front of them and dramatically changed the odds. The 21st were committed, though, and continued to hurl themselves forward.

'The collision was prodigious,' wrote Churchill, 'and for perhaps ten wonderful seconds, no man heeded his enemy. Terrified horses wedged in the crowd, bruised and shaken men, sprawling in heaps, struggle dazed and stupid, to their feet, panted and looked about them.' The charge's impetus carried the troopers through several of the twelve ranks of enemy warriors like a rake through shingle. Then the killing began. For about a minute they set about one another before the 21st burst through. During less than two minutes of fighting, hundreds of Dervishes were cut down; the lancers suffered seventy casualties.

During the late afternoon, the British entered both the Khalifa's capital and, across the river, Khartoum, freeing various chained Christians from the jail. The civilian population, fearing a general massacre, prostrated themselves, or rubbed dust in their hair in a gesture of self-abasement and submission.

The Battle of Omdurman was won with fewer than 500 casualties (killed and wounded) in Kitchener's army. The Dervishes lost almost 11,000 killed (K, with characteristic thoroughness, had the corpses counted) and 17,000 wounded. 'At Last!' wrote Burleigh in the *Telegraph*. 'Gordon has been avenged and justified. The dervishes have been overwhelmingly routed, Mahdism has been "smashed", whilst the Khalifa's capital of Omdurman has been stripped of its barbaric halo of sanctity and invulnerability.' The Queen immediately raised Kitchener to the peerage. He had become a national hero.

In a private letter, Churchill gave vent to his feelings about the cost of it all, saying the victory had been 'disgraced by the inhuman slaughter of the wounded and ... Kitchener is responsible for this'. Some directly accused Kitchener of ordering a massacre of defenceless men, but there is no evidence for such a claim. Rather, it is clear that before the earlier Battle of Atbara (8 April 1898), he gave his troops a mixed message, telling them to show mercy to their enemy but exhorting them to 'Remember Gordon' and saying the men in front of them were Gordon's murderers.

When Churchill wrote his book about these tumultuous events, *The River War*, he did not make any direct accusations against Kitchener, instead recording that large numbers of Dervishes came in near the end of the day, 'as soon as it was apparent that the surrender of individuals was accepted'. This last statement guides us as close to the truth of the matter as we will ever get – implying both that Kitchener's troops were not taking prisoners while in 'hot blood' and that large groups of enemy warriors were mown down, whenever seen, until the end of the day.

Churchill concluded his account of Omdurman with the memorable phrase that it was 'the most signal triumph ever gained by the arms of science over barbarians'. It is apparent, though, from his letters, that he modified the tone of his book for political reasons. He mentioned his need to 'tone down or cut out' his 'more acrid criticism of the Sirdar'. His initial dislike of the general seems to have been based on class prejudice (Churchill told his mother that Kitchener was a 'vulgar common man'), and fed off a general feeling in Cairo, doubtless part envy from other officers, that K did not quite deserve the heroic niche carved for him by the British press.

With the enemy capital captured, Anglo-Egyptian forces moved swiftly through the country, mopping up Dervish resistance. Upon taking Khartoum, Kitchener opened sealed orders from the Prime Minister, and at this moment Lord Salisbury's primary motive for the invasion of Sudan became clear. Kitchener was to head south, in order to frustrate French attempts to seize the equatorial part of the country. Avenging Gordon might play well with the newspapers and army officers, but Downing Street was primarily interested in the great Imperial game. What Salisbury wanted to avoid above all else was a vacuum that would be exploited by the French.

During a tense meeting on the Nile (dubbed the 'Fashoda Incident' by Britain's press) Kitchener convinced the French commander to accept that the British-led Egyptian Army had reimposed its control over Sudan, while avoiding bloodshed. K allowed the French to save face by continuing to fly the tricolour over their post at Fashoda, beside the Egyptian flag, while diplomats in France and London contrived a graceful climbdown.

His victory made him a household name in Britain, a suitable idol for an epoch when science and industry marched relentlessly forward. 'His precision is so inhumanly unerring,' wrote G.W. Steevens of the *Daily Mail*, that 'he is more like a machine than a man. You feel that he ought to be patented and shown with pride at the Paris International Exhibition. British Empire: Exhibit No. 1 *hors concours*, the Sudan Machine.' But the reputation for efficiency had acquired, as its flipside, one for brutality. Shortly after capturing Omdurman, he ordered the Mahdi's tomb destroyed and had his bones scattered. This act, deemed by many to have been one of 'Oriental' cruelty, even upset Queen Victoria.

Early in 1899, Kitchener was made Governor General of Sudan, with a mission to rebuild the country and expunge all vestiges of the Mahdist state. Lord Cromer offered some words of advice that show pretty clearly what he considered to be the strengths and limitations of the 'Sudan Machine':

In the first place, pray encourage your subordinates to speak up and to tell you when they do not agree with you. They are all far too much inclined to be frightened of you. In the second place, the main thing in civil and political life is to get a sense of *proportion* into one's head, and not to bother about insisting on every particular view as regards non-essentials . . . In the third place, *pray* keep me informed and consult me fully. A secretive system will not work so well in civil as in military matters.

Kitchener's rule was short lived (he soon handed the reins to Wingate) but established a stable and reasonably enlightened period for Sudan. The British popular demand for progress was satisfied by banning slavery and allowing foreign businessmen into the country. He wisely prevented Christian missionaries from getting to work soon after the guns fell silent, made sure that the government built munici-pal mosques (banning private ones, where sedition might be preached) and invested enormous efforts in education.

The conquest of Sudan, while undertaken during the Great Power carve-up of Africa, represents a fascinating chapter in light of the current confrontation between the West and Arab militants. Sudan under the Mahdi and Khalifa was, after all, the first example of a militant Islamic theocracy in modern times. In certain respects the lessons learned then are clearly not applicable today: few opponents would ever be as rash as the Khalifa's generals in throwing away the lives of so many devoted followers in a 'stand-up fight'; Victorian public opinion was ready to accept Kitchener's crushing use of force; and satellite TV was not there to inflame the passions of the worldwide Muslim *ummah* or community.

However, some features of Kitchener's campaign are worth remembering now, and indeed give it a meaningful legacy. First, Britain was prepared to wait many years to strike against the Mahdists, during which time the clerics alienated their people with shocking abuses of power (Wingate claimed 8 million Sudanese perished in the fifteen years between Gordon's arrival and Omdurman). Second, these years were used to make careful military preparations and to develop an extensive network of spies, ensuring plentiful intelligence once the 1896 campaign was launched. Third, those entrusted with leadership of the mission were men who had given a great part of their lives to understanding the Arabs and Islam. Fourth, the Anglo-Egyptian Army concentrated overwhelming force. Finally, the overall direction of the campaign was in the hands of diplomatic/political authority (Lord Cromer in Cairo) rather than orchestrated by the usual military chain of command.

So, in his forties, Kitchener had made a mark on history. But it was not his last, nor even his most significant legacy.

When the general's train pulled in at Harrismith on 26 February 1902, his staff followed a well-rehearsed routine. The locomotive drivers let great clouds of steam escape as they cooled their engine. His bodyguard of Cameron Highlanders came clattering down the steps of their carriage, fanning out across the sidings into positions of all-round defence. Officers of K's staff prowled the platform, telling anyone who might fancy a photograph of the great man that their film would be confiscated if they tried. Then the general emerged, a big figure swathed in khaki, exchanging terse greetings and a swift salute as he moved to his charger and mounted up.

Captain Frank Maxwell, a cavalry officer in his early thirties who had won the Victoria Cross saving some horse artillery from the Boers two years before, was one of those who made up the small mounted party. Kitchener called him 'the Brat', but the young cavalier, who lived up to the gentlemanly ideal of sportsman, took it in good part. Maxwell had met his boss in South Africa just over one year earlier. Like many who had not been at Omdurman, the captain had been influenced by K's public image, the purple prose of the popular press and talk of the 'Sudan Machine'.

Although initially in awe of his general, Maxwell evolved ways of teasing Kitchener that almost no other officer dared. The general's nickname suggested a fatherly love for him. Whether Kitchener, who never married, was homosexual, as some historians have suggested, is unclear. It is true that he was more or less engaged to the daughter of a general as a young man (she died before they could marry), but also that bar-room gossip held he had picked up the 'taste for buggery' apparently common in officers serving in Egypt in the 1880s. There is no conclusive evidence – only that he seems to have channelled a great deal of his aggression into his work, and he was a Christian as well as a Freemason who espoused a great belief in chastity.

Maxwell was charmed by the more human side of the man, telling his father, 'K is not the purposely rough-mannered impolite person those who have never seen him suppose. He is awfully shy, and until he knows anyone his manners – except to ladies – are certainly not engaging.'

Maxwell, Kitchener and the others set spurs to their horses and rode away from the railway line, out into the great veld, languishing in the torpor of a southern summer, to watch the British Army at work. On they rode into the landscape with features framed in farmer's Dutch – kraals, kopjes and kops – towards a great mountain called the Platberg. When they reached its flat top, more than 1,000 feet above the plain, they took a moment's rest and then began to survey one of Kitchener's grand designs. 'We had the most glorious and extended view,' Maxwell wrote home to his father: 'the scene was a wonderful one.' The general's party looked to the north, watching British mounted infantry and footsloggers 'crawling about like ants', moving across country in the direction of a line of fortified outposts, blockhouses. They were scouring the veld, stripping away its cattle, wagons and people, while forcing any Boer rebels to flee towards the blockhouses, where the troops inside could open up with all manner of weapons.

Kitchener had arrived in South Africa early in 1900. Initially, he had played second fiddle to Field Marshal Lord Roberts, the two 'heroes' of the Victorian army having been sent out to steady the situation after the Boers had run rings around the British Army during 1899. Kitchener himself had mishandled his one set-piece battle (Paardeburg) in command of the new army, leading to high casualties.

The origins of this conflict lay in the struggle for control of two republics where farmers of Dutch descent formed the majority (Transvaal and the Orange Free State) and for the wealth (including gold) that could be found there. Roberts brought substantial reinforcements into the fight, drove off the Boer field armies besieging outlying British garrisons and eventually took Pretoria, the rebel capital.

In October 1900, writing to Queen Victoria, Kitchener rashly predicted, 'The war is almost over.' But attempts to negotiate an end to hostilities dragged on without result, not least because British politicians, feeling the need to justify the war to a public rankled by the army's initial poor showing, tried to insist on punitive peace terms. Late in 1900, Roberts left and Kitchener was appointed Commander-in-Chief in a war that was rapidly evolving. The enemy field armies, with their excellent long-range artillery, were being scattered, and instead British outposts or supply trains found themselves under attack from flying columns of anything from a few dozen to 1,000 mounted Boer commandos. These guerrilla parties waged hit-and-run raids, acting with aggression and, usually, sound tactical judgement.

Kitchener initially found himself bewildered by this type of warfare. Those who consider him stupid can cite as evidence a comment he made in a letter to a close friend's sons, in which he protested, 'The Boers are not like the Sudanese who stood up to a fair fight. They are always running away on their little ponies.' How anyone could have seen Omdurman as a fair fight or the Boer tactics as anything other than canny under the circumstances almost defies imagination. Evidently, K was a paragon of Victorian values, admiring the 'pluck' of the Dervish and disdaining the 'skulking' inherent in guerrilla warfare. But, although his intellectual horizons were undoubtedly limited, he was not a fool and soon set about designing a solution to the problem of the Boer commandos that would be both innovative in conception and disturbing in execution. Kitchener the machine examined every aspect of the problem and determined to crack it.

The key to defeating the insurgency was to deny the commandos sanctuary. Since the Boer system involved farmers taking their turns at military duty before returning to their homes, Kitchener's plans necessitated waging war on the entire society. Railways were the key to strategic movement, so a programme of building blockhouses to defend the lines started in January 1901. From these trunks, branches, similar chains of outposts, were extended along certain roads or rivers, criss-crossing the areas of Boer settlement. Manning these positions would soak up vast numbers of infantry, but Kitchener had no shortage of men, with more than 200,000 troops under his command. A large proportion of the army consisted of cavalry and mounted infantry, and as 1901 progressed brigade-sized columns of them were used increasingly in drives, acting as a hammer, to strike the Boers against the anvil of fortified lines. It was usually called the 'blockhouse and drive' strategy.

Kitchener's flying columns did not just engage enemy combatants, though. They removed the commandos' means of subsistence, and that often meant uprooting whole communities. Roberts had begun the burning down of farms in reprisal raids, but under his successor such tactics became systematised. These women, children and old folk, 'internees', were put in camps, and as the 1901 campaign progressed they became a source of increasing political difficulty for the government. The fact that the internees received fewer rations than those designated 'refugees' (usually English-speakers displaced by the conflict) rapidly led to accusations that food was being used as a weapon, and even that Kitchener wanted to wipe out the Boers.

A visit to South Africa early in 1901 by Emily Hobhouse, a churchman's middle-aged daughter with a passion for human rights, triggered a series of Parliamentary debates. 'The atmosphere was indescribable,' she wrote after venturing inside the tents at Bloemfontein camp. 'The ration . . . did not come up to the scale, it became a starvation rate.' When she saw destitute Boer families huddled in cattle trucks on a railway siding during one of Kitchener's drives, she wrote that she had witnessed 'war in all its destructiveness, cruelty, stupidity and nakedness'.

These dispatches excited to action MPs who were already calling Kitchener's laagers 'concentration camps'. The term – picked up from Spanish usage in 1890s Cuba – has assumed a completely different meaning since the Nazi era, of course, but at the start of the century the government's critics felt that the high death rates occurring through disease and malnutrition were a stain on national honour. 'I think I shall have a hot time,' the Secretary of War wrote to Kitchener in

March 1901 after some turbulent scenes in Parliament. He asked the general to 'tell me all that will help the defence'. Kitchener couldn't see what all the fuss was about, a response that led quite a few in Whitehall to conclude that he was politically clueless.

In truth, the landscape of power in London had changed significantly during Kitchener's long years of foreign service. Reforms in 1890 and 1895 had established firm political control over the army. The soldiers were still represented on a War Office Council, where they might advise their civilian masters, but under Lord Salisbury's government this body was rarely called together. The hegemony of ministers had been strengthened further by steps to reduce the Crown to a purely ceremonial role. Many officers persisted in seeing themselves as servants of the sovereign rather than of 'tradesmen who had become politicians', but by the turn of the century the monarch did little more than sign their commissions.

As for Parliament itself, by 1898 just 41 out of 670 Members of the Commons were army officers (compared to the high tide of 79 of 558 MPs ninety years earlier). More importantly, in the context of Kitchener's travails in South Africa, those military MPs had been comprehensively eclipsed by the 165 lawyers in the House of Commons. Increasingly, debates about Britain's role in the world emphasised the country's role as a beacon of human rights and fair play.

The general was undoubtedly blinkered and his campaign against the Boers was brutal, but he was also one of the first senior officers to have to cope with a difficult humanitarian situation being exploited for campaigning purposes by an anti-war lobby at home. 'The inmates are far better looked after in every way than they are in their homes,' he insisted in a letter to a lady friend, 'or than the British refugees are, for whom no one now seems to care. The doctors' reports of the dirt and filth in which the Boer ladies from the wilds revel are very unpleasant reading.'

By mid-1901 there were some 65,000 inmates in the South African camps, and 25,000 Boer men who had been shipped to overseas internment. Kitchener was certainly waging war on Boer society as a whole, but the high mortality rate in the camps was an unintended by-product of this strategy. An up-and-coming Welsh Liberal MP, David Lloyd George, campaigned energetically on the issue, saying to the Commons during one of his flights of rhetoric, 'We want to make loyal British subjects of these people. Is this the way to do it?'

This debate marked the emergence of a clearly defined cleavage between military men and a liberal intelligentsia at home; one that has only grown stronger with time. To the critics, operations such as those in South Africa were shameful and obviously counter-productive. To most military men, the 'pro-Boer' Liberals missed the point: Kitchener's strategy was not meant to make 'loyal British subjects' of the enemy. It was meant to break their will to resist with arms. Diverting resentments into non-violent political avenues might do nothing to lessen their sense of grievance, but this was the outcome sought by men in khaki taking the narrow view.

For Kitchener, the more worrying issue as 1901 came to an end was that his drives were not yielding the 'bag' of Boers he had expected. Cornered commandos often managed to break through the blockhouse lines. Sometimes, even worse, they outfought the flying columns sent to hunt them, bagging prisoners of their own and driving off the frightened remnants. Kitchener examined these setbacks with his usual engineer's calculation. If the blockhouse lines could be easily breached, then the intervals between the little fortifications would have to be halved or quartered by a major building programme. The space between them started at 2,500 yards, was reduced to 400 yards and then, in the most threatened sectors, to 200 yards. By the end of 1901 there were more than 8,000 blockhouses, manned by tens of thousands of troops. The number of mounted infantry was increased, with new orders given to try to improve their tactics so that they would not be surprised.

Some of the column commanders believed Kitchener himself was part of the problem, trying to centralise all power and sometimes failing to coordinate the movements of different columns properly. One of the best and brightest of them, an acting lieutenant colonel in the cavalry, the strapping Edmund Allenby, wrote home, 'Lord K of K [Kitchener of Khartoum] tries to run the whole show from Pretoria – and fails. District commanders, with several columns under them, are the only people who could bring the show to a speedy finish.' Kitchener did not devolve power; however, he did respond to the muttering by making increased efforts to travel away from his headquarters so that he could be present at the scene of major operations.

Early in February 1902, a great set-piece drive was launched against a Boer stronghold at Elandskop. Many on the staff were disappointed that just 285 commandos were killed or captured rather than the 2,000 they estimated to be within their net. But the operations continued relentlessly. On 26 February, Kitchener, Maxwell and the staff watched the sweep from Platberg. Heliograph parties, down on the veld with the column commanders, used mirrors to send Morse-type signals, flashes of light to keep the commander posted. 'We hadn't been on the berg ten minutes', wrote Maxwell, 'before from fifty miles away to our right came a twinkle, twinkle message, which spelt out by the signaller read: "400 Boers laid down their arms to me this morning".'

That evening, Kitchener and his party returned to their train, where further reports coming down the telegraph wires could be collated in the carriage that was his mobile command centre. Sometimes he would puff on a cigar or take a whisky and soda before turning in. The routine started all over again at 4.30 a.m. 'K is an extraordinary person,' wrote Maxwell. 'He sleeps and dreams and schemes all night, and in the morning, in pyjamas and dishevelled head, gets you to work . . . and in two hours plans are more or less complete, and orders more or less drafted.' Dispatches would then be sent by messenger or telegraphed and a new drive ordered.

On 31 May 1902 the Boer leaders, ground down by months of British pressure, signed a ceasefire agreement. 'For six months Lord Kitchener fought the politicians who wanted to make a vindictive peace, an "unconditional surrender" peace as they called it,' Kitchener's chief of staff would recall later, but 'he beat them and made his own peace; a generous soldierly peace.' K's 'generosity' consisted of making good much of the damage he had done to the rural economy: giving grants for rebuilding farms and restocking them with animals. Given that the tactics had provoked intense Parliamentary controversy in the first place, it is hardly surprising that partisans of Kitchener and his critics should still be arguing about how the Boers were beaten and how much credit or opprobrium should go to the British general.

For me, the opinions of a young subaltern in the 43rd Light Infantry, John Fuller, hold particular weight. He served for months among jumpy sentries on a blockhouse line and later as an intelligence officer on drives through the veld. He later matured into one of the British Army's all too rare great thinkers (his books being published under the name J.F.C. Fuller). He reacted to the end of the war with this insight:

For nearly a year the Boer cause had been slowly strangled; now it was choking. The blockhouse line had not so much segregated the Boers as split them up. It was impossible for large forces to move about the country without carts and wagons to supply them . . . Though small parties could cross blockhouse lines, large parties could not . . . The blockhouse was in fact a means of striking at our enemy's stomach, and it was far more than the tactical barrier we supposed it to be.

Fuller's acknowledgement of the higher intelligence shaping British operations was qualified, however. He called his memoir, published in 1937, *The Last of the Gentlemen's Wars*. By and large, he believed, it had been a chivalrous affair in which Tommy Atkins and his Boer opponent had evolved 'rules of the game' and casualties had been slight, certainly when compared to those suffered during the First World War. 'What exasperated [the Boers] most was the burning of their farms and the removal of their women and children to concentration camps,' wrote Fuller, adding: 'and it exasperated me also.' As a British officer, he was unhappy to be associated with cruelty towards women. The lesson he drew is an enduring one: 'Do not let us forget that chivalry in war is as important as killing, because on the cleanness with which a war is fought will depend the cleanness of the peace which must one day follow it.'

Britain's campaign in South Africa formed a model for later counterinsurgencies. It is another Kitchener legacy that fifty years later British generals in Malaya removed the civilian population from contested areas and that the Americans did the same when creating hundreds of 'strategic hamlets' in Vietnam. As for 'blockhouse and drive' it was called *quadrillage* by the French in Algeria and has been practised in other conflicts, too.

By the early 1900s, Kitchener's reputation could be summed up succinctly and crudely as: ruthless bastard. His critics might have spat out the words and shaken their heads in sorrow at the suffering of South African farming folk, or what one sarcastically called a 'glorious slaughter of 20,000 Arabs' in Sudan. Admirers, over a gin on the veranda at Simla or puffing a cigar at Whites, might have used the same phrase with a knowing smile to describe a fellow who had what it took to wage war in the industrial age. It therefore should not come as a surprise that when war loomed over Europe in August 1914 so many Britons felt that Kitchener was the right man for high office.

Kitchener was shown in to see the Prime Minister just after 7 p.m. on 4 August 1914. Downing Street has many fine clocks, and it would be hard to imagine a moment of British history when swinging pendulums or a moving minute hand underlined more pointedly the sense of foreboding. German troops had marched into Belgium, on their way to attack France. The British government of Herbert Asquith had given an ultimatum to stop their advance and respect Belgium's neutrality. As Kitchener, sixty-four years old and greying but still an imposing figure, came in and took his seat, there were just a few hours remaining for Berlin to respond.

Time was pressing on K, too. He had been laden with almost every decoration the British state could furnish. Having served as Commander-in-Chief in India, earning the rank of field marshal, there were very few posts in which he could now be employed. After lobbying unsuccessfully for the Viceroy's job in India, it had been tentatively decided to send him to Cairo, in order to 'run' the Mediterranean and North Africa. Asquith, however, had stopped him travelling out. With war imminent there was a general view that Kitchener was needed at the centre of the action, not in some distant sideshow.

The old post of Commander-in-Chief (the titular head of the British Army at Horse Guards that the Duke of York had held during his army reforms of the 1790s) had been scrapped in 1904. It had been replaced by a new office, Chief of the General Staff, but this was not vacant. Military plans to send a British Expeditionary Force (BEF) of six divisions to the Continent were being set in motion, but, once again, Kitchener was not the designated commander.

For several days prior to their meeting, the newspapers had been suggesting that Asquith might employ Kitchener as Secretary of War. Not everyone in Whitehall liked this idea, for it had been another aim of the 1904 reforms to conclude thirty-five years of military changes with civilian political control firmly and finally established over the War Office. What, then, would be the point of handing the top job to a soldier? Looking back at this situation, we might concede that late nineteenth-century reforms designed to make the army more efficient and check its Imperialist firebrands had gone a little too far, and that taking a soldier into the War Cabinet was quite justified in a time of total war.

As for Kitchener himself, he held the army's central bureaucracy in complete contempt and was in the habit of denouncing it as hopelessly inefficient. His fear was that Asquith would ask him to be somebody's deputy or invent some figurehead non-job. But the field marshal could read the papers like anyone else and knew that there was also a possibility of a cabinet post. At their meeting on the evening of 4 August, therefore, Kitchener asked the Prime Minister not to send him to the War Office unless it was with full powers as the Secretary of State for War. Asquith did not offer him the job, but decided to ponder it overnight.

There was palpable nervousness on the streets. Crowds gathered outside Buckingham Palace to cheer the King. Late editions of the papers were snapped up and scanned rapidly in case they carried news of a German climbdown. While many expected the war to be brief and heroic, there was a general understanding that the nation was facing an ordeal more testing than anything it had confronted since the time of Napoleon. Industrialisation and nationalism were about to produce a cataclysm of unrivalled ferocity. German unification had created a superpower in Central Europe and it was on a collision course with France. Allies stood ready on each side. The dread was summed up by a remark of Sir Edward Grey, the Foreign Secretary: 'The lamps are going out all over Europe; we shall not see them lit again in our lifetime.'

On 5 August, Britain was at war. Ignoring Asquith's ultimatum, the Germans were ploughing on relentlessly towards France, and under the terms of the Entente Cordiale, the alliance between London and Paris, the BEF was about to be committed to combat. Asquith therefore wasted no time in offering to make the field marshal Secretary of War. Kitchener was not in any sense a party animal so he made it clear to the Prime Minister that he would take the job only for the duration of the war and could not be expected to operate as a politician, publicly defending the government. 'May God preserve me from the politicians!' he remarked to a friend.

Asquith regarded the appointment of such an ingenue in the black arts of Whitehall as a risk. He was heartened, however, by the positive reaction of press and public. There was simply nobody else trusted to the same degree to face the looming darkness – a general European war – with the same nerve and toughness as Kitchener. Fifteen years earlier, people had said that K had absorbed the 'Oriental' qualities needed to prevail in the Middle East. In August 1914 his legend was reworked by those who felt his machine-like efficiency and toughness in South Africa meant he had the right stuff to beat 'the Hun' at his own game. One wag, observing the indomitable figure of the field marshal at a ball, supposed that he had 'kinship to that old race of gigantic German Generals, spawned by Wotan in the Prussian plains, and born with spiked helmets ready on their heads'.

During the afternoon of the 5th, Asquith hosted a council of war at Downing Street. The Foreign Secretary was there, as was Winston Churchill, who had graduated from the cavalry subaltern Kitchener had met at Omdurman sixteen years earlier to running the Admiralty, and a couple of other senior military officers. During this meeting, Kitchener managed to upset the apple-cart of government strategic thinking completely.

The following morning, as he awaited the summons to Buckingham Palace to receive the seals of his office, Kitchener went to the War Office. Anxious to crack on with the job, he asked for the department's senior officials to be presented. As they crowded into his room, pince-nez specs and winged collars aplenty, they were astounded by almost the first thing he said: 'There is no army!'

At the first few meetings of the cabinet, Kitchener continued to surprise everybody. Unfortunately, cabinet minutes were not formally taken before December 1916, so there is no precise record of what he told them. The following account by Churchill, present at all the key meetings, gives the best sense of how Kitchener deployed his arguments:

Lord Kitchener now came forward to the Cabinet, on almost the first occasion after he joined us, and in soldierly sentences proclaimed a series of inspiring and prophetic truths. Every one expected the war would be short; but wars took unexpected courses and we must now prepare for a long struggle. Such a conflict could not be ended on the sea or [by] sea-power alone. It could be ended only by great battles on the Continent. We must be prepared to put armies of millions in the field and maintain them for several years.

Thus the field marshal blew away the 'all over by Christmas' illusions that even many senior army officers cherished. Of course, it took time for this to sink in, but the singularity of Kitchener's views at this vital moment mark out his historical importance. The Foreign Secretary, hearing the field marshal's assessment that the war would go on for at least three years, disagreed: 'That seemed to most of us unlikely, if not incredible.' That same minister, clearly regarding Kitchener as intellectually limited, later wrote that this remarkable foresight came 'by some flash of instinct, rather than by reasoning', since Kitchener did not predict trench warfare.

There were many reasons why Kitchener may have briefed the cabinet in the way he did, but it seems clear that he was very conscious of Britain's relative importance in the Allied pecking order. He understood the same realities that Marlborough and Wellington had done: an expeditionary corps that formed a small part of a combined army (as was the case with the BEF) would come under someone else's command and gain London limited political leverage. In an age of democracy, however, the deaths of thousands of British troops on French orders or their retreat because the Allies on both of their flanks had fallen back (as happened during the opening weeks of the war) would be all the harder for a British government to justify. He did not doubt victory, and he wanted Britain to have the largest possible say in defining a post-war order.

The consequences of Kitchener's strategy were enormous, and began with an urgent drive to recruit a million new soldiers. Initially, the War Secretary aimed to take the army up to 57 divisions (there were 18,000 men in a British infantry division at the outbreak of war), but by mid-1915 he would plan for 70, and the requirement for new recruits would reach 3 million. A magazine picture of the field marshal pointing at the reader and commanding 'Join Your Country's Army!' was pressed into use as history's most celebrated recruiting poster. Later, when volunteers became more reluctant, an official poster carried the warning that conscription would become necessary if too few men volunteered, as indeed eventually happened.

In August 1914, however, the cabinet resolved that conscription was politically unacceptable. Churchill later differed from the collegial position, arguing of these early meetings, 'It is my belief that had Kitchener proceeded to demand universal national service . . . his request would have been acceded to.' Patriotism provided the drive instead, as 'Kitchener armies' were recruited to boost the army towards its target of seventy divisions by 1916. This degree of national mobilisation was so unprecedented and enormous in its implications that the precise means of raising millions of recruits can be set to one side for a moment. Kitchener's first biographer noted, 'It implied the calling of vast armaments into being, the unlearning of a stereotyped national tradition, the acceptance of a radically novel conception of the whole position and mission of England in the world.'

Kitchener brought Britain into the age of total war. By the time hostilities ended, almost one-quarter of the adult male population,

5.7 million men, would have served in the British Army. It can be argued that some Continental powers had already reached this degree of mobilisation by a series of steps beginning with the French conscription laws of 1794, proceeding through the vast campaigns of Napoleon to Bismarck and his militarisation of Germany. But Britain was the world's most powerful nation, and its abandonment of a centuries-old concept that its army should be small, professional and comprise volunteers was of enormous historical importance.

Obviously, expanding an organisation severalfold in a matter of months was bound to involve all manner of cock-ups and chaos. During one day in September 1914, as the response to Kitchener's call reached its peak, the army had to enlist as many men (over 30,000) as it had during the entire year of 1913. Many of these recruits wore their civilian clothes for weeks and drilled with broomsticks.

Kitchener knew that good professional officers and NCOs would be needed to train these great new armies, so he kept back thousands of soldiers whom other generals were desperate to send to the front. This caused a serious rift between him and some fellow senior officers who, even late in 1914, thought the field marshal's planned seventy-division army ridiculous. When Churchill visited the front he heard complaints about the policy everywhere he went, but later reflected admiration for 'Lord Kitchener's commanding foresight and wisdom in resisting the temptation to meet the famine of the moment by devouring the seed corn of the future'.

Despite holding back experienced soldiers from training establishments, Kitchener faced a critical officer shortage. He excavated from retirement many crusty old warriors in their sixties and seventies quite ignorant of what a European war might require – the army called them 'dugouts'. One twenty-seven-year-old captain noted that his dugout commander was 'quite useless . . . I really ran the brigade and they all knew it.' This ambitious officer was the young Bernard Montgomery.

Equipping the army posed enormous problems, too. By May 1915 the War Office had ordered 27,000 machine-guns, but eventually it gave up with numbers and simply told Vickers it would buy every gun they could make. Kitchener invited the head of America's Bethlehem Steel Corporation to London and ordered a million shells and as many rifles as he could make. The Secretary of War was even more pessimistic in his conversations with the American magnate than he had been with the cabinet, arguing that Britain needed to stock up for *five* years of war.

At times, Kitchener's old faults undoubtedly hindered this process. He jumped to the conclusion that the Territorial Army was useless and it took others months to change his mind, holding back the committal of substantial reserves to the war. He was also, on one key point at least – the commitment of British troops to the disastrous Gallipoli operation against the Turks – open to accusations of being a poor strategist. Kitchener's old inability to delegate produced all manner of hold-ups and confusion at the War Office. The field marshal often refused to share vital information with his officials there, and even with the cabinet, regarding almost every detail as secret. In this respect he epitomised the spirit of the times, because during the run-up to 1914 the British government had finally formulated its concept of official secrecy.

These shortcomings contributed to a political crisis over the supply of shells in 1915, with Kitchener being relieved of authority for munitions production. The main beneficiary from this cabinet punch-up was none other than David Lloyd George, whose 'pro-Boer' attacks on Kitchener's tactics in South Africa had proven so irksome to the War Office many years earlier. During cabinet-room sparring, the Welsh MP (who was Chancellor of the Exchequer as well as the new Minister for Munitions) evidently ran verbal rings around the field marshal. The Prime Minister wrote that in these spats Lloyd George let fly with 'some of the most injurious and wounding innuendos, which K will be more than human to forget'. Kitchener, always the closed book, never really said what he thought of Lloyd George, describing him only as a 'peppery fellow'.

In general, Kitchener was loath to respond publicly to press or parliamentary criticism, believing that this would turn him into a politician, a species into which he certainly did not wish to evolve. On 2 June 1916, just one month before the Somme offensive, however, he tried to answer MPs' concerns about the colossal casualties on the Western Front and the overall course of the war. K went to the Palace of Westminster to brief 200 members. He insisted that this should be confidential, but minutes were taken, and they form one of the few lengthy accounts, in his own words, of what the Secretary of War was trying to do during 1914–16. (One of his biographers suggests that this was one of only four occasions when he spoke publicly during twenty-two months in the cabinet.)

'I feel sure Members must realise that my previous work in life has naturally not been of a kind to make me into a ready debater, nor to prepare me for the twists and turns of argument,' he said, excusing his refusal to appear in open session at Westminster. He talked about the enormous mobilisation and admitted it had been a 'gigantic experiment'. 'I was convinced that . . . we had to produce a new army sufficiently large to count in a European war,' Kitchener then told the hushed MPs. 'I had rough-hewn in my mind the idea of creating such a force as would enable us continuously to reinforce our troops in the field by fresh divisions, and thus assist our Allies at the time when they were beginning to feel the strain of the war with its attendant casualties.'

This notion, that British forces should be on the rise at the decisive period of the war, was a vital aspect of Kitchener's plans – and it is worth underlining that he said this in the summer of 1916 when few others had any idea whether the conflict would go on for one more year or ten. There were many implications in this build-up, as he hinted to the MPs: 'We planned to work on the upgrade while our Allies' forces decreased, so that at the conclusive period of the war we should have the maximum trained fighting army this country could produce.' The timetable was therefore designed at one and the same time to maximise Britain's killing power against the Germans and its political clout vis-à-vis France. Kitchener left the meeting satisfied that he had defused some of the discontent that just a few days earlier had produced an unsuccessful censure motion against him in the Commons. He then prepared to set off on a trip to Russia, where Britain's allies were buckling under the pressure of war.

On 5 June, HMS *Hampshire*, the cruiser carrying the Secretary of War, set sail from Scapa Flow. There were dangers for the fleet, even this close to home, because German submarines had been trying to penetrate British defences. Having surveyed the Royal Navy's usual deployments, the U-boats laid mines. It was the Secretary of War's misfortune that the *Hampshire* struck one just a few hours into its journey. The cruiser went down in minutes and Kitchener drowned as she sank. There was public grief, with many a diarist recording in the sonorous tones of that era the weeping of East End market girls or the grim expressions in their officers' mess. There were tributes aplenty from the field marshal's contemporaries, but I prefer that of A.J.P Taylor, perhaps the greatest historian of the twentieth century, who

16 The appeal for manpower that proved to be Kitchener's principal legacy. He launched this drive for 3 million troops at a time when almost all Cabinet and War Office opinion considered the war would be over quickly.

17 The 21st Lancers' charge at Omdurman. Winston Churchill took part in it as a young subaltern and later wrote about the battle in vivid terms.
18 Allenby in a classic portrait – looking very much the Western Front 'brass hat' who dined in his chateau while his men died in the mud.

19 Royal Horse Artillery in action near Gaza during Allenby's 1917 campaign to break into Turkish Palestine. The open terrain helped the Turks defeat two previous British offensives with machine-gun fire and artillery.

20 A different view of Allenby, arriving at Jerusalem's Jaffa Gate on 9 December 1917. He dismounted and entered the Holy City on foot, a measure of his sensitivity and deference to its inhabitants. The Prime Minister had sent the general to the Middle East with the order to capture 'Jerusalem by Christmas'. Allenby obliged.

21 This painting of the Western Front by C. R. W. Nevinson proved so powerful that a military censor tried to ban it. Its title, *Paths of Glory*, reflected the bitterness of the generation that went to the trenches.

22 'Boney' Fuller pictured as a colonel serving on the Tank Corps staff. Despite the nickname, his superiors spotted early on that Fuller was no great leader of men but possessed a brilliant analytical mind.

23 A British tank pictured as it reared over German defences during the Cambrai offensive in November 1917. These vehicles broke the trench stalemate, leading the Tank Corps to describe their feat as taking them 'through the mud and blood to the green fields beyond'. 24 Hitler's birthday parade in 1939 proved to be a showcase for his *panzer* forces. Fuller was in the audience, revelling in the atmosphere and ignoring a Foreign Office request to stay away.

25 Monty and Ike pictured during a pre-D-Day exercise on Salisbury Plain. Even at this juncture, their relationship was turbulent.

26 German troops advancing during the Battle of the Bulge. This photo was staged for propaganda purposes, as the Nazis made political capital out of their surprise of the Allied armies in the Ardennes in December 1944.

27 Lunching beside the Rhine, the troika who ran Britain's drive to Germany during 1944–5: Churchill, General Alan Brooke (Chief of the Imperial General Staff) and Montgomery. It was during this trip, sensing victory after the long years of war, that Churchill walked to the water's edge and relieved himself into the Rhine.

called Kitchener 'the only British military idol of the First World War'. Certainly, in the public's eyes, he was a soldier without peer.

Kitchener's achievements in breaking the Mahdist state in Sudan and crushing the Boer insurgency were of historical importance, but secondary. It was by the creation of a vast army in 1914 that he left his mark. It can be argued – according to one's prejudices – that he summoned an entire generation of British youth to their doom or that he allowed his country to decide the outcome of the First World War. Either way, it is hard to claim that what he did was insignificant.

The field marshal's entry in the *Dictionary of National Biography* argues that his mobilisation 'not only saved the British empire from destruction, but Europe from German domination'. Many such claims, made in the rosy glow of self-satisfied nationalism, do not stand up to scrutiny, particularly when you examine what a country's enemies were saying. It is therefore worth quoting the views of General Erich von Ludendorff, the man who was at the helm of Germany's war strategy: 'Through [Kitchener's] genius alone England developed side by side with France into an opponent capable of meeting Germany on even terms, whereby the position on the front in France in 1915 was so seriously changed to Germany's disadvantage.'

In evaluating the 20th Century British war machine it is often hard to estimate the value of individuals, however eminent. But it is very hard to credit anyone other than Kitchener with responsibility for Britain's vast national mobilisation in August 1914. The field marshal's 'long war' views put him at odds with everyone else in the Cabinet and, indeed the War Office. It is largely due to this foresight, as General Ludendorff akcnowledged, that Britain and France did not buckle in 1915. In terms of alternative history, a German victory in that year would have opened up some mind – boggling possibilities, not least of checking the rise of Hitler or averting the Russian Revolution. The old empires might not have lasted indefinitely if the war had ended in 1915, but Europe and the world would undoubtedly have developed very differently.

Kitchener was not a pleasant man, and his anti-intellectualism and prejudice against elected leaders make him rather suspect to our generation. At the dawning of an era of total war and industrialised slaughter, he was, however, quite indispensable to his country.

Edmund Henry Hynman Allenby

1861–1936

I had a very big success yesterday, I won all along the line;
killed a host of Boche
and took over 7,500 prisoners.
ALLENBY TO HIS WIFE, 9 APRIL 1917

AT 7.27 A.M. IN ACCORDANCE with the fire plan, smoke rounds began falling in the shell-blasted corridor between the German lines near Gommecourt and Green Street, as the first line of the 1st Battalion, 7th Sherwood Foresters (a Territorial mob known as the Robin Hood Battalion) was called. Ladders were placed against the trench sides, tots of rum downed. Some later claimed the first wave were tipsy, having got a double ration by mistake. They were crouching in a newly hewn assault trench just forward of Green Street. In the main position, Green Street itself, the second and third waves waited, too. Their job would be to push through the first wave, once they had seized the first German fighting trench. Officers eyed their watches nervously. As the minute hands clicked on to thirty minutes past the hour, whistles were blown, and one of the subalterns called out, 'On the Robins!'

Every aspect of this attack was planned to tried and tested formulae. Unfortunately, every aspect of the German reception that awaited the Sherwood Foresters was designed to nullify their sacrifice. The construction of the new assault trench just a few yards ahead of Green Street was a give-away, as was the regulation week-long preparatory bombardment and the practice of attacking on the hour of half-hour. So, as the first British troops went over the top, German soldiers scurried from the deep dugouts (some went down forty feet) where they had endured the Royal Artillery barrage, lined their firing trenches and slapped fresh belts of bullets into the receivers of their Maxims.

The first wave of the 1st/7th assault – perhaps 150 men – was cut down by the machine-guns in a few seconds. Not one of them reached the first German trench, only 100 yards away. After just one or two minutes the second and third waves set off from Green Street, darting through the smokescreen and hail of bullets. Some – perhaps three or four dozen – of these young men from Nottingham found themselves clambering over the moonscape of pulverised soil and enemy wire and staring down into the first enemy trench. They tossed in Mills bombs and followed up with the bayonet. Many of the German defenders fled, getting shot in the back as they went.

Gasping, pumped full of adrenaline, the small group of Robin Hoods prepared to execute a second attack – since the German trench system about Gommecourt, as elsewhere, ran in three distinct lines. For these few men who had made it this far there were hundreds lying wounded from Green Street, across no man's land, where they crawled into shell holes to try to get some cover.

The wounded were duly pulverised as the German counter-bombardment of heavy artillery began. As for those still standing, great salvoes of shells were set to air-burst over the British trenches, for the Germans knew this game well enough; there would be successive waves of British soldiers crowded in Green Street, awaiting the order to go.

British guns, meanwhile, kept pummelling the first German trench, despite the fact that many who were in it were now Sherwood Foresters. They were ahead of schedule and the smokescreen laid at the outset meant nobody knew they'd made it, so the gunners kept firing as ordered. In desperation, some of the British NCOs and officers sent up red flares – an emergency signal to stop the bombardment. These were seen by German artillery observers who knew it was now safe to start ordering fire missions on their own first line. Shells were criss-crossing the sky, creating a maelstrom of flying shrapnel, earth and dismembered flesh.

Somehow, in the midst of this, about two dozen British troops went over the top again and reached the second German trench. These men were promptly hit by a German counter-attack, local reserves having been prepared for this express purpose. For some of the Sherwood Foresters, a German grenade dropping at their feet was the last thing they saw. Others were mown down by Maxim or shrapnel as they fled from the second German trench back to the first. Five British soldiers made it back to their comrades cowering there.

A fourth wave of Robin Hoods – or rather those who had survived the German bombardment of their own forward lines – followed their comrades over the top. 'It was worse than Dante's *Inferno*, worse than hell fire,' Private Alfred Bennett would recall later. 'German machine-guns and shells and all kinds of explosives made no man's land tremble like a jelly, and the air was nothing but blue flame.' The survivors fell into shell holes, desperately trying to save themselves. The Commanding Officer of the battalion had gone forward too, trying to establish what had happened to his attack. It was about 9 a.m. by this point. 'The colonel and I took cover behind a small bank,' wrote another private of the 1st/7th, 'but after a bit the colonel raised himself on his hands and knees to see better. Immediately, he was hit in the forehead by a single bullet.'

With the CO and most of his men dead or wounded, there was no question of any momentum being maintained. The plan to pinch off the German salient at Gommecourt was going nowhere. It only remained for the Germans to eliminate the two dozen or so British survivors who still had the impertinence to occupy their first trench. 'The Germans made a bombing [i.e. hand-grenade] attack, both from the right and the left,' the regimental war diary recorded. 'Our men were unable to offer much resistance, their rifles being in some cases muddy, and having no supply of bombs, eventually those that were left retired.'

Private Bernard Stevenson, among hundreds of Nottingham lads who'd fallen in with the battalion in August 1914, was one of those few survivors who finally gave up the struggle. He knew that it would be suicide to try to reach Green Street in this hideous bombardment, and he recorded his impressions of sitting in a shell hole just a few feet from the enemy's first trench: 'Decide to wait until nightfall and then attempt an escape. Wait 15 hours. British bombarding German trench all day with heavies, whiz-bangs, rifle grenades and trench mortars. Earth keeps falling on us. Can hear Germans talking and firing.' It was 11 p.m. before Stevenson and a few other stragglers made it back to the British line. He was given a mug of tea laced with rum and told to turn in. First he wrote to his mother to tell her he had survived. 'I'm sorry to say Nottingham will be plunged into mourning when the casualty lists are published,' he scribbled. There were indeed 181 Nottingham men killed that day from the two battalions of Sherwood Foresters that were part of the 46th Division assault at Gommecourt.

A couple of miles to the south, the other arm of a British pincer aimed at the same objective, the 56th Division, had fared a little better. They got more men into the first German trench, but then ran out of hand grenades after a couple of hours' fighting and were also forced back. One officer of the City of London Regiment who had struggled to join the advance wrote of this hellish day: 'The whole of the valley was being swept with machine-gun fire and hammered with shells. We got the men organised as best we could – those of us who were left. So many gone, and we'd never even got past our front line trench! And then we found we couldn't get back. The trenches were indescribable! We were simply treading on the dead.'

So, the attack on Gommecourt resulted in thousands of casualties but achieved nothing. It happened on 1 July 1916, the first day of the Somme, the blackest in the British Army's history, when in one twenty-four-hour period the number of killed and wounded reached a staggering 57,470. In much of the army, there was disgust at the stupidity of it all.

Those involved in the Gommecourt fiasco, however, felt doubly aggrieved, for they had been thrown against one of the strongest German positions on the entire Western Front simply to draw off enemy fire from the main Somme attack to their south. 'Unpleasant as it may seem, the role of the 56th Division', wrote the formation's official historian, 'was to induce the enemy to shoot at them with as many guns as could be gathered together.' Thus, on a day in which British generals had sacrificed tens of thousands of men for no good purpose at all, Gommecourt represented a further level of futility, being an attack that wasn't even *meant* to break through.

The divisions involved at Gommecourt belonged to VII Corps, which in turn belonged to the Third Army, under the command of General Sir Edmund Allenby. He had been deeply disappointed not to be given the main push on 1 July and, in the back-stabbing world of the Western Front high command, had to make do with Gommecourt as a consolation prize. The young cavalry officer who had been promoted by Kitchener as the ace Boer War column commander was, by 1916, a fifty-five-year-old brass hat who suspected he had lost the confidence of his Commander-in-Chief (Field Marshal Sir Douglas Haig).

Allenby dined well at the chateau of Bryas each evening, boasting to guests about the French chef he had secured to prepare the dishes and holding court over his hushed staff and ADCs. Physically intimidating (he was six foot two and barrel chested), his explosions of temper were legendary, and he was known throughout the Third Army as 'the Bull'.

He had been dispatched to France in August 1914 as the British Expeditionary Force's top cavalry commander, but his record since then had been distinctly patchy. Finding one cavalry brigade miles from where it should be during the BEF's initial retreat, a general who asked the brigadier what he was doing there received this reply: 'He told me he was getting as far away from the Bull as possible. It was a most scandalous affair, and he was in almost open rebellion against Allenby at the time.' The same unhappy subordinate (Hubert Gough) had come to despise Allenby as Inspector General of Cavalry before the war, finding him an unbearable pedant. 'He had a great regard for regulations and every sort of detail,' wrote Gough. 'When inspecting some unit, if he noticed some small neglect of detail or non-compliance with an order, however trivial, he got excited and sometimes began to shout, and I have seen him rush at an offending officer and threaten him with a stick.' Another of the Bull's critics said of his operational command in France, 'He cannot explain verbally, with any lucidity at all, what his plans are.'

Running an infantry corps and then the Third Army, the ugly sides of Allenby's personality only seemed to worsen. His explosions of temper could be triggered by anything from discovering a split infinitive in some staff officer's paper to finding a corpse in a trench who, said the general, was flouting Third Army's strict order that steel helmets be worn in forward areas at all times. So keen was he on tin hats, and so resentful were his officers at the discomfort of having to wear them all day, that one London hat-maker started selling lightweight papier mâché replicas, with an example in the shop window reportedly being labelled, 'As Worn in the Rear Areas of Third Army'.

After Gommecourt, one of Allenby's generals refused to accept his orders and tried to persuade Haig to remove the Third Army's commander. This gamble misfired and the complainer was dispatched to England instead. By the time of the Somme, even Archibald Wavell, who had joined Allenby's staff in France and become one of his greatest admirers, conceded that frequent outbursts of temper during inspections of the front lines seemed to 'confirm the legend that "the Bull" was merely a bad-tempered, obstinate hot-head, a "thud-and-blunder" general'.

Such was his reputation that it entered popular culture. The novelist C.S. Forester, in *The General*, used a thinly veiled Allenby to represent the brutality of high command in the Great War. General

Wayland-Leigh, wrote Forester, was nicknamed 'the Buffalo' by his staff, being 'a huge man with a face the colour of mahogany and a suspicion of corpulence'. The loyal Wavell called Forester's depiction a 'gross caricature', but it is evident that the author spoke to many veterans and *his* bovine dialogue seems to fit well with accounts of Allenby's behaviour and the realities of the Western Front. Forester's 'Buffalo' tells a new divisional commander that he must never retire and never make excuses, adding: 'Most of the officers in this army want *driving*, God knows why – the army's changed since I was a regimental officer. You drive 'em and you're all right. I'll back you up. And if you don't – *I'll* have to find someone who will.'

The slaughter in the trenches presented political difficulties at home, which in turn sometimes necessitated blood-letting in the high command. Forester wrote of the generals' fears of 'coming unstuck', 'being unstuck' or even 'unsticking themselves'. He caught the atmosphere perfectly, even if Allenby in his letters home preferred the French '*de-gommer*'. Forester's words about 'the Buffalo' after one botched attack apply perfectly to Allenby's situation after Gommecourt: 'Everyone knew that it would be touch and go with him. He might be selected as a scapegoat, and deprived of his command and packed off at any moment, if GHQ should decide that such a sacrifice would be acceptable to the strange Gods of Downing Street.'

Everything in this chain of command was hierarchy. Allenby refused to hear criticism of Haig or GHQ at his dinner table, even though he himself harboured considerable doubts about the way operations were being conducted. Equally, Haig, although not liking Allenby personally, had sacked the Third Army's rebellious major general when he refused to follow the Bull's orders. So the plan that sent so many Sherwood Foresters to their deaths on 1 July had come down from General Headquarters to the Third Army, then VII Corps, 46th Division and finally 139 Infantry Brigade. At each level generals or colonels might have their own ideas about how such slaughters might be avoided, but if they subverted the GHQ plan they were quickly broken.

It is hardly surprising that in this atmosphere the army's best and brightest found the sterility of thinking, with its resulting waste of life, idiotic and obscene. In trench dugouts and rear-area bars, staff captains or bright majors tried to set the world to rights. For the most part, their debates concerned the minutiae of what was going wrong.

Should there be more machine-guns per battalion? Shorter artillery barrages? Longer barrages? More undermining operations? Very few of them were capable of thinking on the strategic level about why warfare had reached stasis and how generals might find a way out of it.

As it happened, the thirty-eight-year-old J.F.C. Fuller was transferred to Allenby's Third Army shortly after the Somme as an acting lieutenant colonel. His Boer War service and Staff College behind him, Fuller had matured into one of the army's most trenchant and perceptive internal critics. He could see the big picture, even if the cavalry and infantry generals refused to acknowledge it: artillery had become the only offensive weapon left. Fuller was already writing about this new reality and grappling with the consequences of change. Such large stockpiles of shells were required for offensives (a million at the Somme) that the element of surprise would usually be lost. The limited mobility of heavy guns made it impossible for breakthroughs to be exploited, because once infantry advanced beyond the range of their supporting guns (rarely more than 10,000 yards) they were finished. Finally, the power of the machine-gun made it pointless to endanger large numbers of infantrymen in the front line.

What, then, did Fuller make of the Bull? Fuller knew his reputation of course, but had to set it aside, calling Allenby 'a man I grew to like and respect'. Fuller quickly came to appreciate that the Third Army's commander was one of very few Western Front generals who was interested in the ideas that percolated up from his planners and logisticians. This, in turn, meant that Allenby's 'staff was the most harmonious I have ever served on'.

Allenby's pedantry and abrasive visits to the front line were unpleasant traits that actually aided his rise in the early twentieth-century army. He was one of the few of the Boer War generation of cavalry commanders that Kitchener had sent to run the army in France in 1914 who had been to Staff College and thought seriously about war. His intellectual curiosity was such that he consumed books on everything from botany to ancient history to the poetry of the Western Front. His mind was certainly open to lateral thinking. Those young staff officers who came quaking into the Bull's presence at his chateau dinner table soon discovered that he was a quite unconventional general. This officer's recollection of being cross-examined by Allenby gives a good flavour of the man:

His keen grey-blue eyes, under heavy brows, search the face while he probes the mind with sharp, almost staccato, questions about everything under the sun except what is expected. He cannot suffer fools gladly and demands an unequivocal affirmative or negative to every query he makes. He has a habit of asking questions on the most abstruse subjects, and an unpleasant knack of catching out anyone who gives an evasive answer for the sake of politeness.

Allenby's personal stake in trying to avoid any repetition of the Somme was as great as any father's in Britain. His son, his only child, Michael, was serving as a subaltern in the Royal Horse Artillery in the Third Army's sector. Allenby's boy was exposed to the same risks as everybody else's and won the Military Cross while saving a wounded soldier under heavy fire. The general knew army life well enough never to intervene in favour of his son's safety, but he was a loving father and husband – no Edwardian archetype of cool detachment – and he could not staunch his own anxiety at what might happen to Michael.

Each evening the officer who compiled the casualty returns at Third Army HQ in the chateau would hear Allenby's boots clattering up the stone flagstones in the corridor outside. The door would be pushed open with a swagger stick, then the general would enter the room and, making no eye contact, stare out of the window. 'Have you any news of my little boy today?' The staff officer replied, 'No news, sir.' Satisfied, Allenby would turn on his heel and leave.

Here was a man who was longing to break the impasse, yearning for the war to be over. All he needed was the right opportunity to show what he could do.

During the early spring of 1917, the Third Army's sector bustled with activity: above the front, British pilots ran the gauntlet of German fire, taking aerial photographs of the Hun's positions; behind it, trainloads of shells were offloaded into the dumps needed to sustain an opening bombardment; beneath the trenches, the catacombs in the Arras sector were being extended by tunnellers, who laid railtrack and electric light as they went.

The Bull remained the Bull, of course, beasting along his troops. But the New Zealand Tunnelling Company of engineers found that, like many of his ilk, the best way to deal with Allenby was to stand up to him. 'A complaint came in from General Allenby that we weren't saluting officers,' wrote one of the Kiwis whose OC 'is said to have asked Allenby whether he wanted discipline or work, telling him that if he insisted on saluting the footage would drop and the caves would not be ready in time. Allenby gave in.'

All of this hard labour was accompanied by the clattering of typewriters in the different sections of the Third Army's staff. Allenby was being given his big show at last, and the view in many quarters was that if things went wrong, he would be well and truly unstuck. But he had listened to quite a few of the bright ideas put forward by his staff, and the operational plans sent up to GHQ suggested none of the caution that might be expected from a man in such a precarious position.

In a memo dated 17 February 1917, the Third Army suggested, 'the artillery preparation for the assault will be of forty-eight hours' duration . . . to obtain the advantage of surprise'. On the advice of his Commander Royal Artillery (Major General A. Holland), Allenby wanted to set aside the usual week-long bombardment. Other aspects of the plan were quite novel too: fresh divisions, a second echelon, would be positioned to exploit any success; careful plans had been laid to control traffic in the rear so that these follow-on forces could get through; new weapons – tanks as well as aircraft – were to be employed; and two whole divisions would be protected from German bombardment by bringing them forward in the underground caverns.

Third Army's plan caused much collective spluttering into tea mugs at GHQ. In particular, they sought to squash the idea of a curtailed opening barrage. The fact that the Germans virtually set their watches when a week-long fire plan began, so that they would know when to expect a frontal assault, persuaded few at GHQ. But Allenby would not give in, so in the end Field Marshal Haig had Major General Holland replaced as the Third Army's artillery chief by someone who believed in the orthodoxy. The Bull finally had to accept a compromise of four days' preparatory shelling.

During March 1917 this debate was interrupted by a remarkable and unexpected occurrence. The German Army voluntarily abandoned a fifty-mile stretch of front, pulling back ten miles to the newly prepared Hindenburg Line defensive belt. This move had profound implications for the Third Army's planned offensive – making impossible, for example, early ideas that British troops using tunnels should emerge *behind* the German trenches. Colonel Fuller, among others, felt the whole plan of attack needed to be reassessed. There was no chance of that, though: GHQ insisted it go ahead. Fuller wrote that Haig 'possessed a stereotyped mind, and, like a deluge or an avalanche, once set in motion, he could not stop because . . . he considered this particular form of stupidity to be the one test of a good general'.

Having picked apart Third Army's plan, but insisted the attack should go ahead anyway, Haig effectively disowned Allenby a few days before it was launched, telling him that he would have to take full responsibility if it all went wrong. Little wonder that the Bull came close to nervous collapse as Zero Hour, 5.30 a.m. on 9 April 1917, approached.

The gods, though, gave Allenby a helping hand. As the whistles blew on that spring morning in northern France, a freak snow shower was blowing across the battlefield from west to east, into the faces of the German lookouts. Men of the 51st (Highland) Division ran across no man's land with the weather on their side and the enemy bewildered by the shorter-than-expected bombardment. By the time the Germans woke up to the seriousness of the situation, there were kilted men clambering through the wire just in front of them and lofting Mills bombs into their trenches. The Maxims opened up.

Sergeant Bill Hay of the 9th Royal Scots recalled years later:

'Above the din of the barrage you couldn't speak. It was Jimmy Adams who tapped me on the shoulder indicating 'Go!' Well, I was first up the ladder and once on top I turned about and put out my hand to assist him up; there was a loud 'Clang!' and his steel helmet went spinning through the air. He was shot clean through the head and fell back into the trench. 'How bloody ridiculous!' I shouted, as if the Germans were listening. 'He was only a boy!'

As the Scots infantry hurled themselves forward, the intensity of the fire directed at them was not as heavy as usual, though. Hay found himself staring down into the German first trench, where the defenders knew the game was up and were shouting, '*Kamerad*,' with their hands in the air. 'Never mind the fuckin' *kamerad*,' came Hay's pithy response, 'let's have you bastards out now!' Scores of prisoners were herded together and sent back across no man's land towards the British trenches. At this point the German artillery fire plan kicked in, dropping dozens of shells among their own prisoners as they crossed between the lines.

Nobody in the 51st Division had much time for sympathy. They had already got hundreds over the first trench line and were pushing deeper into the German position. The British artillery by contrast was doing wonders, the fall of shot moving deeper into the Hindenburg Line as Allenby's footsloggers pressed on just behind the blasts – a tactic called a 'creeping barrage'. By 7.30 a.m., the 9th Royal Scots had reached their objective for the day. The exhausted men flopped down and broke out hard-boiled eggs – it was Easter Monday.

Further south, in Third Army's sector, the 9th Division, another Scottish outfit, pushed forward, one of its brigades being commanded by Brigadier Frank Maxwell. Kitchener's onetime ADC in South Africa, 'the Brat', led from the front, adopting private soldier's clothing and a rifle (to safeguard himself from snipers) as he went over the top with his men. His brigade reached its objective at 9 a.m., and he reported, 'The attack was a procession.'

'This was the most successful attack I took part in,' a corporal in the 8th Royal Fusiliers would recall, 'and I had been over the top five times. Our casualties were not heavy and this was the first time we had seen a travelling barrage. What a brainwave that was! . . . I remember thinking at the time, "Cor, we're getting on top of them at last."'

By the end of the day, Allenby's army had advanced three and a half miles. It was unheard of: the biggest gain by either side since late 1914, when trench warfare had set in. The Bull's letter home to his wife contained a diary of that week's events: '10 April: I had a very big success yesterday, I won all along the line; killed a host of Boche and took over 7,500 prisoners . . . We have, at last, brought off what I have been working on all winter. My staff has been splendid.'

On 10 and 11 April, though, Third Army's attack bogged down. Driving snow and heavy bombardment had created a quagmire that hindered the exploitation that Allenby had planned. But the Bull was loose: he ordered his troops to take risks in the pursuit, sending cavalry through to keep up the gains.

At Monchy, a village five miles east of Arras, Allenby's cavalry attack came unstuck, the horses falling to barbed wire, machine-guns and shrapnel. Hundreds of horse soldiers were killed around this village, and it was eventually taken by three tanks. There were only forty of these new machines involved in the offensive, fewer than had been hoped, and even these were scattered about the Third Army's sector where many bogged down in the cloying mud. However, the following account by Feldwebel Wilhelm Speck of the 84th Reserve Regiment, which found a British tank sitting astride one of its trenches near Monchy on 11 April, gives some idea of the weapon's potential:

The tank crew opened up with a murderous machine-gun fire which was slowly directed along 1st Company trench. Those that were not killed instantly screamed as they lay there wounded . . . Then the panic started, everyone from the 1st and 3rd companies jumped out of the trench and ran the fastest race of his life, pursued by the merciless tank machine-gun fire which cut down many men as if it were a rabbit shoot.

In truth, many of Third Army's problems, and in particular the inflexibility of its attacks, resulted from the inability of advancing troops to communicate with one another. The tanks used at Arras had been supplied with carrier pigeons for sending back messages. In several places, the need to respect the Royal Artillery's pre-planned fire missions prevented the infantry from exploiting early successes. Brigadier Maxwell fumed as he watched the disorganised defenders in front of him, knowing that the Germans got 'two hours' respite allowed by the programme'. When British troops finally pressed forward on 12 April, Maxwell's brigade was largely destroyed. Brave as a lion, Maxwell was later killed leading from the front at Passchendaele.

Field Marshal Haig, taken aback by Third Army's initial successes and then frustrated by its subsequent slow-down, assumed personal command of the sector, pushing Allenby's troops into a number of ill-advised frontal assaults, culminating in a bloody finale on 23 April in which the 51st Division, among others, was virtually shattered.

By the end of the Arras offensive, Third Army had suffered 87,226 casualties. Its losses were, as a proportion of those taking part and given the short length of the operation, the worst of any First World War offensive (there were half a million casualties at the Somme, but it continued for much longer). Allenby had shown flashes of brilliance in the way he had planned and executed the first phase of Arras, but the heavy losses thereafter left a bitter taste among many observers. It is pointless to speculate how much success Third Army might have enjoyed if it had not been hampered by GHQ interference; suffice to say that Allenby's performance had been noticed in Downing Street and would soon result in the Bull being given a show of his own.

The officers in the GHQ of the Egyptian Expeditionary Force in Cairo found their introduction to Allenby was no short, sharp, forty-eight-hour bombardment but an onslaught that lasted for weeks after he assumed command on 29 June 1917. One staff officer who presented him with a great pile of papers for his perusal found them being hurled across the room as trivia unfit for the consideration of a Commander-in-Chief. On another occasion, those in Allenby's outer office, having exchanged knowing looks while the general took apart a colonel behind closed doors, were alarmed to hear a thump and an abrupt halt to the harangue. The colonel had passed out under the Bull's cross-examination.

Allenby's principal act in stamping his authority on his new command during his first week was to order GHQ's relocation. Both Gordon and Kitchener had taken a dim view of British society in Cairo, believing far too many officers pickled themselves in gin and went whoring. Allenby did something about it. He moved his headquarters from the Egyptian capital 300 miles to the east across the Sinai Desert to Rafah, close to the British front lines at Gaza. As the forlorn staff packed up their things and organised their shipment to Rafah, Allenby began a series of journeys hither and thither to the various corners of his command. Bouncing along rutted tracks in cars or trucks, Allenby appeared unexpectedly among the troops from Britain, Australia, New Zealand and India.

This travelling had an immediate and beneficial effect. Fighting soldiers who lived in the desert realised that GHQ was no longer a remote and cushy institution. The Australians, never the easiest troops for a British brass hat to impress, noted the difference. 'A trooper who caught only one fleeting glimpse of him felt that here at last was a man with the natural qualities of a great driving commander,' the Australian official history of the campaign later recorded. 'Within a week of his arrival Allenby had stamped his personality on the mind of every trooper of the horse and every infantryman of the line.'

The Prime Minister, David Lloyd George (he had succeeded Asquith in 1916), had given Allenby his mission: 'Jerusalem by Christmas'. Allenby did not intend to dawdle. There had been too much drift on the Eastern Front, where Britain fought the Turks. Lloyd George was a convinced 'easterner', believing that this theatre offered the chance of knocking out a key German ally and raising morale in Britain. But the result of interventions against the Turks had ranged from outright defeat (Gallipoli) to partial defeat (Iraq) and stasis (Palestine). At Gaza, the gateway to Palestine since ancient times, two attempts to force an entry into that country had been repulsed at great cost. Matters had settled into trench warfare. Lloyd George believed it gross incompetence, fuming, 'In Palestine and Mesopotamia nothing could have saved the Turk from complete collapse in 1915 and 1916 except our

General Staff.' He had a point, because, even as Allenby set out from London, the Chief of the General Staff had been dismissing the relevance of eastern operations and doing his best to limit the forces sent there. But Allenby had been given personal assurances by the PM and as July wore on reinforcements duly arrived and plans were laid for a new onslaught against the Turkish defensive line, which stretched from Gaza to Beersheba.

In the midst of all of this, on 31 July, returning from one of his desert reccecs, Allenby received the most terrible blow of his life. A telegram from his wife contained the news that their son Michael had been killed in action in France. One evening, while alone with one of his staff officers and with tears in his eyes, Allenby recited from memory some lines by Rupert Brooke:

> Blow out, you bugles, over the rich Dead!
> There's none of these so lonely and poor of old,
> But, dying, has made us rarer gifts than gold.
> These laid the world away; poured out the red
> Sweet wine of youth; gave up the years to be
> Of work and joy, and that unhoped serene,
> That men call age; and those who would have been,
> Their sons, they gave, their immortality.

To his wife, Allenby wrote, 'Michael achieved, early, what every great man in the world's history has made it his life's ambition to attain – to die honoured, loved and successful, in full vigour of body and mind.' There is something very touching about the tenderness of Allenby's love for his 'little boy'. The general reminded his wife, 'He was always the same; a friend, on equal terms; and yet, unaffectedly, he always kissed me when we met and parted – as he did when a child.'

Although deeply shaken, the general did not show his grief in public, even as letters of condolence arrived from the high and mighty (including Field Marshal Haig). Instead, he drove himself harder, preparing what lay ahead. 'He went on with his work and asked no sympathy,' wrote Wavell, who had joined his Egyptian staff. 'Only those who stood close to him knew how heavy the blow had been, how nearly it had broken him, and what courage it had taken to withstand it.'

As he immersed himself in the problems of launching his drive on Jerusalem, the general considered the issue from every angle. He studied

Napoleon's campaigns in the Holy Land, and even those of Richard the Lionheart. All aspects of supply were considered, too, since it had already become apparent how difficult providing water to his desert army would be. There were medical problems to be mulled over as well – precautions against the ophthalmia that had bedevilled Napoleon's host, and enteric fever, which sapped at the divisions outside Gaza. 'His interest in anything appertaining to Egypt and Syria which might affect the troops or the progress of the campaign was insatiable,' wrote one eminent eye specialist consulted by Allenby at GHQ. 'Whether it was a fly expert from the British Museum, a railway expert, an expert on town planning, or a naturalist who could tell him something about the flora and fauna of the country, he had them all up and sucked their brains of anything they could tell him.'

One of the men whom Allenby exploited in this way was T.E. Lawrence. A fluent Arabic speaker and natural explorer, he had been sent from his humdrum job on the intelligence staff at Cairo to help stir up anti-Turkish resistance across the Red Sea in Arabia. Allenby backed Lawrence, drew much information from him and promoted him following the daring seizure of the port of Aqaba in July 1917.

Having made every conceivable preparation in the weeks available, Allenby examined an attack plan put forward by one of his brightest young staff officers. What emerged once the Bull had finished with it was a blueprint that in many respects seems remarkably modern: a pinning attack at Gaza followed by a main blow thirty miles to the south-east at Beersheba; a deception plan that included dummy units as well as fake operational plans 'discovered' by the Turks; extensive use of air power; raids by Lawrence's force of Arab irregulars to paralyse enemy transport; tank attacks to break the stalemate at Gaza; and a grand design of deep strikes, using his most mobile forces to sweep around and cut off large bodies of retreating Turks. Zero Hour was set for 31 October 1917.

For the troopers of the 4th Australian Light Horse Brigade, their moment of truth came just after 4.30 p.m. on the first day of the offensive. They had been resting their horses, after a long night march and a morning in reserve, while others took a ridge that dominated the approaches to Beersheba. The general commanding the Desert Mounted Corps (acting as the eastern arm of Allenby's push) ordered the 4th ALH to break into the town and do so with all haste, since there was a great deal of concern that the Turks were about to blow up the wells.

The Turks had been complacent, refusing to believe that whole divisions of cavalry could cross the desert and attack the eastern end of their defensive line, Beersheba. But Allenby had used 30,000 camels to keep his divisions watered, and a thirty-mile night march compounded the surprise.

As the Australian cavalry charged from the east towards the centre of town, the Turkish Maxims opened up, but the tide of horses kept

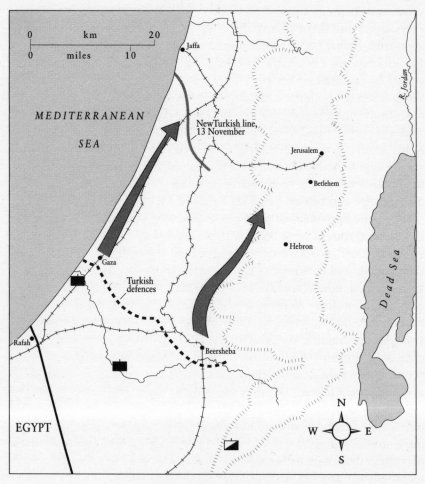

Allenby's push into Palestine, 1917

coming. Many chargers leapt the enemy trenches while some of the light horsemen dismounted, fixed bayonets to their carbines and cleared out the defenders. In no time, the leading squadrons had gone through the centre of Beersheba, and, with darkness falling, secured wells that had been rigged with explosives. The Allies had the water they needed to sustain their drive north.

West of the highly mobile Desert Mounted Corps were two infantry corps. XX Corps assisted with the Beersheba attack but also covered the ground between that dusty town and Gaza on the coast, where XXI Corps mounted the army's third major push on the fortified city. The Gaza attacks went somewhat better than expected and Allenby was very happy for them to exploit their success. Having learned bitter lessons at Arras, he was determined to make sure both that artillery would keep pace with the breakthrough and that communications would be maintained between the advancing echelons. Big guns, like the monster 60-pounders, had to be partially disassembled to move, so the initial emphasis was on horse artillery acting in its historic role. But engineer support had been provided to bridge trenches and reconnect roads so that tractors could haul the guns forward. Similarly, clever arrangements had been made to connect advancing British signallers to Turkish telegraph lines. Large numbers of dispatch riders – on motorcycles and horses – had also been provided.

It became apparent within the first twenty-four hours of the attack that breakthroughs were being achieved in several places. Turkish divisions streamed northwards in disarray, as arguments raged between their *pashas* and the German C-in-C as to whether they should attempt an immediate counter-stroke or fall back far enough to form a strong, new defensive line. Allenby wrote home to his wife, 'The Turks are having an awful hammering. A few pockets of Turks, in isolated trench systems, are holding out east of Gaza. They will be starved out, in time, so I am only shelling them, and not wasting men in attacking them.' During the first ten days of the offensive 10,000 prisoners and 100 guns were taken.

Two weeks after the offensive was launched, about fifty miles to the north Allied troops came up against a new defensive position stretching from the sea just south of Jaffa to the Judean Hills. The experience of riding in a cavalry charge in the age of the machine-gun was recorded by Lieutenant B. Bowyer of the Buckinghamshire Hussars, who took part in an attack to force the Turkish line at al Mugheir.

'Immediately a great clatter of fire starts all along the ridge,' he wrote, describing the moment when they went over the top on horseback at 3 p.m. 'For a moment the shell fire is heavy, as Johnny [Turk] has the range of the gulleys, and an HE drops just between a machine-gun pack horse and its fellow. A few yards in front I have a momentary vision of two horses, a man, and a lot of smoke, flying outwards as I flashed past.' The charge pushed on another half-mile towards the main enemy position: 'I believe the rifle and machine-gun fire got heavier as we neared the slope. Anyhow, several horses and riders turned over in quite the approved battle picture style, and the ground was zipping and spluttering as the bullets hit it.'

At this point, the Yeomanry drew their swords with a cry of 'Forward on!' but their horses had been exhausted by the long gallop and virtually staggered up the final slope to the Turkish position. 'Now we are on top we jump the Turkish trench and sweep over the hill, down the far side, right through a mob of Turks.' Some of the Yeomanry dismounted to take pot-shots at fleeing enemy soldiers running back through the cacti. By dusk the fight was over. 'We had had what every cavalryman longs for,' wrote the elated lieutenant, 'and had been successful against an almost impossible position.' The cost, though, was most of their horses hit, and forty men killed or wounded in the two squadrons that performed the assault.

Allenby drove his advancing troops relentlessly, batting aside excuses or complaints about supplies and the risks of Turkish counter-attack. Early in December, they forced their way up into the Judean Hills, and in coordinated moves to the north and south of Jerusalem moved towards their great prize. Allenby was concerned about the possibility of having to fight for the city and had issued definite orders that artillery should not be used either in the Holy City itself or in Bethlehem to its south. The Turks, however, had no intention of being surrounded and withdrew from Jerusalem, their departure producing a farcical scene as the civic authorities attempted to surrender the prize to the first British soldiers they could find, two sergeants of the 60th (London) Division.

On 11 December 1917, Allenby wrote home, 'Today I entered Jerusalem, on foot.' His decision to walk rather than ride in was seen by the inhabitants as a welcome sign of humility. In his initial proclamation, the general showed his respect for the three great faiths, ordering, 'Every sacred building . . . or customary place of prayer of whatsoever form of the three religions will be maintained and pro-tected according to the existing customs.' He was all too aware of the passions that had been unleashed by the rolling back of Ottoman power and the different positions adopted by his own government about the future of the region. As his Gaza offensive started, the Balfour Declaration (a pledge by the Foreign Secretary to assist in the creation of a Jewish homeland in Palestine) had been issued in London. Knowing the sensitivity of this issue to Arabs, Allenby suppressed local publication of this document for as long as he could. He was also keenly aware that his government had made promises to aid the Arab revolt that had swept up what is now Saudi Arabia into Jordan (with T.E. Lawrence in its midst), with an implied promise of self-rule, while at the same time preparing with Paris a general Anglo-French carve-up of the Middle East (the Sykes–Picot Agreement). Allenby tiptoed through the minefield of Jewish, Christian and Muslim claims, gaining general respect from all three groups. He was helped in this by rumours that raced through the Islamic population that he was a mysterious prophet (*Allah en Nebi*) whom sages had predicted would enter the Holy City on foot. Other actions also bolstered his reputation. Muslim troops of the Indian Army, for example, were sent to protect the sacred sites of their faith. Allenby did not like it at all when he heard anyone using the word 'crusade', and (unlike such figures as Gordon and Kitchener) he was hardly religious. But, of course, the press chose to portray him as the man who had achieved what Richard the Lionheart had failed to do, making him the Christian hero who had liberated the Holy City from 730 years of rule by 'the Turk'. Lloyd George, in any case, had got Jerusalem by Christmas. Allenby's deed also won him great fame in the United States, which had just entered the war on the Allied side.

Among military observers, he had garnered a different sort of noto-riety. His offensive had been one of devastating mobility at a time when the immobile slaughter of the Western Front dominated everybody's mind. One Yeomanry regiment had advanced sixty miles in fifty-four hours. An observer who watched the breaching of the Gaza–Beersheba defences noted, 'Each move in the game was strategically masterful, daring in conception and tactically perfect.'

Rex Wingate, Kitchener's second-in-command at Omdurman, was still in Sudan. He visited Palestine and wrote to Allenby's wife, 'I can only express unbounded admiration for Sir Edmund and his work – when one sees the immensely strong positions of the enemy, the country, and the difficulties which have been so successfully overcome by him and his army. I am confident this campaign will go down to history as one of the finest military achievements on record.'

At year's end 1917, Allenby's army was engaged in a huge logistic catching-up operation. Tenuous supply lines that ran from Egypt had to carry forward large amounts of stores, since the British had not captured a major port in Palestine. A front line had stabilised, running from just north of Jaffa on the coast, up into the hills, north of Jerusalem and deep into the Jordan valley at Jericho. Everybody knew that the war in the Middle East was not yet over.

In London news of the great success in Palestine triggered recriminations between Lloyd George and his Chief of Imperial General Staff. Downing Street felt that the head of the army had been unnecessarily gloomy in his predictions for the campaign. The subtext was Lloyd George's belief in the 'Eastern Front' and the CIGS's equally strong scepticism about it. 'It is very difficult to please Ministers sometimes, as I told the Prime Minister yesterday,' CIGS wrote to Allenby on 14 December 1917. 'If we had underestimated the Turk and had failed we should have deserved to be hung, but because we have succeeded more easily than might have been the case does not seem to justify blaming us for taking every precaution.'

Lloyd George still harboured grand designs about driving on to Turkey. The War Office, by contrast, eyed Allenby's army and saw only troops that were desperately needed on the Western Front. So, in the early part of 1918, two apparently contradictory things happened: the political authorities began examining the conquest of what is now Syria, Jordan and Lebanon while Allenby's army was stripped of some of its best soldiers. The manner in which he reconciled the apparently irreconcilable as these demands were made of him would lead to his greatest campaign.

The morning of 19 September 1918 saw a terrible revelation in Nazareth. The headquarters of the Yilderim Army Group, controlling Turkish, German and Austro-Hungarian troops in Palestine, Syria, Jordan and Lebanon, came under air attack. Bombs felled the telegraph wires running into the town. To the south-west, further air raids hit the exchange at Afula. The air attacks were part of a carefully calculated plan to paralyse enemy communications. 'If Allenby thought a thing was "good",' the Royal Air Force commander in Palestine wrote later, 'it was characteristic of him to use it to the utmost.' Certainly, the C-in-C grasped the value of air power in the most dramatic fashion.

Down on the coast, Turkish forces had suffered a brief but extremely violent artillery bombardment since 4.30 that morning. At one point, 1,000 shells were falling each minute. Allenby's troops outnumbered his enemy's by something like two to one infantry and several times that in cavalry, but the Turks had the advantage of prepared defences, which Allenby intended to nullify by concentrating his own force. Whereas he had used a feint on the coast and attacked inland during his campaign of October 1917, this time he would posture in the hills and strike beside the sea. When the Turks had interrogated a prisoner shortly before the offensive, their C-in-C, German General Liman von Sanders (victor of Gallipoli), refused to believe his information, thinking it another Allenby deception operation.

So, on 19 September, the Turkish XXII Corps, on the coastal plain north of Jaffa, felt the full power of the British hammer-blow. The XXII Corps' 8,000 infantry and 130 guns were assaulted by 35,000 Allied footsloggers after a pummelling from 383 guns. Some 9,000 of Allenby's mounted troops stood by, ready to pour through breaches in the Turkish defences. Not surprisingly, the Turkish front collapsed. The Desert Mounted Corps pushed through the gaps, and by that night was advancing rapidly northwards with a mission to cut off the retreat of as many Turkish troops as possible. This corps combined horsed cavalry regiments with an armoured-car brigade and another of recce troops in unarmoured vehicles. On the 20th, Allied cavalry entered Nazareth, causing complete consternation in the Turkish GHQ, from where General von Sanders escaped only with difficulty.

These advances were so rapid – something like fifty miles in little more than a day – that the cavalry had to double back in places to assist the advance of the British infantry. At El Lajjun (Megido, or Armageddon in biblical parlance) a swift cavalry charge during the early hours of the 21st secured a pass vital to the British advance inland. The main British effort thus turned eastwards, away from the sea, towards Tiberias and Beisan (Beit Shean in modern Israel) in a move that would cut off Turkish forces in the northern part of what we now call the West Bank.

During these first days of the offensive, General von Sanders lost control of large parts of the Yilderim Army Group. Some 20,000 of them

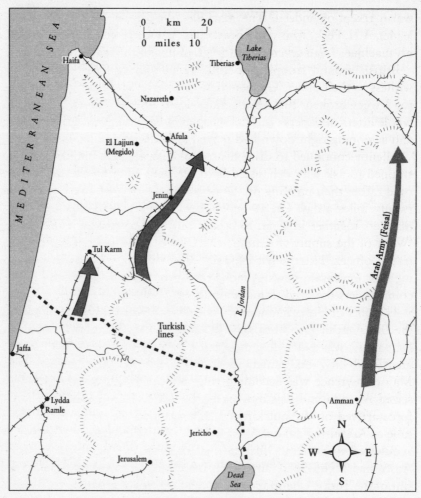

The Megido offensive, 1918

surrendered to the British in the first forty-eight hours. Large columns of demoralised troops were streaming north and east, trying to escape Allenby's trap, and squadrons of the Royal Air Force Palestine Brigade were let loose on them. With the biplanes' strafing and bombing a new kind of warfare was born – what some would later term 'deep battle' or 'air interdiction'. Whole units of Turkish troops were being destroyed or scattered by air attack. 'We used to bomb, diving down line ahead,' recalled one pilot of 144 Squadron. He added that the Turks did not take this punishment passively: 'At Nablus we got a very warm reception indeed. The machine-gun fire was very heavy. Our leader, A.H. Peck, who was a great chap, had forty bullet holes through his machine; I had seventeen through mine, all round me.'

British ground troops who followed up these RAF attacks bore witness to their effect. Gunner M.W. Winslade saw that 'all along the road were broken Turkish wagons, dead horses, bullocks, men and whole litters of papers . . . Our aeroplanes had caught Jacko retreating and swooping right down had played havoc with machine-gun fire.'

Allenby continued to drive his troops forward. On one occasion he stopped to ask why exhausted infantry were lying by the side of the road rather than pressing on. Some of his footsloggers were pounding twenty miles a day. On 26 September Allenby called his corps commanders together in Jenin to confer on the next phase of the battle. 'What of the supply situation?' the C-in-C asked his senior administrative officer. 'Extremely rocky, sir,' came the reply. Apparently ignoring this unpleasant news, Allenby then proceeded to impress upon his commanders the need to maintain the pace of their advance.

The port of Haifa had already been captured on 23 September, and the Daughter of Jacob Bridge, a key point on the road from Galilee to Damascus, was taken five days later. Other eyes were fixed on that great Arab city, too, namely those of the army of Emir Feisal (whom Major Lawrence was accompanying) and an Allied column that had seized Amman and was moving north. Cavalry from Allenby's main force arrived on the outskirts of Damascus on the 30th, at the same time as Arab irregulars of Feisal's army. The following day, the British acquiesced to an Arab liberation of the city, with some elements of Australian Light Horse already pushing through to resume their pursuit of the Turks. Chaotic scenes and a measure of bloodshed followed as Feisal, aided by Lawrence, tried to establish some sort of civic control in the face of opposition. Lawrence, who relished the authority given to him by Allenby, had found himself thwarted on every side until the general himself arrived in the city, when, the angry major wrote, 'I let my limbs relax in [the] dreamlike confidence and decision and kindness which were Allenby.'

The C-in-C was all too aware that the competing ambitions of his own government, France's and Feisal, at the head of the Arab revolt, would focus on Damascus. He simply imposed a curfew, asserted, as he had in Jerusalem, that he could not do anything to decide the future status of the city, and returned to the business of pursuing Johnny Turk.

His army continued its advance, all cohesion having been lost by their enemies. A coastal column took Beirut on 8 October, while an inland force moved up the Beka'a valley, its armoured cars reaching Aleppo on the 26th. In the following days Allied control was extended over much of Syria to the very frontiers of Turkey itself.

Six weeks of fighting had seen advances of 350 miles, with one cavalry division travelling 550 miles. Allenby's troops had captured 75,000 Turks and 360 artillery pieces while suffering around 5,000 casualties. Basil Liddell-Hart, an eminent military theorist of the inter-war years, would write that Allenby's campaign had been 'one of the masterpieces of military history'.

Some have sought to question Allenby's achievement by pointing out that Allied forces outnumbered the Turks by a considerable margin. The exact numbers in the Turkish Army remain unclear, but it is evident that in his 1918 campaign the British general had around double their infantry. On the other hand, few fair-minded observers can dispute that attacking prepared positions, pushing through follow-on forces, advancing hundreds of miles, and all the time policing several captured cities while you go is an operation that requires substantial numbers of troops. The key thing is to see Allenby's campaigns in the context of warfare as it was practised in 1917 and 1918. Turkish troops (stiffened with German and Austro-Hungarian contingents) had shown what extraordinarily tenacious fighters they could be in defence at Gallipoli, and had mounted a credible counter-offensive against British troops in Iraq. They were, then, no pushover. The Maxims, barbed wire and heavy guns that caused hideous stalemate on the Somme had produced the same effect in Gaza. There is no doubt in my mind that had GHQ Cairo continued with 'business as usual' – the lacklustre probings of a C-in-C who knew he had little backing in the War Office – the Turks would not have been driven from the Middle East. However, they got Allenby, a man infused with the desire to break out of the trench-warfare deadlock and rediscover mobility. They also got someone who, by use of irregular forces, air strikes and mechanised units, made the first practical attempt at a new form of warfare. In showing his fluency with all these different arms, while melding together soldiers of many nationalities and faiths, Allenby also has a respectable claim to being what one recent biographer has called 'the first of the modern supreme commanders'.

Allenby was not a politician – although later, out of uniform, he became the arbiter of Egypt's future (and played a key role in convincing Whitehall that that country would have to become independent). His offensives in 1917–18 were carried out on Downing Street's orders, not some initiative of his own. The specific arrangements later put in place to create British-ruled territories in Palestine, Jordan and Iraq were not designed by him, still less the French systems imposed on Syria and Lebanon. It's true he influenced what followed to the extent that his patronage of Feisal's Hashemite tribe made them a suitable choice as the rulers of Jordan and Iraq, and in the latter case this set the scene for decades of domination of Iraqi affairs by the minority Sunnis. But overall, he was evidently a military man who fulfilled the mission given him by Lloyd George.

Having said all of this, though, it is Allenby's role in the creation of the modern Middle East that is his greatest legacy. How so? It was the violence with which he broke up the Ottoman armies that dealt the death-blow to that long-tottering empire. Had a cautious British general advanced a little further into Palestine but been checked in 1917, the Turks would have remained the masters of much of the Middle East. Without the humiliation of Allenby's destruction of their armies and capture of what are now four countries, Turkey's secular revolution under Kemal Atatürk (who had been fighting Allenby) may well never have taken place. The removal of Ottoman power was also the essential prerequisite for the creation of Israel and the coming of age of Arab nationalism.

As for the effect of his campaigns on the British high command and other interested military parties, this is more complicated. He had certainly shown what highly mobile forces could do. In our own lifetime, Allenby's feats were celebrated by the British generals who, from the mid-1980s onwards, sought to infuse the army with what they called 'manoeuvrist doctrine'. But his achievements in this regard were to become mired in controversy during the 1920s and 1930s. Both conservatives and revolutionaries embroiled in the army's internal debate about how best to banish the prospect of another Somme were to claim that Allenby's campaigns proved their point.

As that struggle got under way, it would be J. F. C. Fuller – Allenby's onetime staff officer in Third Army – who would emerge as the most vociferous and subversive critic of military orthodoxy.

John Frederick Charles Fuller

1878–1966

*I knew I should create enemies, yet without a sturdy opposition
it is most difficult to explode deep-rooted absurdities.*
J. F. C. FULLER

Of all meetings between man and machine, the one which occurred on 20 August 1916 in an open field near the village of Yvrench was among the most fateful. Major Fuller and a sapper colleague from Third Army HQ had heard about a demonstration of something weird and wonderful. The Somme offensive ground on within earshot and Allenby was still very much a presence at the nearby chateau HQ that they had managed to leave behind for the day. The weather was balmy, and the sense that they had left behind all sorts of grim labour created something of a holiday atmosphere. 'As we approached the area,' Fuller would write later, 'more and more did it assume the aspect of Epsom Downs on a Derby morning.'

There were hundreds of spectators, from brass hats to staff and humble regimental officers. Some had even brought picnics. The object of their curiosity could be heard humming and clanking some time before it came into view. 'Everyone was talking and chatting, when slowly came into sight the first tank I ever saw,' said Fuller. 'Not a monster, but a very graceful machine, with beautiful lines, lozenge shaped, but with two clumsy-looking wheels behind it.' This petrol-driven leviathan weighed 28 tons, mounted two 6-pounder cannon (or four machine-guns) and was covered in a carapace of half-inch-thick steel armour. It moved very slowly – rarely more than 4 m.p.h. – and its strange parallelogram shape was designed to give it the best chance of crossing ditches up to 10 feet wide and mounting obstacles 5 feet high.

It would be nice to think that this moment – Fuller meets tank – was recorded at the time as the apotheosis that it was. In fact, it took some months, until December 1916, for Fuller to be transferred to the headquarters of the Machine-Guns Corps Heavy Section (a cover name for the new Tank Corps) and for him to realise that this posting would not be some backwater but a turning point in his career that gave him a chance to display his tactical genius.

Once at the chateau of Bermicourt, he and other officers of this new force got to know one another. A fellow pioneer described Fuller perfectly:

A little man with a bald head, and a sharp face and a nose of Napoleonic cast, his general appearance, stature and features earning him the title of Boney. He stood out at once as a totally unconventional soldier, prolific in ideas, fluent in expression, at daggers drawn with received opinion, authority and tradition . . . He was neither an administrator nor probably a good commander, but just what a staff officer ought to be, evolving sound ideas and leaving their execution to others.

Fuller was thirty-eight years old when he began working at Bermicourt, and his trajectory through the army had been neither smooth nor harmonious. Apart from his early experiences in South Africa, his job interested him little during his years as a subaltern. Instead, he had immersed himself in philosophy and developed a fascination with the occult. He found mess rituals tedious or even stupid at times, and even despised much about soldiering in the light infantry. It was largely to escape this routine that he had applied for a place at the Staff College, where at last his formidable brain began to apply itself to the military problems of the day.

It had only taken a visit to an artillery demonstration on Salisbury Plain to set Fuller thinking about the power of heavy guns. Since they and machine-guns could sweep away almost everything, the relative importance of infantry and cavalry would be dramatically reduced – something a hierarchy drawn largely from these two arms simply refused to recognise. As a Staff College student, Fuller dissected such problems with a clarity and lack of tolerance for waffle that disconcerted his instructors. Finding a vague reference to 'the principles of war' in the Field Service Regulations but no definition of what they were, he set out (as someone who'd read the thirty-two volumes of Napoleon's correspondence cover to cover) to define them. This brought him into conflict with the commandant, who told him that it was not his job to rewrite a manual that was the nearest thing the army had to a tactical bible.

It wasn't simply that Fuller couldn't suffer fools, it was that he often chose to mock them, even to their faces. Sent in 1914 to work for a crusty old general moving troops about after the war had started, Fuller was asked by his chief to consider the problems that might be caused by millions of sheep blocking the lanes of southern England in the event of a German invasion. The general told his staff man to order up some signs proclaiming, 'Sheep are not to use this road'. Fuller replied, 'But what if the less well-educated sheep are unable to read them?' This piece of insolence produced a posting to the Western Front. There Fuller developed his ideas, publishing more papers; but on one occasion his ideas about defensive tactics were suppressed by the War Office on the grounds that, if published, they would be useful to the enemy.

The General Staff orthodoxy in August 1914 was that the new weapons made frontal attacks too costly and that envelopment must be tried instead. But the emergence of a long, snaking, muddy front line from Switzerland to the Channel had resulted in there being no flanks to turn. Instead, the belligerent armies grappled for years like exhausted, bloodied, bare-knuckle fighters, with neither able to gain the upper hand.

Fuller began to write about the tactics of penetration – how British troops might punch their way through German trench systems. Much of his early focus, in common with the prevailing discussions in Allenby's HQ, was on preliminary artillery barrages. But by the time he reached Bermicourt, at the end of 1916, Fuller had realised that the tank 'was the unknown x in the equation of victory. All that was necessary was to get people *to see* the problem.'

He was not in charge of the new corps – that honour fell to Hugh Elles, a Royal Engineer. And Elles had brought in several other sappers to help get things off the ground in one of the last great episodes of engineer brains being used to help a befuddled British General Staff embrace the fruits of the industrial age. Fuller's job, though, was pivotal in devising how the new machines would be used. He was able to formulate what armies these days call 'doctrine'. While some visionary documents had already been written about the use of tanks, Fuller wasn't shown them, so he worked with a clean sheet of paper.

The nickname 'Boney' became general at this time, and one suspects there was a measure of mess irony behind it, for although brother officers thought Fuller immensely clever and wickedly funny, he hardly looked like a great leader of men, while he was tackling ideas that would normally be the province of generals. As an ardent student of the Emperor's campaigns, he was flattered by the nickname; it does not seem to have occurred to him that he might only be Boney in the same way that an outsize lummox could be 'Tiny' or a bald recruit 'Curly'.

During the latter part of 1916 and early 1917 the new corps received scores of new tanks and thousands of troops. Elles, Fuller and the others had to train the men to use these new beasts, while getting their generals to understand their potential and limitations. Small numbers had been employed in 1916, and a few dozen joined Allenby's Arras offensive in April 1917, but the Tank Corps people were formulating plans for the new weapons to be used *en masse*.

'Though the Germans gave us a lot of trouble,' Fuller would later declare, 'Sir Douglas Haig and his phenomenally unimaginative General Staff gave us infinitely more.' This might seem like a typically acerbic Fuller jibe, but one example serves to show its justice. Fuller had drafted a manual called 'Training Note No. 16' which set out how the tank should be employed in battle. He saw its main purpose as pushing beyond the enemy's first trench (a job for the infantry) and into the second and third defensive belts, from where the Germans usually counter-attacked, thus making impossible such a counter-stroke. To allow the tanks to do this, the battlefield had to be left free of the huge craters that resulted from prolonged opening barrages, a form of preparation that anyway denied the attacker the element of surprise. 'Experience has definitely shown', said Training Note No. 16, 'that such a bombardment should not exceed 48 hours.' This was precisely the same issue that had caused Allenby's row with GHQ before Arras, and it so incensed Haig's staff that they ordered every copy of Fuller's new manual to be recalled and suppressed. The Tank Corps ignored this instruction, but other HQs obeyed it, which meant that the various corps and army commanders lost their guidance – from the experts – about how the tank could be used to best effect. Since Haig would also not have a tank adviser posted to GHQ (the artillery and engineers were represented there), its ignorance remained almost total.

When the Tank Corps began lobbying during the summer of 1917 to use hundreds of tanks in a 'raid' on the German front, GHQ reacted with suspicion. Haig did not like the idea of Elles having his own show, thinking the new corps was getting ideas above its station. The C-in-C wrote in September 1917, 'In its present state of development the tank is an adjunct to infantry and guns.' He bridled at the Tank Corps' advice about the geographic preconditions for a successful attack (i.e. in terms of the softness of the ground and its moisture), telling them firmly that such considerations would be a 'minor factor' in his determination of where to mount an offensive. It did not seem to occur to the prickly Haig that the tank people were not trying to tell him where to fight his battles, only where he might use tanks to the greatest effect in them.

By late 1917 there were, however, enough corps and army commanders who had heard about the potential of tanks to result in an idea being formulated for a mass use of tanks in a thrust towards the town of Cambrai. Indeed, the emergence of the plan for this offensive can be seen as evidence that Haig had lost some of his control over subordinates who were desperate to try tactical innovations, whether GHQ liked them or not.

Fuller had mixed feelings about this: he was delighted that hundreds of machines might be used in concert, but alarmed that plans originally conceived for a single day's raid across enemy trenches were now being put into effect for a full-scale assault on the Hindenburg Line. The colonel took the unusual step of putting his concerns to Elles in writing. The plan lacked any preparation for a sustained fight, instead throwing all the tanks forward on day one, so Fuller warned, 'To fight without a reserve is similar to playing cards without capital – it is sheer gambling.'

Elles, though, being the pioneering tank-leader he was, had seen his opening and was going to take it. On 19 November 1917 he issued an order to his units massing in the Cambrai sector: 'Tomorrow the Tank Corps will have the chance for which it has been waiting for many months – to operate on good going in the van of the battle.' In a deliberate contrast to usual Western Front generals' practice, Elles signed off, 'I propose leading the attack of the Centre division.' Boney, incidentally, thought Elles was doing the wrong thing by going into battle personally, but later wrote, 'He was right and I was wrong,' a sentiment that one will struggle to find anywhere else in Fuller's vast output of forty-five books and hundreds of articles.

So it was that early on 20 November 1917 Elles and thousands of other crewmen mounted up and 476 tanks moved forward for the first great armoured assault in history.

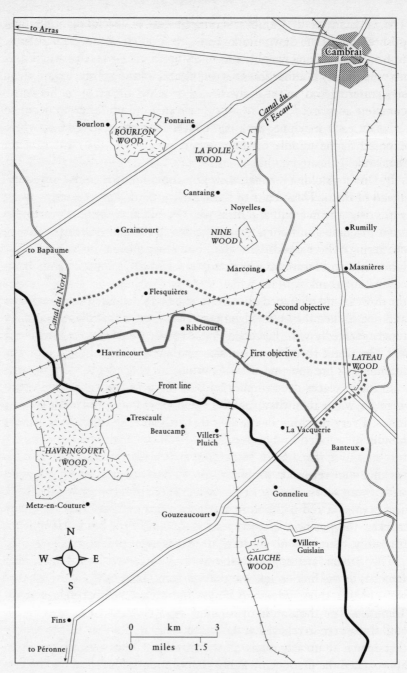

The Cambrai offensive, 1917

The tank attack at Cambrai came, like so many of the war's 'big pushes', out of the dawn murk. Tanks led the advance across six miles of front, there being roughly one every hundred yards. There had been no preparatory bombardment at all, a precaution that prevented excessive cratering and, in the early moments of the attack, gave the British complete surprise.

Inside each machine were eight men. The noise from the engine, exposed in the middle of the compartment, was deafening, and the 'bus' quickly heated up like a bath house, despite the autumn chill outside. Drivers looking through their ports could see the German defences ahead of them. Three belts of barbed-wire entanglements, each twelve yards deep, lay in front, and these were wreathed occasionally in sparks from machine-gun bullets that ricocheted as the Maxims began their chattering. The barbed wire was untouched due to the lack of bombardment, so everything was down to the tanks. Private Bacon, at the controls of a tank with the name 'Early Bird' painted on its side, opened the throttle and ploughed on: 'As we crawled on in front of the infantry and demolished the knife-edged wire entanglements, the bus was spattered repeatedly with hysterical left and right sweeps of machine-gun fire. The whole panorama now was just like a set piece of thousands of fountains of fire spurting from the solid earth.'

In many places deep ditches had been dug beyond the wire. These were far wider than the usual fire trenches and were intended to stop tanks. Every machine in the British first wave, however, had a huge bundle of wooden branches called a fascine lashed to the superstructure just over the driver's head. When they reached the obstacle, the fascines were released, tumbling into the ditch and providing the tanks with a way across. A gunner on each side of the tank opened his hatch and planted a red flag before the machine trundled across. The flags marked the position of the route to drivers of tanks that followed. Certainly, there was no shortage of ingenuity in the attack plans.

The British artillery laid short, sharp barrages on the German trenches as the first attack wave crossed no man's land. These worked well, hitting those who had come out of cover to open up at the Tommies. The thousands of infantry who walked to the rear of the land ships were so relieved at the lack of German counter-bombardment that many lit up cigarettes as they trudged along. When the tanks approached the first enemy fighting trench, those directing the artillery pushed the guns' fall of shot deeper into the German position.

'The surprise had been complete and our artillery overwhelming,' wrote one infantry officer who accompanied the attack. 'The reply of the German guns was negligible. The sight and certainty that they had been taken unawares produced in one a sense of supreme exultation. On the slope opposite tanks showed up like small dull-coloured huts endowed with movement; as they advanced we could see the flashes of their 6-pounders along a line which stretched out of sight both right and left.' This exultation – which one tank officer would write home had him laughing uncontrollably for hours inside his machine – had its counterpart in total demoralisation in the enemy lines. 'Our machine-guns fire incessantly and then rifle and grenade fire is added,' wrote one German officer, 'but [we] must admit all our efforts to stop these tanks ineffective. We can do nothing against them.'

In many places the German infantry broke and ran – it was dubbed 'tank-fright'. Once the first elements were over the first trench and into the Hindenburg Line, the same effect was produced at an organisational level. A British officer sent forward to interrogate enemy prisoners reported: 'Without exaggeration some of the infantry seemed to be off their heads with fright. It was impossible to obtain any clear idea of the situation. There was no chain of command and no orders.'

While this devastating attack unfolded, Fuller spent the morning at Tank Corps headquarters, awaiting reports. Such was his ceaseless industry that he began working, then and there, on notes for a visionary scheme on how tanks could win the war. It would later be called Plan 1919.

British attacks had, by mid-afternoon on 20 November, gained five miles in places. The original operational order had said, 'If . . . we are successful in overrunning the enemy's line of defence, a unique opportunity for the Cavalry action becomes possible.' For the average infantry officer, this was yet another promise of action by a cavalry force that had been pampered through the war and spent three years waiting for a 'unique opportunity'. Since Haig was an old-school cavalry officer, such phrases were always well received at GHQ.

The cavalry 'exploitation' at Cambrai proved to be the same kind of damp squib that it had been in all previous Western Front battles. Fortunately for the men concerned, though, their check was not as bloody as it had been at Monchy during the Arras battle. Instead, the cavalry got over the first German defences (where tanks specially equipped with grapples dragged all of the wire out of their way), but then found themselves blocked by more barbed wire and machine-gun fire, and unable to take villages in the German rear. In one place, a blown bridge put paid to the advance of a cavalry division. One Tank Corps major told his wife he had witnessed 'a great deal of clattering, galloping and shouting, and a lot of our medieval horse soldiers came charging down the street'. In Fuller's new mob, the ordinary soldier's scepticism about cavalry was being refined into a profound contempt.

It will come as no surprise, though, that having suffered such a heavy initial blow, the German high command soon regained its balance and began to reorganise. British attempts to gain more ground started to flounder. At Flesquieres an attack by the 51st Highland Division, supported by tanks, came to grief. The German divisional commander, an artillerist, had trained his field-gun crews in anti-tank firing techniques, and they played havoc with D and E battalions of the Tank Corps. In one engagement a dozen tanks were knocked out in a few moments.

British plans had called for the withdrawal of some tank units after forty-eight hours. In places, they were packing up and leaving as German counter-attacks began. Now the lack of a tank reserve was bitterly felt, as was confusion in the British high command about how the gains at Cambrai should be consolidated. A full-scale German counter-attack on 30 November forced back the British in places. However, the first phase of the Cambrai offensive was judged a success, having gained similar advances to Arras but for less than one-tenth of the casualties. But in many respects it produced an opportunity that was squandered. For a time, Haig's position looked threatened.

In the months that followed, Fuller refined Plan 1919 from an appeal for the production of thousands of new Medium D tanks into a manifesto for revolutionising the army. The document was presented to the War Office in May 1918 and is worth examining at some length since it was perhaps the finest and most influential document Fuller ever wrote.

In 1914 firepower had become so powerful that soldiers could not protect themselves against it, except by skulking in immobile trenches. The tank offered to change everything since it combined firepower, mobility and protection. The petrol engine, wrote Fuller, 'enables men to discharge their weapons from a moving platform protected by a fixed shield'. Since tracked vehicles could travel across 75 per cent of the countryside, 'He who grasps the full meaning of this change, namely, that the earth has now become as easily traversible as the sea, multiplies his chances of victory to an almost unlimited extent.' Fuller knew that his advocacy of tank warfare had already brought conflict with other parts of the British Army – it was, after all, a battle for men and money. In Plan 1919 he admitted frankly that tank warfare, being new, 'has been grafted on to a system it is destined to destroy'. He predicted that infantry 'will become first a subsidiary and later a useless arm on all ground over which tanks can move'.

In order to show that a large-scale increase in the Tank Corps could win the war, Fuller described how massive armoured offensives might be conducted. He identified the enemy command structure as the brain of an opposing force and supply troops as its stomach. The essence of tank warfare should be to strike deep at these vital organs. 'Our new theory should be to destroy "command", not after the enemy's personnel has been disorganised, but before it has been attacked, so that it may be found in a state of complete disorganisation when attacked.'

Plan 1919 was intended to convince generals and politicians, so it used powerful metaphors – whether of naval warfare or describing the enemy army in terms of the body. It also drew on history, Fuller arguing that armoured forces would be used to exploit success and clinch victory in much the same way that Napoleon used his Old Guard. To many in a tradition-bound army, this must have seemed like bare-faced cheek, since it elevated the army's newest corps into the position of its most cherished supreme reserve.

Looking further into the future, Fuller argued that 'infantry will be next to useless', although he allowed them roles of assisting in the initial penetration of an offensive, operating where tanks couldn't go, occupying areas conquered by tanks and protecting rear services. He did not view armoured vehicles as the be all and end all, foreseeing that aircraft would grow rapidly in importance. 'As the mobility of the tank increases,' he suggested, 'so it will have more and more to rely on the aeroplane for its security and protection.'

With plan 1919 Fuller's reputation as a visionary or prophet of war really began to take off. Initially, of course, only a few people in the War Office saw it. But Boney was a tireless advocate, firing off numerous letters and plans as well as lobbying key officers and politicians face to face.

However, as he emerged as the leading tank evangelist, the climate for using these machines on the Western Front suddenly deteriorated. A German offensive in the spring of 1918 caught out the British very badly, and a shaken Haig temporarily abandoned ideas of renewed advances. Even before the enemy blow, which seriously dented British morale, Haig ordered tanks scattered about the lines, with the idea that they could be concealed in pits and emerge to launch local counter-attacks – a concept Fuller derided as turning his beloved machines into 'savage rabbits'.

The last months of Fuller's war were destined to be spent in London in an annexe of the War Office lodged in the National Liberal Club – next to Charing Cross Station. He was in charge of the London staff of the Tank Corps, a post that Elles had convinced him was vital to the corps' future. Fuller's tactics in the bureaucratic fighting were, as one might expect, powerful and innovative, but they also contained many risks for him. After the German spring offensive, for example, he set down in a memo his view that 'our army is crawling with "duds"; though habitual offenders, they are tolerated because of the camaraderie of the old Regular Army: an Army so small as to permit of all its higher members being personal friends. Good-fellowship ranks with us above efficiency.' This chimed in well with the views of many middle-ranking and junior officers, some of whom idolised Boney. It also appealed to a handful of generals who knew it was true. Nevertheless, such invective alienated many senior officers for whom 'disloyalty' was a cardinal offence.

Increasingly, Fuller couched his arguments in terms of scientific truth. This fitted perfectly with the Zeitgeist, and indeed he had been influenced by the writings of Darwin, Hegel and Spencer. These passionate 'modernise or die' polemics excited many but also increasingly stimulated an emotional response from his opponents. Senior cavalry officers saw themselves as engaged in a struggle for survival, and many in the infantry were nettled by Fuller's predictions about their future irrelevance. As the Western Front guns fell silent in November 1918 it could not yet be said that the forces of reaction had quite gelled. But this was largely only because Fuller's intellectual trajectory had not yet reached its zenith, either.

As the war ended, Fuller was challenging an idea that had held sway since Waterloo at least: that the leadership of the army was based on character. Fuller ridiculed the 'good-chap' school of command, arguing that modern war demanded brain power refined through professional education. This proposition provided the subtext for an argument that would break out in the twenties about mechanisation.

Fuller knew he had found his mark when one general burst into his room at the War Office during the summer of 1919, saying, 'Boney! Boney! What *have* you done?' What he had done, as a colonel heading a relatively minor section within the bureaucracy, was write an essay that won the 1919 gold medal at the Royal United Services Institution (RUSI). This body, a sort of officers' club where professional discussions *were* tolerated, had set as its topic the impossibly dry-sounding 'The Application of Recent Developments in Mechanics and Other Scientific Knowledge to Preparation and Training for Future War on Land'. Entries were submitted anonymously, and judged by a panel of senior officers. Fuller's victory ought to have been good news, but there was a good deal of consternation when it became apparent not only that he had won but that his essay had gone far beyond narrow matters of mechanisation. 'To my profound enjoyment the War Office was upheaved,' he wrote later.

The essay began with the motto, 'Racehorses don't pull up at the winning post,' followed by the statement: 'To understand the past and to judge the present is to foresee the future.' Through a series of sections – 'Foresight', 'Imagination' and 'Energy' – Fuller asked the army to think carefully about what it had learned during 1914–18, and to apply it relentlessly. As with Plan 1919, his ability to identify common experience, synthesise it into lessons for the future and then develop these to their ultimate conclusions produced some remarkable insights. His statement, for example, that 'it is fighting power that we want and not numbers of men' can be seen as anticipating the central quest of post-1945 defence policy in Britain and many other countries. Similarly, his conclusion that the power of new weapons necessitated a Ministry of Defence to concert the efforts of Admiralty, War Office and newly formed Air Ministry preceded the actual event by decades.

By advocating wholesale change – the creation of a New Model Army, no less – Fuller, though, threatened to touch off open conflict between different empires within a contracting organisation. His essay was also laced with barbs about the army leadership, its shallow learning and its failure to digest the war's lessons. It reads oddly today only where Fuller gives vent to his enthusiasm for chemical warfare and predicts its widespread further use.

The First World War had finally ended because of German exhaustion. The Allies, notably France and Britain, had been able to endure a little more punishment and had been aided in the last stages by (limited) American intervention. But the USA was one of the few societies to emerge with its self-confidence enhanced by the European holocaust. The stresses of massive mobilisation and the loss of millions of young men proved to be a wrecker of the old social order. German and Ottoman empires had been dissolved. Russia had buckled, and the Tsar had been overwhelmed by a revolution. In France and Britain the old systems of authority had been shaken to their foundations.

One reason why Fuller's writings gained him a wider reputation so quickly was that they resonated with a wider public feeling of alienation from the army leadership. This also produced a popular reluctance, lasting many years, to spend money on war preparations. The country had lost 744,000 dead and, due to the unprecedented call-up required to keep the war going, great swaths of society had for the first time become familiar with the way the army was run. Familiarity had bred contempt for the generals. Of course, Fuller was no pacifist, offering to abolish war, but he was at least promising smaller armies, faster wars and lower casualties.

When the vast conflict had ended in 1918, the War Office had collapsed, in Fuller's memorably pithy phrase, 'like a jelly thrust into a hot oven'. Its energies were taken up with demobilisation, and little had been done about what shape of forces the draw down would finally produce. Summoned in front of one committee of worthies, Fuller was asked questions that he considered facile. When one general enquired, 'How many hours a day can a tank run?' Fuller's reply, deadpan, was 'Thus far we have never exceeded twenty-four.' Some considered him an arrogant upstart, but what a pleasure it would have been to be a fly on the wall at that meeting, as he treated the committee with all the contempt of some real-life Blackadder.

The apparent inability of the War Office to contemplate its own future seriously produced a campaign of what Fuller termed 'propaganda' for his new ideas. 'I knew I should create enemies,' he wrote later, 'yet without a sturdy opposition it is most difficult to explode deep-rooted absurdities.' Those in the General Staff who considered him a pain knew that the danger presented by Fuller's revolution was that some politician (like Churchill, an important early advocate of the tank) or some foreign army might embrace it. This is precisely what happened.

When the French Army ordered Fuller's prize-winning essay to be translated and given to every senior commander, tension inside the War Office rose. So impressed were the French with it that they invited Fuller to join their intellectual elite, as a member of the Academy. 'The fat was now fairly in the fire,' wrote Boney. 'I was forbidden to accept the honour and simultaneously forbidden to refuse it, because that might insult the President of France.' Someone with a lesser sense of mischief might have been tempted to lie low for a while, but not Fuller.

He entered – anonymously, of course – the next RUSI naval-essay gold-medal competition, and won. Inevitably, there was shock that a magisterial *tour d'horizon* of future war at sea had been written not only by an army man (who had the nerve to put as his motto at the beginning '*Veni Vidi Vici*' – 'I came, I saw, I conquered') but by Fuller, of all people. Pressure within Whitehall had reached the point that the RUSI refused to publish the essay or award the colonel his second gold medal.

While all this was going on, and just to keep the army pot boiling, Fuller had written an article for the *Cavalry Journal*. By his standards, it was quite tactful, but its message that senior officers of that branch were guilty of 'mental lethargy' – and evidently needed a tank man to do their thinking for them – produced a vigorous response. A debate had now been joined in earnest. For instance, one cavalry officer argued that Allenby's skilful use of divisions of horse soldiers in Palestine showed they could still be effective on the modern battlefield.

In an attempt to clear the air, a debate on the role of tanks was held in December 1920 at the Senior Officers' School in Woking. Churchill, no less, was in the chair as Fuller matched wits with Lieutenant General Philip Chetwode, who had been Allenby's smartest corps commander in Palestine. While there was no winner as such, the audience went away impressed by the quality of both speakers. Allenby himself did not weigh into this controversy, although it can be argued that his campaigns in the Middle East made him eminently qualified to pontificate about mobility or air power. Instead, Archibald Wavell became Allenby's military evangelist, a moderniser who avoided rhetorical extremes, and later, in the North African desert, (initially) showed himself a skilful commander of mechanised forces.

All of this, though, lay well ahead in the early 1920s, when the government formally adopted a doctrine that assumed it would have at least ten years' warning before a major war. Fuller carried on building his reputation, at home and abroad, as something of a military celebrity by publishing a book on tanks in the Great War in 1920 and another on his broader ideas about the future of conflict called *The Reformation of War* in 1923. In the latter he argued that 'The true purpose of war . . . is to enforce the policy of a nation at the least cost to itself and the enemy.' Many of his concepts about mobility and the profound effects of mechanisation were laid out again in this work. He also unveiled a general scheme of operations, 'the defensive-offensive', declaring that the most efficient form of fighting was to allow your enemy to develop their attack up to the point that they had shown their intentions and committed themselves before launching your own main effort. With *The Reformation of War*, his visionary ideas would reach many people who had been ignorant of Plan 1919.

Although there were many generals who disliked Fuller and his tactic of publishing his ideas to both military and civilian audiences, it is important to note that even in 1923 his trajectory was still upwards. He was appointed Senior Instructor at the Staff College early in that year, and three years later Military Assistant to the Chief of the Imperial General Staff. Both of these were jobs for army high flyers.

The First World War's catastrophic loss of life had produced a yearning for change in the middle levels of the army, and a crisis in confidence at the top. Whatever Fuller's barbs about the leadership, some of them supported him, and Britain still possessed in its Royal Tank Corps an armoured force that no other nation could match. It was not as if Germany and Russia were, in 1923, turning out vast numbers of tanks (or, indeed, any at all). In many ways, then, Boney's early years in the Tank Corps demonstrated how open the British Army was to new ideas, even if its leading exponent was a troublemaker. After his 1926 appointment, however, his career began to unravel.

While still teaching at the Staff College, Fuller had been refused permission to publish his lectures on theoretical matters as a book, *The Foundations of the Science of War*. He requested an interview with the Chief of the Imperial General Staff, who explained that he did not want serving officers publishing books that might undermine the army's manuals. 'This small incident,' Fuller reflected later, 'more so than any other, brought me to realise how far I had outgrown the Army.' Increasingly, this feeling became mutual.

Field Marshal Lord Carver, a tank officer who wrote Fuller's entry in the *Dictionary of National Biography*, considered that sending him to Staff College had been a 'disastrous posting', because it removed him from practical matters and allowed his writings to become 'more theoretical, complicated, less likely to be implemented'.

When *The Foundations of the Science of War* was eventually published in 1925, it provided Fuller's growing band of enemies with an excellent opportunity to cut him down to size. The book contained a series of theoretical propositions about the nature of war, and claimed that it could be studied as a science in which certain absolute truths could be deduced. It aroused a vitriolic attack in the *Army Quarterly* in the form of an unsigned review (written by Brigadier John Edmonds, a staff officer who would later write the official history of the 1914–18 war). Edmonds began, 'The danger of such a book is that the young should take it seriously,' and continued, 'He who can, does; he who cannot, teaches.' Fuller had made a great mistake in confusing lecturing with writing, Edmonds believed: 'The mental acrobatics, striking paradoxes and funny epigrams necessary if a teacher of little personality is to keep the attention of his hearers are out of place in an argumentative work.' As for the principles elaborated by Fuller, Edmonds considered them either statements of the obvious or complete balderdash.

Captain Basil Liddell-Hart, himself an up-and-coming theorist of armoured warfare, wrote to the *Army Quarterly* to complain about the hatchet job. The journal's editor allowed Liddell-Hart to defend Fuller's book with an unsigned article in the next issue, but added his own damning endorsement of Edmonds, writing: 'Colonel Fuller has the knack of making simple things appear difficult, and the ordinary man has neither the time nor patience to puzzle his brain.'

Many officers of conservative cast were delighted with the exposure of Boney's ideas as, appropriately enough, the emperor's new clothes. General Archibald Montgomery-Massingberd (destined to take over as Chief of the Imperial General Staff in 1933) wrote to Liddell-Hart, 'I hope someone will stop [Fuller] making such an ass of himself.' Even within the Tank Corps support for him began to falter. One senior officer writing in 1925 noted, 'He is inclined to "lecture" – or rather one gets the feeling that he is under the impression that no one else has thought about tank tactics at all.' A few years later, an erstwhile member of Fuller's 1917 team at Bermicourt commented bitterly, 'Having done so much to get the Idea going, he has dropped completely out of the work of turning that Idea into reality.'

The post-war freefall in the army's self-confidence had been checked. New blood and new ideas were required for war in the industrial age, but many senior officers came to the conclusion that Fuller's insistence that 'character' be replaced with 'intellect' in army promotion was a false alternative. The prime quality that was needed was 'efficiency': men with good minds but able to cooperate fruitfully with their colleagues. Prima donnas were not required, and increasingly that's how Fuller was seen. The new wave was represented by types like Wavell at the senior level and Montgomery in the middle. Indeed, the latter followed a couple of years after Fuller as an instructor at the Staff College. Monty was gaining a reputation as a great 'trainer', someone who could enthuse ordinary soldiers with understanding and a sense of purpose in their mission.

As for the more theoretical stuff, increasingly it was to Liddell-Hart that many tank pioneers looked. Having left the army in 1924, he became a highly influential newspaper correspondent. His thinking – in many ways quite as clever as Fuller's – remained applied to the nitty-gritty of mechanised war. Many of his ideas arose from his basic concept of the 'indirect approach', which castigated Great War generalship for attacking the strongest sectors of the enemy line and argued instead that armoured forces should bypass the opponent's chosen fighting grounds, using superior mobility to flow along the line of least resistance.

Through a combination of intellectual vanity and pursuit of ideas to their logical conclusions (up and up from tank tactics to strategy, military science and the stratospheric heights of policy and even futurology) Fuller, by contrast, dissipated his support and made himself irrelevant to the future of tank forces in his own army. Boney's career effectively ended when the Chief of the Imperial General Staff (in whose office he worked) offered him the plum job of commanding a new mechanised experimental force in December 1926. When Fuller tried, under threat of resignation, to renegotiate the terms under which he would accept this task, his boss replied, 'Don't be silly,' and effectively wrote him off.

Fuller had seen the experimental force as being of equivalent importance to the future of the army as the Light Brigade formed in Shorncliffe in 1804. Incidentally, he had knocked off a book on Sir John Moore's training methods during his time at the Staff College. At one point, he even complained that he was not being given permission to fire officers as Moore had been in 1804, but this was no more than petulance, for Boney did not measure up to Moore (let alone his nick-namesake) as a leader of men and the Chief of the Imperial General

Staff could, after all, reflect that the army had moved on somewhat in its management of officers' careers. It is only worth noting that in the 1920s there was no all-powerful patron, as the Duke of York had been, for new tactics. Fuller should have learned enough from his study of history to appreciate the difference between his own position and Moore's in the early nineteenth century.

As a prolific author, with admirers in many foreign armies and in academia, Fuller had forgotten what made him special in the first place – his unique grasp of the effect of advances in weapons technology on tactics and organisation. The sense of acclaim his ideas inspired from those in the wider world had, however, been lost by the great majority of British officers. Many had never liked him; others were alienated by his arrogance, inflexibility and sarcasm. Thus he lost the chance to remain an influential player at precisely the time that armoured warfare was about to become vitally important once more. Fuller, who had married in 1906 but remained childless, lost his sense of perspective, and was indulged by his wife as he increasingly struck the poses of intellectual martyr and middle-aged grump.

Between his bungling of the experimental force appointment and his retirement from the army in 1933, Fuller commanded an infantry brigade, was promoted to major general and refused a second-rate job in India. His cue to leave the army was the appointment of Montgomery-Massingberd as CIGS. The latter was an utter reactionary in the debates over modernisation and command, having commented, 'Character is more important than brains.' It was particularly unfortunate for the army that someone like him should have taken over just when a new commitment to tank warfare was most needed.

In 1932, the British Army had ordered just nine tanks – and even these were pathetic little affairs, weighing less than four tons. Racehorses, Fuller had written in 1919, don't pull up at the winning post. Britain's knackered runner in the armoured warfare race found itself riderless. Fuller turned his back on his own army, giving himself over increasingly to right-wing extremism, rejection of parliamentary democracy and bitter reflection of what might have been.

For Fuller, 20 April 1939 was a memorable and delightful day. The Foreign Office had urged him not to go to Berlin at such a sensitive time, but bugger them. As an honoured guest of Adolf Hitler, Boney had been given an excellent seat from which to watch the morning's procession of Germany's reconstructed army. It had been so impressive that the only issue was one of stamina. 'For three hours', Fuller wrote breathlessly, 'a completely mechanised and motorised army roared past the Führer.' Ensigns carrying the colours of every regiment had been formed into a great phalanx of fluttering standards, dipping them in homage as they marched past Hitler's stand. Fuller watched from directly opposite as the pageant to celebrate the Führer's fiftieth birthday reached its crescendo.

The Nazis were masters of such displays, laying on something stirring for everyone. For many patriotic Germans it was the military oompah bands. Committed Nazis, on the other hand, revelled in the party regalia of swastikas, brown shirts and, afterwards, beer-cellar songs. Fuller shared in some of this ideological excitement, describing fascism as 'a universal philosophy', but it was the tanks that really sang to him. Hundreds of them had come past the reviewing stands, assaulting the senses with their rumbling weight, revving engines and diesel smell.

That afternoon, at the Chancellery, the British general was lined up with other foreign dignatories and admirers, as the Führer received them. Hitler seized Fuller by the hand and, knowing what he would have enjoyed in the parade, asked, 'I hope you were pleased with your children?' Fuller replied, 'Your Excellency, they have grown up so quickly that I no longer recognise them.'

Fuller's intellectual journey to Berlin was the ultimate example of the way in which he followed his ideas to their conclusions, even if it ruined him. Frustration at the way the War Office was run in the twenties led him to examine decision-making at the highest level. Fuller became convinced that the constraints imposed by Britain's noisy democracy made it impossible for the army to be modernised. His longing for strong leadership and contempt for Parliament drew him ever further to the right. He had joined the British Union of Fascists in 1934 and harboured an ambition to be Minister of Defence in a government under its leader Oswald Mosley. By 1939, the possibility of such a regime being voted into power in Britain was nil, and one can only shudder at the thought of what would have happened if Hitler had conquered the country and looked for collaborators.

Boney had entered into the fascist idea without reservation. His contribution on the 'Jewish question', published in a fascist magazine in 1935, was entitled 'The Cancer of Europe'. One of his biographers has suggested, 'The proliferation of these [anti-Semitic] distortions and smears was no doubt the price Fuller thought he had to pay for the power and influence which the establishment of a fascist state would have given him.' This is a very generous conclusion, because the facility with which Fuller made anti-Jewish jibes in letters and books suggests pleasure rather than duty.

The embrace of fascism and the journeys to see Hitler cost Fuller a great deal. The *Daily Telegraph* had rejected his services as military correspondent because of his politics; his friendship with Liddell-Hart dried up; and when the war finally began, an attempt by the then Chief of the Imperial General Staff (an old patron of Boney) to bring him back into uniform as a deputy chief was swiftly vetoed by the government.

In 1939 and 1940 Fuller published two volumes of military history, *Decisive Battles of the Western World*, which marked his last important intellectual legacy. He wrote many newspaper articles, but his wicked pen was so well suited to attacking the orthodoxies and leadership of the forces that once the tide of war turned his inspiration seemed to dry up. In general, though, he sat out the Second World War as a spectator and lived out of the public eye until his death, writing just the occasional newspaper column to supplement his pension.

Not long after the war began, the US military attaché in London invited Fuller to lunch. The American brushed aside an MI5 health warning, evidently wanting to meet the grand old man of mechanised warfare for himself. He was disappointed, though: 'Fuller is now a very little, old, wizened-up man, who is bitter and outspoken against the War Office, the British government, and the way the war is being conducted.'

Fuller's historical legacy lies in his influence. It is, of course, very hard to be certain how and why people change their minds, for they are often unaware of it themselves. The position is further complicated with Fuller by the fact that much of what he wrote, for instance between 1916 and 1923, about the effects of mechanisation on armies has become received wisdom. As if this is not enough, as Fuller's mind brewed up stranger, less palatable stuff in the 1920s, Liddell-Hart took up the business, making his own vital contribution to blitzkrieg theory. The gritty malt of Fuller's original propositions therefore became blended with the product of another man's intellectual ferment.

The simplest and most poignant truth about Fuller is that he had ideas about tanks that were better applied by the German Army than by his own. This is the stark reality behind Hitler's comment in 1939 that his new panzer armies were 'Fuller's children'. General Heinz Guderian, architect of the mechanised army that crushed Poland in 1939 and France in 1940, wrote that in the 1920s, when he was conceiving his plans, 'It was principally the books and articles of Englishmen, Fuller, Liddell-Hart and Martel [another Tank Corps veteran], that excited my interest and gave me food for thought. These far-sighted soldiers were even then trying to make of the tank something more than just an infantry-support weapon.' In the early 1920s Germany's senior officers dreamed of tanks, and they did so because of Cambrai and Fuller. He had shown them what tanks were for.

Later, during the 1930s, Guderian had to defend his corner against German infantry and cavalry generals who had their own views about the future of armour. Undoubtedly, at this stage, when he and like-minded officers in every other major European army were trying to create armoured divisions and prevent tanks being scattered in penny-packets for infantry support, Liddell-Hart became the more influential guru.

Some of those who have questioned the validity of Fuller's vision have also pointed out that the German blitzkrieg army of the early war years was far from being the all-tank force that the Englishman had advocated. In fact, it was only slightly mechanised. When Hitler's army invaded Poland, it was sustained by 199,000 horses. Even in 1945 the great majority of German divisions were unarmoured. However, this is not too relevant to the question of Fuller's legacy, for, in my view, it is wrong to see the Germans either as the ultimate exponents of tank warfare or to think that the kind of vision spelt out in Plan 1919 was ever fully realised by Hitler.

History's greatest tank force was the Red Army. It built and utilised them in vastly greater numbers than the Germans, and used them to bury Hitler's regime. In their later offensives – for example, against the Japanese in Manchuria – Stalin's hordes came closest to realising Fuller's vision of war. The British officer's influence on the Red Army way of war can be traced through the person of Mikhail Nikolayevich Tukhashevsky. In 1931 he wrote the introduction to the Russian edition of Fuller's The Reformation of War, and he was the Red Army's principal theorist of armoured warfare. His patronage of Fuller's ideas was a factor of the greatest importance.

'Fuller's great merit', wrote Tukhashevsky, 'is that he does not just study past experiences but, by keeping track of technological advance, endeavours to indicate a direction for the structure and equipment of land forces as a result of which future war might take new, more effective forms.' The Russian general thought Boney a hopeless social reactionary, too obsessed with chemical warfare and not interested enough in paratroops, but he urged Russian readers of the British book to 'pay particular attention to the actions of tanks in the enemy's rear, which, together with a simultaneous frontal assault, must undoubtedly result in more intensive manoeuvre and more decisive tactical action'.

Tukhashevsky had little time for Fuller's more theoretical ramblings, and it is amusing to see the no-nonsense way in which he urged his tank men to bypass this intellectual boggy ground and press on towards more profitable ideas. 'Fuller loves to give his theories of war a philosophical basis,' noted Tukhashevsky. 'However, the philosophical aspect – in fact Fuller's weakest spot – is extremely confused, and there is no point in examining it critically.'

The Soviet moderniser was far more successful in achieving the outcome he wanted than either Fuller or Guderian. By the time he was purged by Stalin and shot in 1937, his country was already engaged in the huge industrial change required to make real the vision of a mechanised army. The following year, the Soviet Union manufactured 2,270 tanks, Germany 812 and Britain just 408. Throughout the war, and despite the disruption of losing many factories in the western USSR, the Soviet tank industry outproduced the German by a significant margin.

One other point of contrast with the Germans must be made: the two armies' tank philosophies. Guderian's practice of bypassing centres of enemy resistance was certainly inspired by Liddell-Hart's concept of the indirect approach. Fuller, however, gave greater emphasis to decisive battles – taking the bull by the horns and destroying the main concentrations of enemy forces. The Soviet sledgehammer that bludgeoned its way to Berlin was closer to that design.

After the Second World War, the Soviet Army finally matured into the kind of all-mechanised force predicted in Plan 1919; even its airborne divisions were armoured, with light tanks dropped by parachute! It remained a very large army, but Marshal Tukhashevsky had been quite explicit back in 1931 that he did not consider Fuller's idea that mechanisation would produce smaller forces to be applicable to the

Soviet Union. The marshal wanted his armies huge *and* mechanised, greedy man.

The giant tank armada that sat across the Iron Curtain, threatening Europe for four decades, was therefore the truest fulfilment of Fuller's dream, made real by Tukhashevsky and his successors. Britain, by contrast, kept the majority of its infantry on their feet and unarmoured throughout the post-1945 period.

As for the actual use of all-mechanised armies (as opposed to the partially petrol-driven ones of the Second World War), the salient examples lie in the Middle East. Fuller died in 1966, a year before Israel's extraordinary defeat of the Arab armies in the Six-Day War. It would have been a nice historical irony for Boney to have witnessed the Jews he despised applying his ideas so successfully. The echoes of Boney's ideas could also be detected in the 2003 American 'shock and awe' campaign against Iraq.

Of course, we have in time realised that armour has all sorts of limitations: it is not quite as mobile off-road as many people believe (as I learned to my cost years ago, bogging my tank on more than one occasion during my brief service in the Royal Tank Regiment, modern descendants of Elles and Fuller's corps); when facing guerrilla fighters in built-up areas, the tank can be a distinct liability, as the Russians discovered in Chechnya in 1994; and in an age of global media the tank can easily come to symbolise, as in Tiananmen Square, the perversion of brute power.

One biographer has called Fuller 'the most intellectually gifted soldier ever to serve with the British army'. That is overstating it. There are a couple in our own generation who might better deserve that label. Where also, one might ask, should such great captains as Marlborough and Wellington fit in this estimation, since they undoubtedly possessed a genius for war and the way generals *applied* their intellect must be considered, rather than just trying to estimate brute mental firepower. The epitaph Fuller deserves is of most intellectually *influential* officer ever to serve in the British Army.

His writings were snapped up by the general staffs and officer schools of France, Germany, the Soviet Union and every other significant military player. Frankly, the 1920s were the only time in its existence that the British Army exercised worldwide leadership in military thought. In the eighteenth century European military gentlemen considered a knowledge of Vauban or Turenne and later de Saxe or Frederick indispensable; during the nineteenth century it was Clausewitz or Jomini. Fuller and Liddell-Hart are Britain's only real claimants for such laurels. Two came along at once after centuries of waiting because of the alienation felt by the Western Front officer corps and as a result of Britain's status as a pre-eminent industrial power at the time.

It is somewhat invidious to have to choose between these two British thinkers, but Fuller exercised personal influence over the birth of the Tank Corps as well as its early operations, published his ideas first, reached the rank (symbolically important for this book, at least) of major general and – before he succumbed to pretentious, self-referential theorising – laid the foundations of what we would now call military science. The fact that it took the Germans, the Red Army, the Americans and even the Israelis to bring his ideas alive simply confirms in hindsight his own conclusion that he outgrew the British Army.

Bernard Law Montgomery

1887–1975

*Our British soldiers are capable of anything
if they are well led.*
BERNARD LAW MONTGOMERY

THE 3RD DIVISION'S MARCH of 10 May 1940 was a picture of regularity. The columns of its constituent brigades and battalions flowed across the border from France into Belgium, heading east towards the River Dyle and the city of Louvain. Traffic-control parties regulated the great move; air sentries scanned the horizon for signs of the Luftwaffe; and staff officers searched out Belgian headquarters so that everything might be coordinated efficiently.

The British Expeditionary Force had been sent to France in 1939, where, for the most part, its commanders had frittered away the months that passed between the declaration of war (over Hitler's invasion of Poland) and the arrival of blitzkrieg close to the Channel and Britain itself. The places on the BEF's maps were familiar to any student of the army's campaigns, its usual fighting ground in 1915, 1815 and indeed 1415.

The 3rd Division's commander, Major General Bernard Montgomery, had not been idle, though. His formation had been honed during five major exercises that had emphasised all of the operations it was about to carry out – from advancing to defend a river line to breaking contact with an enemy and falling back towards the coast. As events unfolded, Montgomery's staff were struck by his prescience, one reflecting, 'Although Monty made no predictions about the course of the battle, it followed almost exactly the way he had anticipated in his exercises.' Unfortunately for the army, the 3rd Division was the only part of the BEF that had rehearsed to this degree.

For months, British forces had been held back in France. The Belgians remained neutral until invaded by Germany, when they finally allowed Britain and its French allies to assist in defending the country.

Montgomery had therefore been unable to practise one thing: namely, how the 3rd Division would fit in with the Belgian forces already in place at Louvain.

By the morning of 12 May, Montgomery was able to report to his corps commander, Lieutenant General Alan Brooke, that his division was deployed and ready to defend the Belgian city. Brooke was pleasantly surprised, having found the Belgians mulishly obstinate. His subordinate explained that he had simply reported to the local general, placing the 3rd Division under Belgian orders. 'But what are you going to do if the Germans attack?' Brooke asked. 'Oh,' replied Montgomery, 'I then place the [Belgian] divisional commander under strict arrest and I take command.'

This was Bernard Montgomery epitomised: cheerful, practical, professional and utterly ruthless. Standing just five foot seven, already fifty-two years old, he shared with many of his illustrious predecessors the grey-blue eyes that could fix an underconfident subordinate and cause him to quake in his boots. His rise through the army had not been rapid – he was too outspoken, too convinced that his own ideas were right. On several occasions he had come close to following J.F.C. Fuller in ruining his prospects. Montgomery's most recent gaffe had been shortly before the move to Louvain itself, when he had signed an unusually frank and descriptive divisional order aimed at preventing venereal disease. It caused outrage among his superiors.

Once the shooting started, the army was to discover that Montgomery's skills outweighed his failings. In particular, he had an instinctive understanding that the amateurish bumbling of the peacetime officer corps was simply unacceptable to the wider British public. They were supplying an army of citizen soldiers while trembling at the prospect of a repeat of the First World War's slaughter. 'Our British soldiers are capable of anything if they are well led,' Montgomery had announced to his subordinates in April 1940. 'No officer is of any use as a leader unless he is mentally robust, and has that character and personality which will inspire confidence in his men. All officers who fail in this respect must be removed from the Division at once; if their names are reported to me I will do the rest.'

On 13 May, as German troops reached Louvain, its Belgian defenders ran away, so Montgomery was spared the unpleasant business of locking up their commander. A couple of days later, the 3rd Division beat off some German probing attacks with ease. As the pressure ratcheted up,

Montgomery decided that it was important to preserve his faculties by having regular meals and plenty of sleep. While many of his fellow British commanders succumbed to nervous exhaustion, the 3rd Division's leader was usually tucked up in bed by 10.30 p.m. 'The more I saw of him, the more I came to admire his superb control,' noted Brian Horrocks, a lieutenant colonel who took command of one of the 3rd Division's machine-gun battalions during the Louvain action. 'He went to bed early and slept peacefully all night, with the result that he arrived back at Dunkirk as fresh as when he had started.'

The 3rd Division's fight on the Dyle, though, was to prove a short-lived highlight of the campaign, for with French forces falling back on either side of the BEF, there was no choice but to withdraw. A miserable 250-mile retreat from one river line to the next had begun, and it would culminate, by 30 May, with Britain's expeditionary army penned in against the sea at Dunkirk. On that day, General Brooke, having been ordered to return to Britain for a new assignment, went to bid farewell to Montgomery.

Standing among the dunes of the seaside town as Stukas and German artillery flayed the British defences, the two men considered the lost campaign. Brooke had throughout been struck by Montgomery's good spirit and professionalism. At this dire moment, his own resolute front collapsed and Brooke began sobbing. Montgomery put his arm around his superior's shoulder and led him away from their staff. 'I knew it meant his friendship was all mine – and I was glad to have it that way,' Montgomery wrote later. Brooke, indeed, was to prove a fantastic mentor, having lobbied for Montgomery to get the 3rd Division (they had met at Staff College in the twenties), mopped up the damage caused by Monty's brutal directness and later served as the buffer between Britain's top field commander and the cabinet.

When Montgomery left the Dunkirk beachhead, his 3rd Division was, by common consent, the best-organised and most complete remnant of the BEF. Both he and Brooke were clear that their overall commander, Lord Gort, had failed in a way that brought back many bad memories of the Western Front. The propaganda about little boats and the army's rescue may have inspired the public, but Montgomery knew that the absence of proper planning and leadership had been scandalous. The army – 338,000 members of it – had to be rescued by the Royal Navy and civilians. They left behind more than 68,000 casualties and prisoners, 63,000 vehicles and half a million tons of stores.

Arriving in London, Montgomery requested an interview with the Chief of the Imperial General Staff, seeing him on 2 June. Montgomery told the army's head that 'events of the past few weeks have proved that certain officers were unfit to be employed and should be retired'. The angry divisional commander noted in his diary, 'I gave it as my opinion that the BEF had never been "commanded" since it was formed.' Expressing views more pungent than any CIGS would expect from a mere divisional commander, Montgomery urged the appointment of Brooke as Commander-in-Chief for the Home Defences.

This frankness was quite out of kilter with the usual behaviour of the officer class. Gort himself had said that Montgomery was 'not quite a gentleman', and he was right. Beating Hitler required something different, and, unlike Gort, Montgomery had a habit of being right. Sweeping changes were made in organising Britain's home defences. Brooke was the man to do it, and soon gained the confidence of Winston Churchill. This, in turn, was to produce Monty's opportunity to make history.

The day was already ebbing away as Brigadier 'Pip' Roberts picked out the first panzers manoeuvring across the desert in front of his position. Roberts was in command of 22 Armoured Brigade, equipped with Grant tanks, dug in to position on Point 102, a low hill that sat between the Germans and the principal piece of strategic geography in those parts, the Alam Halfa Ridge. 'On they come, a most impressive array,' Roberts wrote, 'and now they are swinging east and look like passing our more forward positions.'

As the brigade commander looked out that evening, the tanks passing in front of him were the hammer-blow of Erwin Rommel's assault, an upper-cut that was designed to drive out of the desert interior towards the coast and knock out the British defence. For a moment, Roberts worried that this formation, the 21st Panzer Division of the Afrika Korps, would carry on past his carefully prepared fighting positions, but then, with a churning of sand, they slewed around, northwards, towards Point 102. As one of the best and brightest Royal Armoured Corps commanders, Roberts observed with professional admiration and apprehension the leading echelon of the steamroller that had so recently forced British troops to retreat hundreds of miles: 'It is fascinating to watch them, as one might watch a snake curl up ready to strike.'

Then the bark of German tank guns shattered the silence. Roberts's 22 Brigade had the best tanks left in the Eighth Army, but – it became the familiar story of the Second World War British tankie – they were outgunned. In a few moments, a whole squadron of Grants was hit. The sequence in each case was similar: a flash and shower of sparks as the armour-piercing round struck; sometimes cries from those inside followed by a few of them bailing out; then the first signs of flame darting out of the hatches, leading, a few minutes later, to secondary explosions as the ammunition inside went off and the whole machine was ripped apart.

Was the plan, enunciated with such confidence by the army commander who had taken over just three weeks earlier, in trouble? As 21st Panzer closed on his position, Roberts began to worry whether he could hold on. 'Artillery is the only thing I have available to stop them,' he recorded, 'so we bring down all we can and again they are halted.' The brigade commander also rushed forward his reserve tank regiment. It was a matter of throwing everything into the fight.

As darkness fell on 31 August 1942, the all-out British effort began to wear down Rommel's best division. The field artillery stopped some; anti-tank guns probably rather more; even the Grants managed to account for some. A few hundred yards to the front of 22 Brigade, the flickering light of burning panzers was illuminating the desert.

The following day, when German signallers sent in their casualty returns, the cost of 21st Panzer Division's failed assault on Point 102 emerged. They had started the day with 124 working tanks and ended it with just 72. These figures were sent back using Engima cipher machines, but due to Britain's Ultra breakthroughs, the messages were quickly cracked and reported at Eighth Army headquarters. Rommel's attack was losing momentum, and with British forces on three sides of 21st Panzer and the minefield they had breached to their rear, it was the German general who started worrying. His plan to end the North African war by a bold push into Egypt had been checked by Montgomery.

By the time it was getting dark on 1 September, Rommel resolved to pull back his exposed armoured division. He was short of fuel, knew his men had taken a bloody nose, and expected any British general worthy of his rank to counter-attack shortly.

Montgomery was absolutely determined to retain control of his first great battle as an army commander. He had given strict orders against local armoured counter-attacks. He wanted to retain his armour for use in an offensive battle that would begin at a time of his own choosing. So, instead, on 3 and 4 September, infantry were used to counter-attack. The battle, though, was petering out, and Rommel conceded, 'There is no doubt that the British commander's handling of this action was absolutely right and well suited to the occasion, for it had enabled him to inflict very heavy damage on us in relation to his own losses, and to retain the striking power of his own force.'

When Monty had addressed the staff at Army HQ on 13 August, he had told them, 'The bad times are over.' He had insisted, '*Here* we will stand and fight; there will no further withdrawal. I have ordered that all plans and instructions dealing with further withdrawal are to be burned, and at once. We will stand and fight *here*.' At Alam Halfa he had demonstrated before the month was out that these were not idle boasts.

Montgomery had hit the British Army in Egypt like the proverbial mailed fist. Shortly after arriving in Cairo, he set down his impressions of the Middle East HQ brass. The chief of staff was 'quite useless', the vice-chief 'a menace', the directors of military operations and intelligence, 'in my opinion, quite unfit for their jobs'. His arrival at Eighth Army HQ had followed a similar pattern to his 3rd Division as well as his corps and army commands in England. Huge problems were diagnosed and many individuals condemned as useless. His memos and directives all carried the message, often barely concealed: only Monty had the answers.

It will come as no surprise that this alienated many people, including thrusting professional officers in much the same mould as the commander himself. Michael Carver, a desert veteran since the outbreak of the war, noted, 'We were not particularly impressed with this self-assured white-kneed expert from Britain. He was needlessly offensive to some of the older officers and infuriated one or two in particular.' One of the intelligence officers who had listened to his speech at Army HQ on 13 August thought it corny, like something from a public-school prize-giving.

The roots of Montgomery's drive and rudeness lay in his upbringing. Much of his childhood had been spent in Tasmania, where his father was the Anglican bishop, and his mother had ruled the household with a rod of iron. The general would later describe these years, baldly, as 'unhappy', and he clearly bore a grudge about his mother's beatings and myriad petty regulations, for he declined to attend her funeral. He benefited at least from an excellent education at St Paul's, the first of several respects in which his life mirrored that of the Duke of Marlborough. The rules and restrictions of army life suited him, and he soon became dedicated to his career, sublimating, just as Gordon and Kitchener had, sexual drive into an ardent desire for promotion. When Monty married, some saw even this step as one he felt necessary for advancement. But the early thirties proved a period of real domestic happiness for him, during which he became father to one son. His wife's death in 1937, caused by blood poisoning following an insect bite, caused him to plunge once more without reservation into his army career.

The man who toured about the desert in August 1942 was therefore a profoundly lonely figure who sought love through impressing superiors and gaining the affection of his soldiers. As he gave his pep talks to junior commanders and ordinary soldiers, an unmistakable change came over Eighth Army. One war correspondent who watched it described how, 'insistently and steadily, hour after hour, the orders went out, and a great commotion spread across the desert'. Monty acquired an Australian bush hat and, as he toured the regiments of his desert army, added their cap-badges to it. A speech that might have sounded corny to one of the intellectuals at headquarters went down just fine with the grimy sappers, Kiwis and tankies: they just wanted to know that their chief was somebody who had a workable plan to beat Rommel and get them home alive.

Alam Halfa had been a battle very much in the style of Wellington, serving the same purpose as Bussaco. It was fought on 'ground of our own choosing' to exhaust the enemy and break his confidence, while the Allied army gathered strength. Monty, like the Iron Duke, ignored the clamour of those who thought he had not followed up Alam Halfa aggressively enough, since he simply could not afford to have a failure. The campaign would have to develop to his timescale. The Eighth Army commander knew that the delivery of hundreds of new Sherman tanks and several weeks of brisk desert training would change the terms of his next contest with Rommel, an offensive battle at El Alamein.

The Eighth Army's greatest battle began at 9.40 p.m. on 23 October 1942 with a barrage of 1,000 guns. If this enormous concentration of firepower was reminiscent of someone like Allenby in the First World War, then it was for good reason. The Axis army (Germans and Italians) occupied a very strong position, secured to the north by the Mediterranean and to the south by the Qattara Depression, a sea of soft sand unsuitable for vehicles. Rommel's positions sat atop commanding ridges, able to observe the Allied advance across open desert, and protected to the front by dense minefields, barbed wire and all manner of field works.

Montgomery therefore had no choice but a frontal assault, and it is for this reason that his superiority in men (195,000 versus 54,000 Italians and 49,000 Germans) can be regarded as a necessity rather than a luxury. The Allies also had more tanks and serviceable aircraft. The German tanks, though, were technically superior and their defences were thickened by eighty-six of the dreaded 88mm flak guns – designed for use against aircraft but deadly against tanks, even at a couple of miles.

Eighth Army's attack plan directed the main blow to fall on the Miteiriya Ridge, at the north of the Axis position. A corps of veteran infantry – South Africans, Australians, New Zealanders and the 51st Highland Division – would make the initial push, breaching the enemy minefields at night before moving onto the ridge. Two armoured divisions would then be pushed through them. Montgomery knew from Ultra intelligence that Rommel's tanks were scattered along his position in 'fire brigade' detachments. The British general's aim was to trigger local counter-attacks which would be defeated (he called it 'crumbling' the enemy defences), leaving British armour concentrated on the Miteiriya Ridge, ready to turn the tide once Axis forces had exhausted themselves. A large deception operation using dummy units was mounted to keep as many enemy troops as possible in the south.

Monty undoubtedly expected a drawn-out slugging match. Brigadier Freddie de Guingand, his chief of staff, recalled that in talks given to units a few days before the battle, '[Monty] touched on the enemy situation, stressing their weaknesses, and said he was certain a long "dog-fight" or "killing match" would take place for several days – "it might be ten". He drummed in the need never to lose the initiative, and how everyone – *everyone* – must be imbued with the burning desire to "kill Germans".' Certainly he got this kind of battle, but it developed in some ways he had not foreseen.

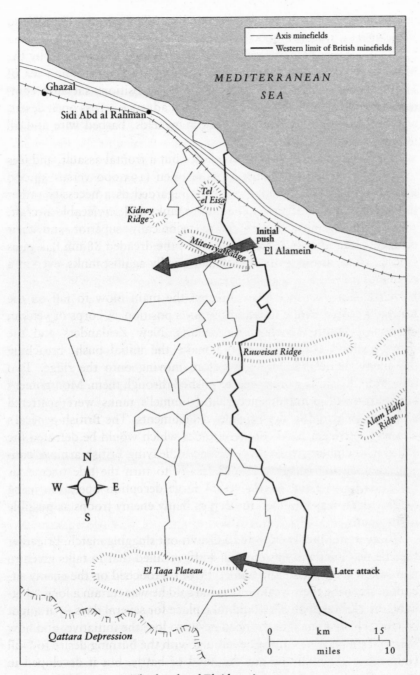

The battle of El Alamein, 1942

The difficulties became apparent on the first full day, 24 October, as British tanks, mingled with the infantry, faced stronger than expected German resistance. One day followed another with the two armoured divisions stalled. An officer of the Seaforth Highlanders who found himself in the middle of a tank battle on the Miteiriya Ridge described it vividly: 'At dawn our tanks came up and began fighting their battle right among us, manoeuvring for position and firing while it seemed like every tank and anti-tank gun in the Afrika Korps fired back. Solid shot was ricocheting all over the place, and there was HE, too. The whole show was fantastic.' Montgomery soon realised that the armoured division commanders, claiming his orders were impossible, were afraid of heavy losses. He regarded them as ignorant of how best to combine their tanks with artillery and infantry. As the offensive slowed down it was noticed even at the cabinet table in London. General Alan Brooke, by then Chief of the Imperial General Staff, defended his protégé against furious attacks from Churchill, noting in his diary on 29 October: 'I was met by a flow of abuse of Monty. What was my Monty doing now, allowing the battle to peter out (Monty was always my Monty when he was out of favour!)'

Out in the desert Montgomery himself evolved what was to become a trademark response to political pressure: emphasising over and over, 'The battle is going exactly to my plan.' On the same day that Churchill was venting his spleen, though, the commander of the Eighth Army chose to adopt a suggestion made by HQ in Cairo to switch to an attack in the southern sector of the front. This action, evidently a departure from Montgomery's original blueprint, began early on 2 November and sealed Rommel's fate.

During the 3rd and 4th the Axis forces were overwhelmed. Armour was brought in to reinforce the Eighth Army's southern breakthrough, while the original attack force, close to the sea, was also able to make some progress. In twenty-four hours Rommel's army lost 200 tanks. Late on the 4th the Axis commanders were trying to disengage after a ten-day 'dog fight' that had whittled down and exhausted their troops. At this moment Eighth Army's numerical superiority really came into play, since it retained divisions that had fought little during the preceding days and were ready for the chase. During the following weeks, Rommel's men were hustled along the North African coast, unable to consolidate and make a stand. By the end of 1942 they had been driven back more than 1,000 miles, from Egypt to Tunisia.

Some of Monty's subordinates suggested that he was not ambitious enough in his pursuit and could have annihilated much of Rommel's force with some deep envelopments during the early days of November. There is probably some justice to this, for, like Wellington, Montgomery did not want to jeopardise his success by rushing forward. He wanted a methodical advance (in large part so that the supporting Desert Air Force could get new airfields and maintain top cover) and knew that his offensive battle had been an emphatic reversal of fortune for the British Army after its terrible defeats in earlier campaigns.

The Eighth Army Chief of Staff commented, 'Without [Alamein] one frankly cannot imagine the feats which were subsequently achieved. Behind us stretched a pathetic catalogue of bungled efforts and ultimate failures.' In addition to causing great losses to the Axis forces, the Eighth Army scored the propaganda coup of capturing General von Thoma, commander of the Afrika Korps (Rommel was von Thoma's boss, in charge of all Axis forces). Montgomery commented, 'I doubt if many generals have had the luck to be able to discuss with their opponent the battle that has just been fought.' It was, indeed, a rare distinction, inviting comparison with Marlborough's feat of capturing Tallard at Blenheim.

In Britain there was exultation. One BBC radio announcer abandoned customary restraint when beginning the news headlines, telling listeners, 'There's some cracking good news coming in.' It took a few days before the newspapers started to focus on Montgomery. Instead the initial emphasis was on the humiliation of the 'Desert Fox', the German general who was loathed but respected in virtually every household in Britain. 'Rommel Routed, Huns Fleeing in Disorder', the *Daily Mirror* trumpeted on 5 November, picturing below not Monty but the German commander with the caption, 'He Couldn't Take It'.

Many later writers regarded Monty as something of a disaster in matters of politics: he was too abrasive, he did not seem to understand that in a democratic set-up it was ministers who had the power to be ego-maniacs, not their generals. Certainly, he was often not good at day-to-day dealings with politicians (or, indeed, other Allied generals), but his frequent failure to adopt the best means of civil/military dialogue was less significant than his profound understanding of the *ends* of war and how to attain them in a democracy. Montgomery grasped a simple reality: the people of Britain were looking for a man capable of beating Rommel. His predecessor had been so overwhelmed by this idea, and had such a poor purchase on the wider political context, that he had banned mentions of Rommel's name in British Army orders, pathetically ending his diktat with the words 'p.s. I am *not* jealous of Rommel'. Monty had said from his first talk to Eighth Army HQ on 13 August that his aim was to beat the German general. On the eve of El Alamein his message to the troops began, 'When I assumed command of the Eighth Army I said that the mandate was to destroy *Rommel* . . . We are ready *now*.'

In America, where they liked a winner, El Alamein was an important propaganda coup as well. After the fall of Singapore and Tobruk, there had been much disparagement of the British Army, but now, the *Daily Express* correspondent in the States noted, 'Overnight that talk has been swept away by the great victory in Egypt . . . There is little talk about America's elections today; it is all about the defeat of Rommel. Montgomery has driven the election off America's front page.' This fame in America initially gave Montgomery an advantage when dealing with the commanders of the US forces that entered the North African war with amphibious landings in Algeria just a few days after El Alamein. Dwight Eisenhower, an American general with little practical experience, had been placed in charge of this new front. This changed everything.

Comparisons with Blenheim are particularly apposite at this point. Marlborough's victory was the first great British triumph, and El Alamein was to prove the last. Back in 1704, on the upward curve of power, the British Army had escaped the gravitational pull of its Dutch allies and become a European force to be reckoned with. In 1942, with substantial American forces entering the war, Britain, having passed its zenith of Imperial glory, was being drawn inexorably into the orbit of the new colossus.

As the numbers of troops tipped more and more in favour of the United States, the implications for those who commanded them would have been obvious to Marlborough, Wellington or Kitchener. British soldiers were going to play the role of auxiliaries of a greater power. There would be a great deal of British denial about this (indeed, there is still some), but Churchill and Brooke understood perfectly what was happening and spent the rest of the war driving the best possible bargains that they could with Uncle Sam. While Montgomery's head was able to grasp this truth, in his heart, or rather his gut, he found it difficult to accept that someone else was going to be telling him how to fight his battles. In Monty's mind the question of who made the decisions had to have something to do with ability, and, of course, he was quite convinced of his own. The greatest test of this conviction would come in Normandy in July 1944.

It was not the kind of morning call even the veterans were used to. The noise attracted the interest of everyone in the three armoured divisions that were crammed into their forming-up points. 'At 0500 hours a distant thunder in the air brought all the sleepy-eyed tank crews out of their blankets,' according to one crewman from the Guards Armoured Division. '1,000 Lancasters were flying in from the sea in groups of three or four at 3,000 feet. Ahead of them the pathfinders were scattering their flares and before long the first bombs were dropping.' Heavy bombers had been drafted in to play the role usually performed by artillery, and unthinkable destruction was about to rain down on Normandy.

The Allied landings on D-Day had been an enormous success, but for weeks they had fought foot by foot to expand their narrow beachhead. The cost of this frustrating battle had been considerable: 37,000 US and nearly 25,000 British (including Canadian) casualties before the end of June. As the transports kept unloading men and *matériel* through the beaches, by the same date 875,000 soldiers and 150,000 vehicles had been squeezed into a coastal strip a few miles deep.

Under the complex division of responsibilities agreed by the Allies, Montgomery had been given command of all ground forces for the first phase of the operation, although Eisenhower remained Supreme Commander of the theatre as a whole, and was slated to take over the land role, too, just as soon as American forces built up to army group level. There had been plenty of applause for Monty when the landings – the biggest amphibious operation in history – had gone well, but as one week followed another without a breakthrough, politicians on both sides of the Atlantic had grown impatient.

As the total of landed troops neared a million, questions were asked about how 400,000 Germans could stop so many Allied divisions moving forward. On 6 July, Churchill complained bitterly about Montgomery's lack of progress, leading General Brooke to an uncharacteristic explosion of temper: 'I flared up and asked him if he could not trust his generals for five minutes instead of continuously abusing them and belitting them.'

On 18 July these frustrations were visited upon the Germans sitting on top of the long ridge south of Caen. By coincidence, a stretch of this front was being held by 21st Panzer Division, effectively destroyed in North Africa but re-formed in France under its old master Rommel. Werner Kortenhaus, a crewman in the divisional tank regiment, looked up at the same armada of Lancasters that moments before had passed over the British Guards. He could not quite believe what he was watching: 'We saw little dots detach themselves from the planes, so many of them that the crazy thought occurred to us: are those leaflets?' Seconds later, dozens of 500-and 1,000-pound bombs started raining down on them. 'Among the thunder of the explosions,' Kortenhaus would recall, 'we could hear the wounded scream and the insane howling of men who had been driven mad.' So terrible was the ordeal which tossed tanks about or buried them in earth that a couple of panzer soldiers killed themselves rather than endure it.

Carpet bombing the Normandy countryside was an inefficient procedure, for the great majority of the ordnance fell into woods or fields. In places, though, whole battalions were devastated. The 503rd Heavy Tank Battalion – a key German formation for the defence of this sector, being equipped with Tigers and King Tigers – had 145 bombs fall into its hides. One tank ended up on its roof; others were written off or badly damaged. One company (normally around a dozen tanks) ended up with a single machine operational. The greatest effect of the bombardment, though, was the trauma to those on the receiving end. 'Dazed and shaken figures rose from the uncut corn and attempted to give themselves up to the leading tanks,' wrote Major Bill Close, commanding A Squadron of the 3rd Royal Tank Regiment, as they advanced through enemy positions. 'Other Germans squatted in their foxholes staring stupidly, completely demoralised as we passed.' Major Close and his regiment were part of the 11th Armoured Division, which, led by 'Pip' Roberts (promoted to major general at the tender age of thirty-seven), formed the spearhead of Operation Goodwood, Monty's latest attempt to break out of the beachhead.

In typical fashion, Monty had insisted during the weeks before Goodwood that his operations were proceeding entirely to plan. Those at Eisenhower's HQ (SHAEF, or Supreme Headquarters, Allied Expeditionary Force) who had grown tired of this mantra pointed out that Montgomery had still not captured Caen, something he had originally intended to do during the first twenty-four hours after D-Day.

Montgomery was, however, justified in asserting that he remained true to his vision for the Normandy battle: that a British army occupying the eastern side of the beachhead would draw as many German divisions on to itself as it could, while to the west an American one (US First Army, under Lieutenant General Omar Bradley) secured the Cherbourg peninsula and then broke out to the south.

By mid-July the British had still not captured all of Caen and the Borguebus Ridge to its south, dominating ground that the British commander needed as the hinge-point for the great door-like movement he intended to make. Bradley, meanwhile, had done little better on the western flank. Monty had however drawn twelve German divisions on to the British sector (six of them armoured), while eight (three of them armoured) remained opposite the Americans. The British general knew he was asking troops from his own nation to die so that Americans might get the glory of a breakout, telling the commander of the British Second Army, 'Go on hitting, drawing the German strength, especially some of the armour, on to yourself – so as to ease the way for Brad.'

Around lunchtime on 18 July, however, things were looking up for Monty. His great armoured punch around the eastern side of Caen and to the city's south had advanced several miles. Major Close and his tanks were approaching the Borguebus Ridge. But now the Germans had recovered from their morning pounding and they started manning anti-tank guns which opened up on Close's squadron; 'within moments there were five or six tanks brewing up'. The major reacted as British officers tended to when confronted by tough resistance: he called on the flexible firepower of the Royal Artillery, shouting to his forward observer, 'For Christ's sake, get a stonk down as quickly as possible.' In minutes, shells were bursting in the enemy-held village, scything down the anti-tank-gun crewmen.

A couple of miles to the east of Major Close, in Cagny, another village fortified for defence, Lieutenant Freiherr von Rosen, a young officer from the 503rd Heavy Tank Battalion, arrived on the scene. Having survived the morning's bomber strikes, he had dodged his way through dozens of British tanks advancing through the fields. In Cagny he found a Luftwaffe officer in charge of a battery of four 88mm flak guns. They were effectively surrounded by advancing tanks of the 11th Armoured Division, but their commander insisted they were there for anti-aircraft defence only. 'I took my little pistol,' recalled von Rosen,

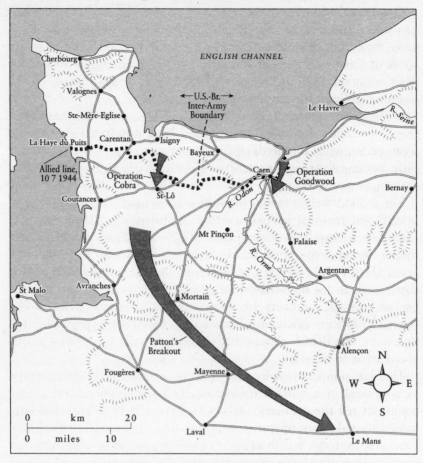

The Normandy breakout, 1944

'and asked him whether he would like to be killed immediately or get a high decoration. He decided for the latter.'

Pip Roberts would later realise that an order to bypass Cagny in the interests of maintaining the speed of his advance was the worst mistake of his career. When the 88s began firing, dozens of British Shermans were set ablaze like so many torches. 'I see palls of smoke and tanks brewing up with flames belching forth from their turrets,' said an officer of the worst-hit regiment. 'I see men climbing out, on fire like torches, rolling on the ground to try and douse the flames.' The German defence coalesced, and a bitter contest was joined in earnest.

Goodwood was effectively over by 20 July. The British Army had 413 tanks knocked out, thousands of casualties, and had gained just seven miles. On the plus side, the armour had got to the high ground south of Caen, and the Canadians completed their capture of the city itself. Monty had got the 'hinge' for his breakout at last, and drawn the last uncommitted panzer division in Normandy on to the British front, too. The Americans surely could not complain since their element of all this, codenamed Operation Cobra, had been postponed due to bad weather. So, while hundreds of British tanks burned, Bradley did very little. Yet this was the moment when the British general's enemies made their move against him.

The groundswell in favour of sacking Monty came about for several interrelated reasons: he had oversold Goodwood to the point that Eisenhower as well as others expected a *British* breakthrough rather than a further preparation for an American one; senior air commanders at SHAEF (RAF officers, in fact) held a grudge against Monty that dated back to his high-handedness in North Africa and resented the use of strategic bombers for tactical effect; he had alienated key American officers (including Eisenhower) by rudeness to them; and, unusually, the British general had misled his own troops and public about what to expect.

This last point is worthy of examination first, since Montgomery, as a general in a vibrant democracy, faced an awful dilemma. He could not tell the ordinary soldiers that the aim of Goodwood (and indeed several major operations that preceded it) was to draw as many Germans on to the British as possible so the Americans could have the glory of liberating large parts of France. This was too much like asking them to die in a diversionary attack on the first day of the Somme. 'There was by definition an almost insuperable problem, because you could not be totally frank with people about what was going on,' noted one officer 'in the know' at Monty's HQ. 'If you *had* been, they would have said . . . "I'm not bloody well going to do that."'

As events unfolded, with exciting initial gains on 18 July, the tangled web woven at Montgomery's headquarters gained another dimension: the press were briefed and duly reported a 'breakthrough'. This was all well and good in terms of military logic, since it would further encourage Rommel to commit his last reserves to the Caen sector, and perhaps even denude the defences facing the US First Army, which would imminently launch Operation Cobra. In political terms, however, it was disastrous, since the newspapers soon had to retract their highly optimistic initial reports.

Montgomery's offensives in late June and through July to Goodwood may be regarded as an inspiring piece of coalition generalship. British lives were deliberately sacrificed in the common good. Monty knew how tired the British people were of war, but it was American urgency that had really begun driving the coalition, and Washington increasingly defined what the common good was. Montgomery was therefore the first field commander to bring Britain's army into line with these new geopolitical realities.

The greatest tragedy of the Normandy breakout was how little the Americans appreciated the sacrifice of Goodwood and other British battles. Only Bradley, who had been told by Monty to take as much time as he needed for his own push, Cobra, really understood what had been done, and, alas, Monty later managed to alienate him as well, so when the time came to write memoirs, the US First Army commander hardly extolled his boss's strategic brilliance.

Eisenhower, it seems, could not grasp Montgomery's plan at the time, despite it all being spelled out very clearly in documents sent to SHAEF. Furthermore, he had been angered by Monty's manner, early on in their relationship. The British general stopped Ike smoking the first time he briefed the American. Then, in North Africa, Monty's insistence on collecting his 'winnings' (a Flying Fortress and crew to be loaned as his personal runabout) after he won a bet to clear the Germans out of the continent further upset Eisenhower, who had considered the wager no more than a joke. Brooke described the Flying Fortress affair in his diary as another episode where Montgomery demonstrated his 'usual lack of tact and egotistical outlook which seemed to prevent him appreciating other people's feelings'.

Monty had worked satisfactorily with his American boss through the remainder of the North African campaign and during the invasion of Sicily, partly by convincing himself that he himself was really in command. Churchill, too, made the most of the military credibility gained at El Alamein in order to convince the Americans that the Allies should attack Italy in order to knock it out of the Axis alliance. In time, though, the power political realities of the relationship reasserted themselves. Many in Washington began to see Italy as a costly diversion of effort. This tension found form at Allied HQ in a clamour from Ike's American colleagues to do something about excessive British influence on strategy and to cut Monty down to size.

Eisenhower was politically adroit enough to understand the momentous implications of sacking a British commander as popular as Monty. As July wore on, though, such a step became possible because of Churchill's frustration and the machinations of Eisenhower's deputy at SHAEF, Air Marshal Arthur Tedder. Having a senior RAF officer leading the 'Monty must go' chorus made it look less like an American vendetta and gave Montgomery's enemies the necessary top cover to make a move. From the evening of 19 July, when Montgomery started withdrawing British armour from the Borguebus Ridge and consolidating his positions with more infantry, Tedder, seeing this as an admission that Goodwood had failed, began calling for a change in command. One of Eisenhower's aides noted a couple of days later that Tedder had come to the Supreme Commander's office in order 'to pursue his current favourite subject, the sacking of Monty'.

News of this plot, detected by the ever-vigilant Alan Brooke, soon reached Monty at his tactical headquarters, or 'Tac'. Montgomery had, from early on in the war, preferred to avoid the throng of staff officers, dispatch riders, cooks and bottle-washers that gathered about a major HQ, running his battles instead from closer to the action at Tac, a small group of caravans where his 'gallopers', young staff officers sent out on fact-finding missions, would report back to him each evening. He did not like going back to Britain to brief his superiors and, increasingly, as the Normandy battle became more fraught, he resented having visitors at Tac, too.

Brooke considered matters sufficiently serious that he flew to Normandy during the afternoon of 19 July and told Montgomery about Tedder's scheming and the Prime Minister's fury at apparently being banned from visiting Normandy. Brooke noted that he 'warned [Monty] of a tendency in PM to listen to suggestions that Monty played for safety and was not prepared to take risks'. He then dictated a note to Churchill, which Montgomery signed, inviting the Prime Minister to visit.

The next day, Eisenhower descended on Tac to see Montgomery, and the day after that, Churchill finally came, too. It was, recalled one staff officer, 'common knowledge at Tac that Churchill had come to sack Monty'. How could the general have forgotten that his own appointment in 1942 to command Eighth Army had followed a similar prime ministerial visit to clear out the senior brass in Egypt? It was, without doubt, the greatest crisis of Montgomery's career.

The general responded to the pressure with his usual sang-froid and confidence. Since notes do not survive of the briefings he gave inside his caravan on successive days to Eisenhower and Churchill, we can rely only on Monty's own suggestion that, having been told that everything was still going according to a master plan, the PM 'understood at once'. Some insight into the magnetism displayed during these talks is afforded by Brian Horrocks who, having been severely wounded, returned to the command of XXX Corps in Normandy early in August. He feared his old master would have been subdued by all the criticism, but as a lengthy one-on-one briefing began in the caravan, 'It was soon obvious that he was in top form,' Horrocks recalled. 'As Montgomery talked to me I began to feel more and more guilty at ever having doubted his capacity to shrug off criticism like water off a duck's back.'

However, what Montgomery had won on 20 and 21 July was not a great victory but a temporary reprieve. He had been lucky, too: the meeting with Churchill was undoubtedly more convivial due to the timely receipt of intelligence of the attempt to assassinate Hitler the previous day. But everything still depended on what happened with Bradley's Operation Cobra, which was finally launched on 24 July.

Cobra, in one sense, was the reverse of Goodwood in that it started wretchedly but became a triumph. The initial heavy bombardment by Flying Fortresses dropped short in places, killing 111 and wounding 490 US troops – such was the magnitude of 'friendly fire' incidents just a generation ago. The Americans, though, pressed on with élan, smashing the Panzer Lehr Division, making their way to their initial objectives and pushing through with barely a pause. There was an aggression and relentlessness about the US advance which would be hard to imagine in a similar British operation. Of course, the commander of 21st Army Group had done much to make it possible: Monty's great design had given the Americans a local preponderance of more than two to one against the Germans. Bradley had followed Montgomery's advice to attack on a concentrated front (Eisenhower tended to favour simultaneous pressure all along the line) and reaped the rewards. Monty was, in fact, an excellent commander of American troops: in later testimonials he enthused about their great drive (implicitly acknowledging the British Army's limitations), while he could provide a creativity that was lacking in many US generals.

By the evening of 25 July it was apparent that Cobra was going very well. Three days later, after spectacular gains, Eisenhower wrote to his British chief of land forces, 'Am delighted that your basic plan has begun brilliantly to unfold with Bradley's initial success.' Even this qualified language, though, would be discarded as George Patton's Third Army was unleashed to exploit Bradley's breakthrough and moved in a great arc around the German left and, increasingly, behind them.

During the first days of August, Montgomery directed a huge battle of annihilation, trying to prevent the escape of several German divisions by closing their exit from Normandy, the Falaise Gap. Military logic would have dictated that the Germans evade from this encirclement, but Hitler, by one of his infamous personal interventions, would not hear of retreat. 'He refused to face the only sound military course,' Montgomery wrote later. 'As a result the Allies caused the enemy staggering losses in men and *matériel*.' There were recriminations, though, that the Falaise battle did not achieve even more. Patton blamed the British for failing to advance with similar alacrity and perform their part in it. But by 22 August, the end of this battle, although some 20,000 Germans had escaped through the gap, 60,000 had not. The Normandy campaign was effectively over.

Between their 6 June landings and the end of the Falaise battle, Allied forces had engaged in warfare on a vast scale. The price of the bitter fighting through the hedgerows and villages of northern France was 209,000 casualties (just under 40,000 of them dead). But the cost to Hitler was considerably more, with 25 out of 38 divisions destroyed, 240,000 casualties and a further 200,000 troops captured or missing. By the end, the Allies had more than 2 million troops ashore and advancing towards the Reich.

Whose victory was this? Eisenhower was the Supreme Commander and would doubtless have been blamed, particularly if the landings themselves had gone horribly wrong. But Montgomery was the leader of the land forces, the man who actually planned and commanded the business. Even Eisenhower, it must be remembered, considered Monty to be the author of 'the plan'. 'Ike knows nothing about strategy and is *quite* unsuited to the post of Supreme Commander,' Brooke wrote at the height of the rear-echelon rowing in late July. 'It is no wonder that Monty's real high ability is not always realised. Especially so when "national" spectacles pervert the perspective of the strategic landscape.' Credit for the conduct of the Normandy battle is fairly given to Montgomery by writers like Carlo d'Este, Eisenhower's most recent American biographer. But the ever-perceptive Brooke had touched on something quite critical in his diary – the factor of national rivalry that would shape the perceptions of players in an Allied war effort.

Suspicion had long been a feature of multinational campaigns – just look at the arguments about the Prussians at Waterloo. By 1944, though, the features of total war, waged by huge populations of voters who derived their information from mass media, changed completely the nature of higher command. For many people, national factors or fame counted for more than sheer military ability. Generals like Patton were in any case both skilled at war *and* American. Monty's big mistake, as the war moved to its final phase, was to allow his unassailable self-belief to blind him to certain new realities. Politics would not allow him to carry on giving the orders to great armies of Americans simply because, in his view, he was better than their generals.

On many occasions during these turbulent episodes he relied on the support of General Brooke. Montgomery understood how valuable it was, but at times he did his patron no favours. As the Normandy battle reached its final phase, Brooke replied to a letter of thanks, telling his field commander: 'You can go on relying on my firm support, my dear old Monty . . . There are people who don't understand you and I have had some pretty stiff battles on your behalf at times . . . Waging war may well be difficult, but waging war under political control becomes at times almost impossible.'

On 1 September Eisenhower took the baton of land forces command from Montgomery. The armies at play were so large that tiers of command unrecognisable from Wellington's day had evolved. Under the Duke, the British Army had been organised into divisions for the first time in 1809. Groups of two or more divisions formed a corps, and by the First World War the British were using multi-corps formations called armies. These could reach 250,000 troops, and rarely fell below 100,000. In Normandy Montgomery commanded a collection of them, designated the 21st Army Group, a truly vast war machine embracing US, British and Canadian armies as well as smaller contingents from many other nations.

During the breakout battle, 21st Army Group (i.e. Monty) had directed all land operations. Eisenhower's SHAEF, sitting back in England at that stage, had provided overall coordination with naval and air forces, and the logistic back-up. But with British manpower exhausted while American troops were pouring in, Bradley's First Army had been combined with Patton's Third in a new US 12th Army Group. Under the deals cut between Churchill and President Roosevelt, the 2-million-strong host heading for Germany needed yet another tier of leadership, one that was superimposed on a *group* of army groups. Hence SHAEF moved to France and took control of the land forces operations.

Churchill tried to soften the blow by making Montgomery a field marshal, 'to mark the approval of the British people', said the PM, 'for the *British* effort that had led to the defeat of the Germans in France'. However, such was Monty's popularity and global celebrity by this point that Churchill himself began to worry about it. On learning that the King, during a visit to France, had not presented the 21st Army Group commander with his new field marshal's baton, Churchill was suspicious. 'Monty wants to fill the Mall when he gets his baton! And he will not fill the Mall!' he shouted at Brooke that autumn, evidently having conjured up a mental picture of hundreds of thousands of cheering Britons in front of Buckingham Palace greeting their most famous soldier. Brooke reassured the Prime Minister that there would be no reason for Montgomery to grandstand in this way. 'Yes,' an unconvinced Churchill bellowed back, 'he will fill the Mall because he is Monty, and I will not have him filling the Mall!'

Although he had lived a sort of monastic life at his Tac HQ for months, it is clear that Monty's pride swelled after the Normandy battle, and he never completely recovered from having to accept the backseat behind Eisenhower. He had little respect for the Supreme Commander's judgement and they were soon arguing about whether the advance towards the Rhine should be pursued on a 'broad front'. (Eisenhower's policy) or in a concentrated thrust. Ike listened to Monty's noisy interventions with a good deal of tact, but some of the other US Army leaders were more outspoken. Bradley had got on well enough with Montgomery when serving under him, but once promoted to command of the US 12th Army Group, their relationship became more fraught. 'Monty is beginning to believe in the Monty legend, that he is a great man of history,' one of Bradley's staff had written during the Normandy battle. Increasingly, such sentiments would poison the relations between the three key figures – Eisenhower, Bradley and Montgomery – as the Allies pushed towards Germany.

The conference between Eisenhower and Bradley on 16 December 1944 was meant to be a routine affair. The latter had travelled back from his front to the opulent surroundings of Versailles, where the vast SHAEF staff made its home close to the pleasures of Paris. He was anxious to get more battle-casualty replacements for his divisions, many of which were still understrength because of losses suffered during the Normandy breakout.

Some early reports reaching the two men suggested the Germans had attacked that morning in the forests of the Ardennes, on the Belgian–German frontier. Bradley was sanguine about this, feeling it might be a spoiler designed to distract him from launching his own operations. As the day went on, though, the jocular front initially maintained by both

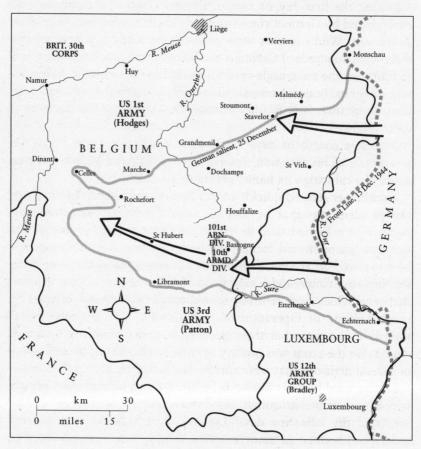

The battle of the Bulge, 1944

generals disappeared. Staff officers struggling to find out what was going on could not get through to many of the frontline units; phone lines were down everywhere. Ominously, there were indications that many German divisions not previously thought to be in the Ardennes sector were involved.

The American Army had in fact been taken horribly by surprise. Some 200,000 German troops and 1,000 tanks had been massed without being detected. A combination of effective deception plans and rapid movement by rail had thwarted the Allied intelligence machine with its Ultra decrypts and superior aerial reconnaissance. Hitler had launched a great thrust designed to punch through Bradley's depleted divisions and head for the Channel.

During the first day or two of this onslaught the confusion was exacerbated by German commando raids, some using men dressed as Americans. Wild rumours were passed from one GI to another that there were hundreds of Germans behind their lines, that they were able to fool even the most eagle-eyed sentry as they went about their sabotage missions. Fears of assassination resulting from these early reports kept Eisenhower and Bradley confined to their HQs during most of what followed.

It took a couple of days for Bradley, in particular, to realise the seriousness of his situation. A large German salient had been created, giving the campaign its name, the Battle of the Bulge.

Eisenhower reacted quickly by rushing reinforcements to the scene. His problem was that he had very few of them. The broad-front policy meant he had tried to be strong all along his line and so had very few uncommitted formations left. Two armoured divisions had been ordered to the most threatened sectors, but apart from them the Supreme Commander could only call upon the 82nd and 101st Airborne, which were refitting 100 miles from the front following the tough fighting of Operation Market Garden. The airborne moved smartly into action, but their inability to stem the enemy onslaught meant that the 101st was quickly bypassed in Bastogne, becoming one of several divisions that were surrounded or overrun.

Having used his only available forces to try to prevent the Germans widening their breakthrough, Eisenhower had little influence over the events of the following days. Locked up at SHAEF, he issued few orders and seemed in many respects to have been overwhelmed by events. There was one more important act he had to perform, though.

The German 'bulge' had cut right through Bradley's 12th Army Group sector. His First Army, to the north of the salient, had been out of communication with him for forty-eight hours by the evening of 19 December. The First Army commander had gone to pieces under the strain and, one observer noted, sat at a desk with his head in his hands while his Chief of Staff tried to coordinate resistance using the army's three remaining divisions. During these early days of the German offensive, 25,000 American soldiers were taken prisoner.

Despite the seriousness of the situation, it took two British staff officers at SHAEF to wake the (American) Chief of Staff to Eisenhower, General Walter Bedell Smith, on the night of 19–20 December. They suggested that since Bradley could not even communicate with his First and Ninth armies, Montgomery, whose entire 21st Army Group lay north of the bulge, should take command of them. Bedell Smith denounced the men who had woken him as 'sons of bitches' and 'limey bastards', shouting, 'Whenever there is any real trouble, the British do not appear to trust Americans to handle it efficiently,' and sacked them.

Bedell Smith may have been prejudiced and ill tempered but he certainly wasn't stupid. The following morning, he acted on the staff officers' suggestion and reinstated them, saying, 'I knew you were right. But my American feelings got the better of me.' Eisenhower told Montgomery to assume command of the First and Ninth armies (totalling eighteen divisions) on 20 December.

Circumstance had therefore forced the Supreme Commander to do something very close to what Monty had been arguing for since August: to give one army group priority for the drive towards the Rhine and to make it (surprise, surprise) the northern one (i.e. his). Bradley knew this only too well, and when Eisenhower rang him to inform him that he had ordered the British field marshal to assume control of something like 200,000 American troops, there was an explosion. Bradley shouted down the phone, 'I cannot be responsible to the American people if you do this. I resign!' Eisenhower, often derided by critics for taking the views of the last person he'd spoken to, proved on this occasion to be the mouse that roared. As Supreme Commander, he pointed out, it was *he* who was responsible, so, 'Your resignation therefore means absolutely nothing.' After more spluttering from his army group commander, Eisenhower terminated the call with 'Well, Brad, those are my orders.'

Hearing in London of this tumult, General Alan Brooke must have shared in some of Montgomery's satisfaction. But being the wise Chief of the Imperial General Staff he was, and knowing the characters he was dealing with, he instantly saw danger in this new situation. He sent a message to Monty on 21 December, acknowledging the field marshal's prescience but continuing, 'You should not even in the slightest degree appear to rub this undoubted fact in to anyone at SHAEF or elsewhere.' Brooke had not, of course, heard the words used by Bedell Smith and Bradley, but to us, today, they are powerful evidence of how far American national pride influenced these players.

When Montgomery appeared at the US First Army HQ to take over the defence of the northern sector, it was, as one observer noted, 'like Christ come to cleanse the Temple'. He galvanised the Americans with his self-confidence and tactical advice. However, it wasn't always easy to get these ideas across, since the doctrinal differences between British and US armies were very evident during the Battle of the Bulge.

British officers sometimes compared US practices to Western Front generalship in the First World War, and indeed it can be likened to the French variety of it. The Americans shared a belief in offensive action, all along the line, all of the time. During the dark days of December 1944 this meant not only that they had almost no reserves, but that most of their divisions had no training in defensive fighting. There was also something of the Western Front in the American commanders' refusal to relinquish ground, even in the face of high casualties.

Montgomery's orders, therefore, on taking command, were to abandon the American-held salient of St Vith, shorten defensive lines and create a reserve corps that would be used to launch a counter-attack as soon as circumstances were right. These commonsense directives were greeted with relief by the US commander in St Vith, who credited Monty with saving his division from annihilation. The general in charge of the 82nd Airborne noted a changed atmosphere at First Army HQ: 'The staff spoke of Montgomery with amusement and respect. They obviously liked him and respected his professionalism.'

As a precaution, Monty deployed XXX British Corps behind the American First Army, in defensive positions along the River Meuse. This was a wise contingency plan but was the source of later bad feeling: some Americans appear to have resented the implied lack of confidence in their own ability to hold out – shades of British troops standing with fixed bayonets behind US ones. The XXX Corps' deployment (they did almost no actual fighting) would also be used by Montgomery, in the view of some Americans, to exaggerate the British role in stabilising the Ardennes front.

The goal of containing the German advance had in fact been achieved by Christmas Day, and the bitter tenacity of American resistance was at last repayed. Actions like the 101st Airborne's defence of Bastogne were to become mythical episodes for the American public. Fuel shortages and air strikes robbed the Germans of any momentum, and they became vulnerable to counter-attack. Patton began striking hard from the south at the German salient, while all the time suspecting Montgomery was being too slow to do likewise from the north. Although there were many days' hard fighting ahead, the crisis had passed.

Montgomery had wasted little time in launching a personal counter-offensive, too. He returned to his familiar theme that Eisenhower could not personally run the land battle, writing to him on 29 December, 'You cannot possibly do it yourself.'

After the unbearable tension of the Battle of the Bulge, Monty's return to his 'there must be an Allied ground forces supremo and it must be me' line was the last straw for the Supreme Commander. Eisenhower decided that the field marshal's behaviour was tantamount to insubordination and, once again, the mouse roared. He decided to tell the US/UK combined chiefs of staff that either he or Montgomery would have to go . . . but it wasn't going to be him. At this point General Freddie de Guingand, Monty's devoted chief of staff since Alam Halfa, entered the fray, pleading with the Supreme Commander for time before flying back to 21st Army Group HQ. When de Guingand told Montgomery that Eisenhower wanted to replace him, the field marshal 'looked nonplussed – I don't think I had ever seen him look so deflated. It was as if a cloak of loneliness had descended upon him.' Somebody, at last, had managed to puncture Montgomery's carapace of cockiness and brought home the consequences of his behaviour.

Montgomery stepped back from the brink by signing de Guingand's draft of a grovelling signal to Eisenhower: 'Very distressed that my letter may have upset you and I would ask you to tear it up.' He signed off, 'Your very devoted subordinate, Monty'. The field marshal thus finally abandoned his struggle to reclaim the role he lost at the end of the Normandy battle and, after the Bulge crisis had passed, Bradley resumed control of the US First Army. By this point, there were thirteen British divisions fighting in northern Europe and seventy-two American ones. Such were the realities of the power relationship as the war moved towards its end.

The political sensitivity of command arrangements was such that the Allies had kept secret for many days that much of Bradley's army group had been under Montgomery's command during the Ardennes battle, but Monty himself happily announced this at a press conference on 7 January. By this stage of the war, the correspondents at army group headquarters had become virtual cheering sections for their own countries. One of Bradley's staff called the 7 January briefing 'a cataclysmic Roman holiday in the British press . . . The troops are referred to as "Monty's" troops in a palavering gibberish that indicates a slavish hero devotion on the part of the British press.' Bradley duly responded with his own briefing on 9 January to an American press corps which played a similar national role. In his dealings with Bradley, Eisenhower and the British press, Montgomery had therefore ignored Brooke's injunction not to 'rub in' his role in turning around a battle that could have been an even bigger disaster.

On 2 May 1945 in a tent pitched on Luneberg Heath, Montgomery accepted a German surrender. It wasn't *the* surrender; that was handled by Eisenhower three days later. Rather, the solemn occasion in Monty's tent, at which enemy forces in northern Germany capitulated, was one of those cleverly evolved pieces of Allied showmanship that allowed the British public to believe that, after six years of suffering, their man was the one who had finally put Hitler's goons in their place.

So ended Monty's career as a wartime general. He had won epic victories at Alam Halfa, El Alamein and in Normandy. During the Battle of the Bulge, he showed exemplary leadership, averting a crisis while many other generals were ineffective or went to pieces. He had also suffered disappointments.

The failure of Operation Market Garden, his attempt in September 1944 to open a highway into Germany's industrial heartland by using paratroops to seize a series of bridges, was not a serious stain on his record. In the first place, much of the public, after the success of the Normandy breakout, hoped that the war might end by Christmas 1944. Montgomery, usually criticised by fire-eaters like Patton as over-cautious, took a risk in order to try to shorten the war. At Arnhem, the 'bridge too far', British paratroops paid a heavy price for this gamble, but while many detailed criticisms of the operation can be made, in principle it was certainly worth trying.

Montgomery's failure to make proper plans for the capture of Antwerp, a port vitally important to the logistical support of the final push on Germany, was a more serious failure in my view. Since this sin of omission did not carry the same spectacular consequences as the fighting at Arnhem, though, it has received little attention from the public or historians. Nevertheless, constraints of supply – notably the lack of a major port near the head of the Allied advance – certainly slowed the push into Germany in the autumn of 1944.

As for his mark on history, Monty's, like Wellington's, lay in winning such spectacular victories in the sideshow (in Monty's, case, North Africa; in Wellington's, the Iberian peninsula) that it bought him and Britain a key role in the main event – the final defeat of the Nazis. Britain thereby became the main European player in the post-war settlement (to the west of the Iron Curtain anyhow). As Deputy Supreme Commander of NATO after the war, Montgomery then shaped the forces that had to confront the Soviet Union. His main influence on the organisation was to insist on constant, realistic training.

In the British context, his determination in applying to the whole army the methods – major exercises, study days and so on – that had brought his 3rd Division to such a peak of efficiency in 1940 defined the post-war professional force. One of its generals, writing in the eighties, argued that Monty 'dominated the collective consciousness of the British Army' during the Second World War and this proved to be the case to a large extent after it as well.

Of Monty the man we need not say too much, since the qualities necessary to galvanise the peacetime army to the point when it could confront the architects of blitzkrieg made him a very prickly customer indeed. Certainly, his personal unpopularity led many officers in the post-war army to look to other examples of leadership, notably William Slim, whose command of the 14th Army in Burma is still considered inspirational. Slim won many battles against the Japanese under shockingly difficult conditions, but Burma was another sideshow, and the objective of his campaigns (turning back the Japanese from the gates of India) makes them something of a historical oddity, since he and many others knew that the Raj was on its last legs.

Perhaps Montgomery's lack of popularity in the army is also testimony to his exceptional abilities. Churchill, in typically pugnacious mood after the war, told one officer, 'I know why you all hate him. You are jealous: he is better than you are.' Certainly, the peacetime British Army was often more comfortable with charming mediocrity than with Monty's brand of conceited excellence. Churchill evidently recognised in Monty somebody with a shared understanding of what high command in an age of total war required: simple messages, like 'I am here to beat Rommel', were needed to galvanise citizen soldiers; wobbly politicians had to be constantly reassured that 'the plan is working'; and the wider public responded to the showmanship he displayed in front of the cameras. Some might argue that Montgomery's behaviour towards the Americans or his gaffes on numerous subjects showed him to be a disastrous political general. I disagree. He had a powerful sense of what was needed to beat Hitler, it chimed in very closely with what the public expected and in the end this gave him a powerful, intuitive bond with Churchill. Although Alan Brooke did sterling work constraining the Prime Minister's wilder ideas about strategy, and indeed protecting his friend in the field, Montgomery was alone among British generals in exciting Churchill's envy.

The last and most important element in Montgomery's legacy concerns his role in defining Britain's future military relationship with America. There were many difficult episodes in this process, but in the end, even if it took Eisenhower's threat of sacking him to do it, Monty understood the realities perfectly well, and he went on to serve Ike post-war as his deputy at NATO. However, even before the showdown between those two men in December 1944, Montgomery's conduct of the Normandy breakout, paying for American success with a British battle of attrition, showed an underlying grasp of the new power relationship.

At Blenheim and Waterloo, British generals had commanded armies made up largely of foreigners. These arrangements were forged through clever military diplomacy, having a C-in-C who had shown great skill in the field and through a shared understanding (often aided by British cash) of who outranked whom in the league of European powers. It was this last factor that had changed profoundly as the Second World War came to a close. Montgomery had finally been forced to acknowledge that 'American public opinion, and, ultimately, Roosevelt,' in the words of Carlo d'Este, 'made it impossible for a British general to command the final battles of World War II'.

Montgomery's personal struggle against accepting Eisenhower's authority over the drive into Germany echoed that of his nation about

American strategic leadership. When Monty finally signed his chief of staff's telegram to Ike on the last day of 1944, thereby abandoning his pretensions to overall command, a tipping-point was reached. Britain was forced to acknowledge it had been displaced by a greater power. The age in which British generals directed great armies in major wars was over.

Of British Generals . . .

It MIGHT SEEM IMPOSSIBLE to find threads that connect the lives of ten men separated by centuries, but they certainly exist. Those who mastered their circumstances prevailed; those who did not left the worst kind of legacy. Some would answer that is obvious, so it is important to explore the peculiar characteristics of military leadership in Britain. Much was determined by the country's geographic position as an island; by the early flowering of free speech, personal liberty as well as democracy; by the social realities, be they of class or industrial progress; and finally by the fact that men wishing to rise to positions of power within any organisation – and, in particular, the army – have to master its peculiarities. Those British generals who left a great legacy combined military skill with a mastery of politics, of dealing successfully with the civilian holders of power. In the cases of George Monck, the Duke of York and Herbert Kitchener, this second factor was even more important than winning great battles. Those who failed, by contrast, were those who miscalculated, who failed to understand the set-up in the palace or Downing Street.

This lesson is particularly important since the professional army, for the past century at least, has reserved particular contempt for so-called 'political generals'. When used around the officers' mess dinner table, the term covers a broad array of sins from sycophancy to ruthlessness. At the heart of such distaste is a sense that the seamy business of political dealing cannot sit well with adherence to a gentleman's code of honour in which truthfulness and loyalty rank high.

These values were all very well for those who did not aspire beyond command of their regiment in peacetime; indeed, these days it is reassuring that so many people still live by them. But we should be under no illusions: the British standing army came into being following a military coup and right until the moment 285 years later when Churchill feared Monty was overtaking his own popularity, the best man to lead it was a general with a sound grasp of politics.

As for the rules of sound political generalship, they are as vaguely defined as the smoke-shrouded contours of some eighteenth-century battlefield. John Churchill, the Duke of Marlborough, was without doubt a consummate player at court for many years, but in the end he overstepped the mark, tried to grab too much power and fell from grace. Arthur Wellesley, the Duke of Wellington, clearly learned by this example and played his cards very carefully indeed during his long years of campaigning. However, later in life, in gratifying his ambition for the prime ministership, he ended up with a liability on the historical balance sheet.

The British undoubtedly prefer their military leaders not to aspire to the very apex of power, and they are perennially suspicious of smooth-talkers. In *Much Ado about Nothing* Shakespeare wrote of Claudio, 'He was wont to speak plain and to the purpose, like an honest man and a soldier,' and it is interesting to see how often this archetype of a military man, as someone straight, better at deeds than words, re-emerges from Monck to Kitchener and Edmund Allenby. The irony is that frequently great British generals have lied or at least cloaked their real intentions in order to reassure nervous civilians and overcome political obstacles.

When it comes to fighting wars with coalitions of allies – Britain's usual practice, given the small size of its standing army – it is worth noting how often commanders-in-chief have had to adopt the diplomats' modus operandi (being sent abroad to lie for their country). Marlborough's barefaced dishonesty when telling the leaders of the Netherlands where he was taking their army in 1704 is only the most spectacular example. It is certainly the case that Britain's need for friends in arms required from its commanders skills of tact, persuasion and sometimes skulduggery that were usually unnecessary in those leading the armies of great land powers, be they Louis XIV's French force in the eighteenth century, Russia's in the nineteenth, or the US Army in the twentieth.

I am not setting out to prove that high command required *daily* dishonesty, but rather that in the British Army the successful Commander-in-Chief has invariably been somebody who combines a certain ruthlessness with an acute sense of the political landscape and a good measure of military ability. In this sense, 'non-political generals' have always come second or been disasters.

In understanding where these men sprang from and how they changed the world, we must never lose sight of that most basic geographic fact – Britain's insularity. This physical reality made the navy top dogs, of course. Since invasion was prevented in the first analysis by the fleet, there was a seriousness about naval preparations, and a fear of the consequences of disaster, that meant the admirals were more often heeded by monarchs and ministers. Even the army's amateurish ethos and lack of professionalism – factors that drove to distraction would-be reformers from the Duke of York to J.F.C. Fuller – can be attributed in some ways to the fact that soldiering was simply not the kind of national life-and-death enterprise in Britain that it was in Russia or France.

For many countries, failure of the army meant pillage, rape and occupation. Since the British Army could not even be truly tested until after the Royal Navy (and, later, the Royal Air Force) had already failed, the stakes were commensurately lower. There can be little doubt that the lack of respect among the Georgian public for its army stemmed from the conviction that it was a second-rate operation, attracted few people of talent and was basically regarded as a mechanism for skimming undesirables off the street to go and die somewhere overseas.

During the early days of Britain's standing army, certainly from 1680 to 1815, its amateurishness produced a distinct lack of confidence about soldiering in society at large. This was why those few aristocratic families intent on a military career for their sons usually sent them abroad to learn it. It is also why so many Britons were unsurprised when military disasters unfolded or became near hysterical with gratitude when somebody like Marlborough, who could beat the continental experts at their own game, emerged. At sea, since 1588, there had always been greater confidence about the outcome.

The consequences of soldiers playing second fiddle to the sailors permeated many aspects of British life in the eighteenth and nineteenth centuries. Britain, for example, only needed conscription (in its full form) 120 years after France introduced it. The maintenance of a small professional army placed few strains on society, requiring neither absolutism nor militarism. George Orwell put it eloquently: 'A navy employs comparatively few people, and it is an external weapon which cannot affect home politics directly. Military dictatorships exist everywhere, but there is no such thing as a naval dictatorship.'

But if a small standing army suited Britain and its internal politics very well most of the time, there have, of course, been some moments of existential danger when it did not. The obvious examples are when Napoleon and Hitler threatened invasion.

At these times, the symptoms of the British Army trying to get itself organised were familiar and depressing enough to produce the aphorism about it beginning every campaign with a defeat. However, at moments of real danger the dramatic expansion of the army drew in a much greater variety of people – many of them brighter and more open to innovation than its usual fodder – and the organisation was being transformed. This applied almost as much to what the Duke of York did in the 1800s as to Kitchener's colossal mobilisation more than a century later.

Once the danger had passed (and great victories been won by the legions of mobilised men) insularity became the dominant paradigm again, and the loss of direction, intellectual drive and sense of purpose is equally palpable from accounts of 1816, 1919 and 1946. All of this meant that a class consisting of what one writer calls 'those prolific lowbrow families whose sons officered the army' resumed command. What was more, this same unpromising material would be expected to produce the generals for the next war.

As the adjunct of a great sea-going power, the army's duty during centuries of Empire consisted of garrisoning pestilential spice islands or the back-countries of trading ports. Often it proved very hard for these garrisons to find naturally defensible boundaries as they pushed further into Africa, the Indian subcontinent or China. So, within a few years, the Victorian army suffered three epic disasters, essentially because the army, carried along by Imperial hubris, strayed too far from the Royal Navy and encountered more opposition than it could cope with – Isandhlwana (South Africa), Maiwand (Afghanistan) and the Gordon relief expedition (Sudan).

Colonial soldiering, with its penny-packets of troops scattered about, usually deprived the army of the chance to think and train on the scale needed for operations in Europe. It stunted the way it grew both physically (the regiment being the prime focus of its organisation) and mentally, contributing to the slow development of a British general staff. The redcoats' fate as glorified marines produced many other vices but also some virtues, such as fostering leadership among junior and non-commissioned officers, as well as educating them in the need for sensitivity to local customs.

The British system of long professional service, and the soldiers' exposure to combat in policing operations around the world, resulted in an extremely professional body of men. The high quality of the British rank and file through most of the period 1660–1945 and the army's limitations in major warfare were therefore two sides of the same coin.

The security provided by the British Isles affected the political development of the country, which in turn further constrained the army. England emerged from its civil war as an anti-militarist society in which great importance was placed on freedom of speech and belief. From the outset, Britain's professional soldiers found themselves barracked: from the Puritan sectaries in Monck's day to the Whigs who taunted Marlborough and the Radicals who brought down the Duke of York. At a very early stage, then, soldiers learned the respect for Parliament and popular sentiment that is essential in a democracy.

From Marlborough onwards, the occasionally violent partisanship of Parliament made it vitally important for British military commanders to avoid failure. Setbacks seemed to confirm all the critics' instincts that Britain was a second-rate military power and should not be indulging in adventurism overseas. A defeat, when frankly admitted at Westminster, could bring down a coalition, or at the very least provide a handle for those who wished to deride the government of the day. This produced the caution – or, to put it more pointedly, the lack of offensive spirit – that became a common denominator in the thinking of so many British generals, from Wellington to Montgomery. It is evident even in the colonial campaigns of Kitchener.

The dread consequences of admitting defeat often aroused a self-justificatory or defensive technique in the writing of official dispatches. Wellington at Quatre Bras, Haig at the Somme and Monty during the early days of the Normandy breakout would all stick doggedly to the line that they were masters of the situation and had not suffered a reverse. Great British generals have had to learn the art of defending their actions to the home audience through the most *careful* use of words.

Legends about 'undefeated generals' have particular resonance in the English-speaking world, whereas in those countries steeped in land warfare there is more open acknowledgement that battle plans, like all forms of human endeavour, sometimes go wrong. Field Marshal Blücher of Prussia, to give one example, suffered his share of drubbings at the hands of Napoleon, but his sovereign accepted that he was skilful as well as uniquely aggressive in command, so 'Old Forwards', as his men called him, remained in place to share with Wellington the glory for Waterloo.

Elsewhere in Europe, a lack of derision for miscarried military plans was part of a whole with absolutism and the use of armies to coerce or awe their own people. Violence against civilians was used in Britain and Ireland, of course – particularly during the years when redcoats policed the country – but to a lesser degree than on the Continent. Orwell thought that this difference manifested itself in the way armies paraded, noting, 'Beyond a certain point, military display is only possible in countries where the common people dare not laugh at the army.' Certainly, the number of occasions when the British Army has driven phalanxes of tanks through the streets of London can be counted on the fingers of one hand, whereas in Paris (where the threat of military coup was palpable even in 1968) such display of heavy metal is still an annual event. And few would claim that the British people since 1660 have been afraid to laugh at their army.

While it is true that Britain has generally been an anti-militarist society, there was a period, at the zenith of Empire in the late nineteenth century, when campaigns resulting from blatant nationalism and a crude desire for revenge were unleashed, for example in Sudan and Afghanistan. This epoch was comparatively short lived (perhaps forty years), and was produced by a highly unusual combination of factors, whereby certain people in the army – such as Charles Gordon – used the press to excite public support, thereby outmanoeuvring the elected politicians of the day.

The situation exploited by Gordon and Lord Wolseley ended as soon as politicians emerged who were better judges of the public mood and how to shape it than their generals, and tighter political control was exerted over the army. The Boer War was a turning point in this, displaying the army's limited competence when facing a skilled 'European' enemy, and prompting the emergence of populist critics, such as David Lloyd George, who were more articulate than the generals. Nevertheless, the Gordon episode was significant because it underlined that Britain was the first country in which the power of the newly enfranchised and their newspapers was a factor in the decision to wage or abandon military campaigns. Just as the need to keep allies onside turned British generals from Marlborough onwards into skilled diplomats, so developments in the early twentieth century demanded that Allenby and Montgomery become excellent PR men. But while these soldiers understood the need to maintain public support during major wars, the landscape was very different in peacetime.

For many Britons from the eighteenth century onwards, suspicion of standing armies and ridicule of soldiers dovetailed neatly with their desire not to pay higher taxes. This reluctance to spend money on naval or military preparations had its benefits, many historians have argued, in allowing the country to race ahead of its Continental rivals in economic development, particularly industrialisation. This, in turn, created new inventions for the armed forces.

During the years of Britain's greatest power (from the 1790s to 1918, perhaps), the army was extremely good at assimilating new technology. Whether it was Major Shrapnel's shells (first used by Wellington in Portugal), the firepower unleashed by Kitchener at Omdurman or the tanks at Cambrai, new inventions could be pressed into action with impressive speed. Often the effect on an enemy was devastating. The army may have been more conservative than society at large, but it undoubtedly benefited from the free flow of ideas and economic liberalism of wider British society. Thus Wellington – aristocrat, social reactionary and High Tory – became an enthusiastic patron of rifles and new light infantry tactics.

It was only when the Empire became preoccupied with the idea that it was in decline, particularly after the First World War, that this interaction went wrong, with the result that near-fatal mistakes were made in failing to mechanise. It was no coincidence that during these years the gentry that had provided the bulk of the army's officers for centuries became, under the pressures of early twentieth-century class politics, utterly reactionary and anti-intellectual. Fuller evidently misjudged both the nature of his own society and the limits of how far the army could modernise itself, becoming a fascist pariah in the process. Montgomery, although possessing a far lesser intellect, found more practical ways to make the changes necessary while not alarming the senior commanders he derided so frequently as 'useless'.

Monty's example takes us to the last big factor in defining what British commanders could – and could not – achieve: namely, their success as political generals, not in the party sense, but in the business of rising to the top of their own organisation. These men had to be driven, of course – and many had unhappy childhoods or difficult relationships with their mothers (Wellington, Gordon, Kitchener, Fuller and Montgomery all stand out). But this trait is shared by many high achievers; it is hardly something specific to the British Army.

A more interesting aspect of their characters, particularly those who were great successes of one sort or another, was the degree to which they were outsiders who considered themselves in conflict with those at the top. Of course, the Duke of York, the King's second son, can be excluded from this group, but even Wellington, with his aristocratic background, often felt himself at odds with the army hierarchy. As for the others, Gordon, Kitchener, Allenby, Fuller and Montgomery all entered the army with limited financial means and saw themselves as fighting bitter personal battles for advancement.

In some of these careers, the sense of being an outsider was definitely linked to sexual longings that were considered shameful. Gordon, Kitchener and Montgomery all seem to have been either practising or latent homosexuals, and they possibly even shared a common desire for sex with boys. The suggestion that they remained usually celibate, channelling their aggression into the army, emerges as a common factor in accounts of them. Certainly, they all avoided a scandal. But they and the wider group of outsiders could not escape the prejudice that derived from the army's particular class and social assumptions. So, while an unhappy childhood or sexual guilt may have driven certain men, their success within the army required them to master the conventions of an institution that saw itself occupying a specific place in the British national hierarchy.

A combination of lowly family circumstances and great personal drive easily excited snobbery. Marlborough was initially regarded as an *arriviste*, Kitchener called (by Churchill) a 'vulgar common man', and one of Montgomery's superiors wrote that 'in dealing with him, one must remember that he is not quite a gentleman'. There is no doubt that a general who wished to spur a British Army to efficiency, let alone victory, had to be thick skinned when dealing with class prejudice as well as a willing inconoclast.

Conversely, those officers who had the family credentials to rise effortlessly, such as William Howe, almost always disappointed in command because they had no interest in challenging the army's arcane ways. They could also look down upon less fortunate officers who tried to rise by zeal alone, using various devices to advance over their heads the more socially acceptable types. It is salutory to note that vitally important steps to ease the path of ambitious outsiders could only be imposed on the officer corps by the ultimate insider, the Duke of York. Nobody could accuse him of championing merit in officers' promotions or education because he was 'not quite a gentleman'. The Duke, though, is the exception that proves the rule about iconoclasm being a quality for the path to greatness in this particular organisation.

If someone like Allenby seems an improbable troublemaker, as he followed Douglas Haig's orders for countless futile assaults on the Western Front, we must not forget that the officer corps' initiative had been so stifled in 1917 by GHQ's pedantry and micro-management that even arguing for a two-day artillery barrage rather than a seven-day one had come to constitute a kind of sedition. Sticking – quite literally, in this case – to one's guns and overcoming holders of received opinion were vital qualities for successful commanders.

During the largest expeditions, those required on European campaigns against highly professional opponents, the scale on which brother officers were cajoled, sidelined or sacked increased in proportion. Wellington, Kitchener, Allenby and Montgomery shared an ability to ride roughshod over subordinates again and again without apparently entertaining a moment's guilt about it.

British armies, in order to meet the challenge of large-scale operations, required a tough leader and had to allow him several years in which to hand-pick his subordinates. So, even in 1942, after two and a half years of war, General Sir Alan Brooke, Chief of the Imperial General Staff, fumed in his diary: 'Half our Corps and Divisional commanders are totally unfit for their appointments, and yet if I were to sack them I could find no better! They lack character, imagination, drive and power of leadership.' Brooke put this down to the terrible losses of the First World War, but I think it also had a lot to do with the values of the officer corps, summed up by Fuller when he wrote, 'Good-fellowship ranks with us above efficiency.' The British Army was truly world class, then, only when an exceptional general had been given years in which to bring his forces close to perfection in leadership and training: Marlborough at Blenheim in 1704; Wellington at Salamanca, 1812; Monty in Normandy, 1944.

If we look, by contrast, at campaigns in which things went badly, we see either hostilities ending before the work was done (the Boer War), a long war with an incapable Commander-in-Chief (such as Howe in America, 1775–8) or a combination of poor generals and truncated campaigning (the Crimea). In each of these cases there was soul-searching afterwards as to what had gone wrong, but a reversion to peacetime rules of good-fellowship in the officer corps that prevented effective remedies.

The army's 'culture' – to use a deliberate anachronism since I am writing about its ethos before 1945 – was therefore one in which the fighting efficiency needed for a war against equals could come about only under exceptional circumstances. An individual had to rise to a rank sufficiently high that he could break many of the usual rules of officer behaviour that he himself had adhered to in order to climb the promotion ladder in the first place. The reward from superiors or politicians grateful for success on the battlefield was further promotion, honours and public acclaim – but also a good deal of resentment from fellow officers.

Stellar C-in-Cs broke careers, but they also disturbed their peers' self-image. Others argued that the ambitious 'climber', in ruthlessly getting to the top, must have cloaked his real designs or dissembled to some degree. In this sense, dealing with the internal challenge of promotion to the highest ranks required the same qualities as dealing with ministers or the wider public – political generalship, a way of waging war with words or gestures that sat badly with the chivalrous self-image of many regimental officers. Montgomery evidently felt this dilemma, which is why, in the interests of avoiding accusations of personal dishonesty, he was blunt to the point of insult with many of his colleagues.

As time has gone on, the need for such qualities as 'being good in committee' has increased compared to the days when sound generalship required a man not to duck cannon balls or let his wig slip. In writing during the 1930s about Marlborough, Winston Churchill argued that modern warfare had diminished the Commander-in-Chief:

There are no physical disturbances; there is no danger; there is no hurry . . . In the height of his largest battles, when twenty thousand men are falling every day, time will hang heavy on his hands . . . His personal encounters are limited to an unpleasant conversation with an army commander who must be dismissed, an awkward explanation to a harassed Cabinet, or an interview with a representative of a neutral press . . . It is not true that the old battle has merely been raised to a gigantic scale. In the process of enlargement the sublime function of military genius – perhaps happily – has been destroyed for ever.

It is interesting to contrast this passage with those penned a few years later in the Second World War diary of General Sir Alan Brooke. He evidently considered that a great part of the 'military genius' required of a wartime Chief of the General Staff consisted of managing Winston Churchill. 'He knows no details, has only got half the picture in his mind, talks absurdities and makes my blood boil to listen to his nonsense,' wrote the general after a particularly infuriating meeting with the Prime Minister in September 1944. 'I find it hard to remain civil. And the wonderful thing is that $^3/_4$ of the population of the world imagine that Winston Churchill is one of the Strategists of History, a second Marlborough, and the other $^1/_4$ have no conception what a public menace he is and has been throughout the war!'

Between these statements, by a future PM and his long-suffering CIGS, there lies an obvious truth about generalship as it evolved during the nineteenth and twentieth centuries. It was no longer possible, as it had been in Marlborough's or Wellington's time, for a commander to be seen by tens of thousands of his troops personally leading them onto the battlefield. For Whitehall warriors like Brooke, or C-in-Cs of major forces in the field such as Monty, skill in the black arts of managing ministers or public opinion became increasingly important. Moral courage might be required to stand up to someone like Churchill, but the premium on its physical variety was reduced as commanders-in-chief directed their operations from bunkers or HQs many miles from the front. Undoubtedly, this change provided the subtext for the army's internal debate, early in the twentieth century, about the increasing importance of 'intellect' and 'efficiency' and the corresponding decline in 'character' as the prime qualification for promotion.

The disdain expressed for politicians and politics by Kitchener as he himself was appointed to the cabinet as Secretary of War in 1914 can be seen as a peculiarly intense form of denial by a senior representative of a bewildered officer class. Indeed, terms such as 'climber' and 'political general' became widespread in the early twentieth century at exactly the time when it became apparent that ruthlessness, drive and brain power were simultaneously indispensable for senior generals and incompatible with the 'good chap'/'good sport' ethos of the officer corps. Even those who were most committed to burying these old ideas about what made a great general became sentimental as they wielded the shovel, with Boney Fuller calling the Boer conflict the 'last gentleman's war'.

Military genius was not lost, as Churchill suggested, but rather it had to be applied quite differently in the age of tanks and universal suffrage. Nowhere did it take longer for the need for such change to be accepted than within the officers' mess. The great wars of the twentieth century demonstrated that old-fashioned blood and thunder would simply be regarded by brother officers as thud and blunder. Skills of subtlety, intellect and professional commitment, which had always been necessary for the army's dealings with wider society, became prerequisites within it for high rank.

There are many reasons why it has not been possible to find a post-1945 subject for this book; not least that the army's story after the Second World War is essentially one of decline. There were several sterling figures directing the British Army during this period, but the story of graceful exits or judiciously applied spending cuts is hardly on a par with those of earlier centuries. These decades after the defeat of Hitler revealed a society learning to accept that it had become a lesser player, and even acknowledging that there have been some fascinating episodes in military intervention during the post-war years, we cannot yet claim the benefit of historical hindsight when the events concerned occurred in the 1980s or later. So Montgomery stands as the last general to lead great British armies in battle, and he personifies Britain having to yield to the reality of new power relationships.

Some British politicians would speak in the Cold War years of there being a 'blood price' for Britain's special relationship with the United States. Montgomery made the first hefty downpayments in the battles for Caen. What began with the Royal Armoured Corps' 'death ride' of 18 July 1944, during Operation Goodwood, culminated almost six decades later in the statement in the 2003 Defence White Paper that operations in any full-scale war 'involving intervention against state adversaries . . . can only plausibly be conducted if US forces are engaged, either leading a coalition or in NATO'. In the intervening years there had been all sorts of denial about Britain's role vis-à-vis

OF BRITISH GENERALS . . .

America, from politicians fostering the delusion that an equal voice in places such as the United Nations Security Council would deliver an equal say in the direction of the Western alliance to Foreign Office diplomats repeating their mantra about punching above our weight.

After El Alamein, though, in any matter of large-scale warfare Britain's army became auxiliary to the Americans' in the way the Dutch performed for Marlborough or the Portuguese for Wellington. I don't think that acknowledging this reality insults any of the parties. Britain's small, professional army is highly competent, particularly in the small wars that it has found itself engaged in since 1945. It has given the Americans plenty of lessons, just as the Dutch had much to teach the late seventeenth-century British. As for paying with blood for the US–UK alliance, the Portuguese, after all, did so handsomely for Wellington.

Talk of the Dutch or Portuguese is only fitting when charting the ebb and flow of empires. Britain, as a seaborne power, eclipsed those earlier ones and has been obliged to yield in its turn to the USA. After Monty, there may have been great British generals, but the country's interests and the size of its armies were both scaled back to such an extent that the power of any of those men to change the world, except perhaps through ideas, ended in 1945.

When examining the way British armies were led during these three centuries, then, we see how extraordinarily difficult it was for the right man to create the right circumstances at the right moment to change the world. Since the army was an appendage of such a great sea-going and trading power, however, those who managed the apparently impossible task of satisfying civilian politicians, impressing a sceptical public and galvanising an officer corps of gentlemen amateurs can be regarded as truly great generals. Little wonder that their legacy was more durable than that of those who commanded armies for despots or autocracies that have been buried by the forces of history. There is the rub. Since the British Army formed part of a singularly successful system of power, someone who could lead armies skilfully under Britain's peculiar constitution was by definition someone great enough to leave a legacy that can still be seen today.

Bibliography

General Works

Bagehot, Walter, *The English Constitution*, London, 1873
Barnett, Corelli, *Britain and Her Army*, London, 1970
Fortescue, Hon J.W., *A History of the British Army*, 13 vols, London, 1935
Orwell, George, *The Lion and the Unicorn*, London, 1941
Spiers, E.M., *The Army and Society, 1815–1914*, London, 1980
Strachan, Hew, *The Politics of the British Army*, Oxford, 1997

George Monck

Albemarle, George, Duke of, *Observations upon Military and Political Affairs*, London, 1671
Ashley, Maurice, *General Monck*, London, 1977
Braybrooke, Richard Lord (ed.), *The Diary of Samuel Pepys*, London
Chandler, David (ed.), *The Oxford Illustrated History of the British Army*, Oxford, 1994
Denton, Barry, *Regimental History of the New Model Army – Lloyd's Regiment – Monck's Regiment*, London, 1994
Firth, C.H. (ed.), *Scotland and the Commonwealth, Letters and Papers Relating to the Military Government of Scotland from August 1651 to December 1653*, Edinburgh, 1895
Gumble, Thomas, *Life of General Monck*, London, 1671
Hobbes, Thomas, *Behemoth, or the Long Parliament*, [1671], ed. Ferdinand Tonnies, London, 1884
MacKinnon, Colonel, *Origin and Services of the Coldstream Guards*, London, 1833
Peachey, Stuart and Turton, Alan, *Old Robin's Foot*, London, 1987
Skinner, Thomas, *The Life of General Monck: Duke of Albemarle*, London, 1724

Walton, Colonel Clifford, *History of the British Standing Army 1660 to 1700*, London, 1894
Warner, Oliver, *Hero of the Restoration*, London, 1936

John Churchill

Bishop, Matthew, *The Life and Adventures of Matthew Bishop, Written by Himself*, London, 1744
Chandler, David, *Marlborough as a Military Commander*, London, 1973
Churchill, Winston S., *Marlborough, His Life and Times*, 4 vols, London, 1933
Dumont, Monsieur, *Histoire Militaire du Prince Eugene de Savoye, du Prince et Duc de Marlborough, et du Prince Nassau-Frise*, 3 vols, The Hague, 1729
Manley, Mary Delariviere, *Secret Memoirs and the Manners of Several Persons of Quality of Both Sexes from the New Atlantis, an Island in the Mediterranean*, London, 1709
Murray, General the Rt. Hon. Sir George (ed.), *The Letters and Dispatches of John Churchill, First Duke of Marlborough, from 1702 to 1712*, 4 vols, London, 1845
Walton, Colonel Clifford, *History of the British Standing Army 1660 to 1700*, London, 1894

William Howe

Anderson, Fred, *Crucible of War*, London, 2000
Anderson, Troyer S., *The Command of the Howe Brothers during the American Revolution*, New York and London, 1936
Boatner, Mark M., *Encyclopedia of the American Revolution*, Mechanicsburg, Pa., 1966
Colley, Linda, *Britons: Forging the Nation, 1707–1837*, New Haven, Conn., 1992
Ewald, Captain Johann, *Diary of the American War*, New Haven, Conn., and London, 1979
Jones, Maldwyn, 'Sir William Howe: Conventional Strategist', in George Athan Billias (ed.), *General Washington's Generals and Opponents*, New York, 1964
Knox, Captain John, *Historical Journal of the Campaigns in North America*, Toronto, 1914
Mackesy, Piers, *The War for America 1775–1783*, London, 1964
Mowday, Bruce E., *September 11, 1777, Washington's Defeat at Brandywine Dooms Philadelphia*, Shippenberg, Pa., 2002
Schecter, Barnet, *The Battle for New York*, New York, 2002

Ward, Christopher, *The War of the Revolution*, 2 vols, New York, 1952

Willcox, William B. (ed.), *The American Rebellion: Sir Henry Clinton's Narrative of His Campaigns 1775–1782*, Hamden, Conn., 1971

Wood, W.J., *Battles of the Revolutionary War 1775–1781*, Chapel Hill, NC, 1990

Frederick, Duke of York

Berry, Paul, *By Royal Appointment*, London, 1970

Bunbury, H. E., *Narratives of Some Passages in the Great War with France (1799–1810)*, London, 1927

Burne, Alfred H., *The Noble Duke of York*, London, 1949

Calvert, Harry, *Autobiography of General Sir Harry Calvert*, unpublished MS, c. 1806.

Clarke, Mary Anne, *The Rival Princes*, New York, 1810

Glover, Richard, *Peninsular Preparation: The Reform of the British Army 1795–1809*, Cambridge, 1963

Gurwood, Colonel (ed.), *The Dispatches of Field Marshal the Duke of Wellington during His Various Campaigns*, 8 vols, London, 1852

Harcourt, Edward, *The Harcourt Papers*, Oxford, 1880

Haythornethwaite, Philip J., *The Armies of Wellington*, London, 1994

Le Marchant, Denis, *Memoirs of the Late Major General Le Marchant*, London, 1841

Thoumine, R.H., *Scientific Soldier – a Life of General Le Marchant 1766–1812*, London, 1968

Urban, Sylvanus (ed.), *The Gentleman's Magazine*, June 1799, February and April 1809

Verner, Willoughby, *History and Campaigns of the Rifle Brigade*, London, 1912

Verney, Sir Harry (ed.), *The Campaigns in Flanders and Holland in 1793–4*, London, 1853

War Office, 'General Orders' and 'Circular Letters', files at the National Archives, 1795–1809

Watkins, John, *A Biographical Memoir of Frederick, Duke of York and Albany*, London, 1827

Arthur Wellesley

Blakiston, Major John, *Twelve Years' Military Adventure*, London, 1829

Grattan, William, *Adventures with the Connaught Rangers*, London, 1902

Gurwood, Colonel (ed.), *The Dispatches of Field Marshal the Duke of Wellington during His Various Campaigns*, 8 vols, London, 1852

—— (ed.), *Wellington's Supplementary Dispatches*, Vol. IV, London, 1854

Haythornethwaite, Philip J., *The Armies of Wellington*, London, 1994
Hofschroer, Peter, *1815: The Waterloo Campaign*, 2 vols, London, 1998
Longford, Elizabeth, *Wellington*, 2 vols, London, 1969
Muir, Rory, *Britain and the Defeat of Napoleon 1807–1815*, New Haven, Conn., and London, 1996
——, *Salamanca 1812*, New Haven, Conn., and London, 2001
Napier, *History of the War in the Peninsula and in the South of France* [1835], 6 vols, London, 1992
Oman, Charles, *A History of the Peninsular War*, 8 vols, Oxford, 1902
——, *Wellington's Army 1809–1814*, London, 1912
Sherer, Moyle, *Recollections of the Peninsula*, London, 1824
Siborne, W., *History of the Campaign of Waterloo*, London, 1990

Charles Gordon

Chenevix Trench, Charles, *Charley Gordon: An Eminent Victorian Reassessed*, London, 1978
Churchill, Winston S., *The River War*, London, 1899
Cromer, Earl of, *Modern Egypt*, 3 vols, London, 1908
Egmont-Hake, A. (ed.), *The Journals of Major-Gen. C.G. Gordon at Kartoum*, London, 1885
Gordon, Henry William, *Events in the Life of Charles George Gordon*, London, 1886
Hamer, W.S., *The British Army, Civil–Military Relations 1885–1905*, Oxford, 1970
Harries-Jenkins, Gwyn, *The Army in Victorian Society*, London, 1977
Jenkins, Roy, *Gladstone*, London, 1995
Pollock, John, *Gordon: The Man behind the Legend*, Oxford, 1993
Robson, Brian, *Fuzzy Wuzzy: The Campaigns in the Eastern Sudan 1884–85*, Tunbridge Wells, 1993
Strachey, Lytton, *Eminent Victorians*, London, 1918
Wilson, Andrew, *The Ever Victorious Army*, London, 1878
Wingate, F.R., *Mahdiism and the Egyptian Sudan*, London, 1968

Horatio Herbert Kitchener

Arthur, Sir George, *The Life of Lord Kitchener*, 3 vols, London, 1920
Burleigh, Bennet, *The Khartoum Campaign 1898*, London, 1899
Churchill, Winston S., *The River War*, London, 1899
——, *The World Crisis, Vol. I: 1911–1914*, London, 1923
Cromer, Earl of, *Modern Egypt*, 3 vols, London, 1908
Fuller, J.F.C., *The Last of the Gentlemen's Wars*, London, 1937
Grey, Viscount, *Twenty Five Years*, London, 1932

Maxwell, Charlotte, *Frank Maxwell, Brig. Gen.: A Memoir and Some Letters*, London, 1921
Pakenham, Thomas, *The Boer War*, London, 1979
Pollock, John, *Kitchener*, London, 1998
Simkins, Peter, *Kitchener's Army: The Raising of the New Armies 1914–16*, Manchester, 1988
Steevens, G.W., *With Kitchener to Khartoum*, London, 1898
Surridge, Keith, 'More than a Great Poster', *Historical Research*, Vol. 74, 2001

Edmund Henry Hynman Allenby

Carver, Field Marshal Lord, *The Turkish Front 1914–1918*, London, 2003
Cave, Nigel, *Gommecourt: Somme*, Barnsley, 1998
Forester, C.S., *The General*, London, 1936
Fuller, J.F.C., *Memoirs of an Unconventional Soldier*, London, 1936
Gardner, Brian, *Allenby*, London, 1965
Hughes, Matthew (ed.), *Allenby in Palestine: The Middle East Correspondence of Field Marshal Viscount Allenby*, Stroud, 2004
Nicholls, Jonathan, *Cheerful Sacrifice: The Battle of Arras 1917*, London, 1990
Perrett, Bryan, *Megido 1918*, Oxford, 1999
Travers, Tim, *The Killing Ground: The British Army, the Western Front and the Emergence of Modern Warfare, 1900–1918*, London, 1987
Wavell, Field Marshal Viscount, *Allenby Soldier and Statesman*, London, 1946

John Frederick Charles Fuller

Fuller, J.F.C., 'The Application of Recent Developments in Mechanics and Other Scientific Knowledge to Preparation and Training for Future War on Land', *Journal of RUSI*, Vol. 65, May 1920
——, *The Reformation of War*, 1923
——, *Sir John Moore's System of Training*, London, 1924
——, *The Foundations of the Science of War*, London, 1925
——, *Memoirs of an Unconventional Soldier*, London, 1936
——, *The Last of the Gentlemen's Wars*, London, 1937
——, *Decisive Battles of the Western World*, 2 vols, London, 1954
Guderian, General Heinz, *Panzer Leader*, London, 1952
Holden Reid, Brian, *J.F.C. Fuller: Military Thinker*, London, 1987
Liddell-Hart, Basil, *The Tanks*, 2 vols, London, 1959
Macksey, Kenneth, *To the Green Fields beyond*, London, 1965
Simpkin, Richard, *Deep Battle: The Brainchild of Marshal Tuckhashevskii*, London, 1987

Trythall, Anthony John, *'Boney' Fuller: The Intellectual General 1878–1966*, London, 1977

Woollcombe, Robert, *The First Tank Battle – Cambrai 1917*, London, 1967

Wright, Patrick, *Tank*, London, 2000

Bernard Law Montgomery

Alanbrooke, Field Marshal Lord, *War Diaries 1939–1945*, London, 2001

Badsey, Stephen, *Normandy 1944*, Oxford, 1990

Borthwick, Alistair, *Battalion*, London, 1994

Carver, Michael, *Out of Step: The Memoirs of Field Marshal Lord Carver*, London, 1989

Daglish, Ian, *Operation Bluecoat*, Barsnley, 2003

——, *Operation Goodwood*, Barnsley, 2004

d'Este, Carlo, *Eisenhower*, London, 2003

Hamilton, Nigel, *Monty*, 3 vols, London, 1981

Horrocks, Sir Brian, *Corps Commander*, London, 1977

Liddell-Hart, Captain Sir Basil (ed.), *History of the Second World War*, 6 vols, London, 1966

MacDonald, Charles B., *The Battle of the Bulge*, London, 1984

Montgomery, B.L., *El Alamein to the River Sangro*, Berlin, 1946

——, *Normandy to the Baltic*, Berlin, 1946

——, *The Memoirs of Field Marshal the Viscount Montgomery of Alamein*, London, 1958

Orwell, George, *The Lion and the Unicorn*, London, 1941

Index

Abu Klea, Battle of, 177, 178, 179
Abyssinia, 187
Act of Union 1707, 55
Adams, Jimmy, 224
Adjutant General, 104
Admiralty, 169, 206, 254
Adowa, 187
Afghanistan, 159, 306
Afrika Korps, 272, 278, 279
Afula, 234
Air Ministry, 254
Alam Halfa Ridge, 272, 275, 296, 297
Albany, 84, 86, 88, 90–1
Aldgate, 22
Aleppo, 238
Alexander the Great, 6
Alexandria, 164, 165
Allenby, Edmund
    cavalry, 256
    Egypt, 226–7, 229, 239
    Fuller and, 221, 246
    General, The and, 219–20
    hierarchy, 220
    intellectual curiosity, 221
    Kitchener and, 201, 218, 221
    Lawrence, T.E. and, 229
    legacy, 239
    mentioned, 276, 302, 308, 309
    Near East campaign, 229–38
    patchy record of, 219
    PR, 307
    son, 222, 228
    Third Army, 219–26
Allenby, Michael, 222, 228

Allied landings, 281
American Civil War, 160
American First Army, 295
Americans
    Breed's Hill, 71–3
    Bulge, Battle of the, 293–6
    D-Day, 281
    French and, 86, 88, 91
    Howe and, 75
    lessons from British, 313
    Montgomery and, 299
    New York, 77–80
    Normandy, 281–91
    North Africa, 280
    strategy against, 76–7, 85
    Ticonderoga, 84
    war with, 75
    Washington's strategy, 81, 86–7
    Westminster factional support, 74, 88
    White Plains, 80
Amherst, General Sir Jeffrey,
    Canada won, 70
    Commander-in-Chief, 103
    Howe and, 71, 75, 77
    innovatory battle formation, 69
    mentioned, 72, 86
Amman, 237
Anabaptists, 9
Anglo-Egyptian Slave Convention, 164
Anne, Queen, 45, 56, 57, 59
Anse au Foulon, L', 65
Antelope, High Wycombe, 104–5
Anti-Slavery Society, 163
Antwerp, 298

'Application of Recent Developments in
    Mechanics and Other Scientific
    Knowledge to Preparation and
    Training for Future War on Land',
    254
Aqaba, 229
Arabs
    Balfour Declaration, 233
    Damascus, 237
    Kitchener and, 188, 190
    Lawrence, 229
    nationalism, 239
    Six-Day War, 265
    Sudan, 195–6, 203
Ardennes, 292–3
Armageddon, 235
Armée du Nord, 99, 102
Army Quarterly, 258
Arnhem, 297, 298
Arras, 225–6, 231, 246, 250
Asquith, Herbert, 204, 205–6, 227
Assaye, 123, 124, 127, 131, 137, 159
Atatürk, Kemal, 239
Atbara, Battle of, 194
Athlone, Earl of, 43–4
Australians, 227, 230, 276
Austria
    Blenheim, 52
    Britain compared to, 112
    Herzeele, 97
    lack of democracy, 103
    Marlborough in support of, 46
    Marlborough warns, 44
    struggles against French, 102
    subsidies to in 1809, 128
    Tourcoing, 99
Austro-Hungarians, 234, 238
Axis, 276, 278, 279, 286
Axminster, 35

Bacon, Private, 249
Bailen, 128
Baker, Valentine, 170–1
baksheesh, 163
Balfour Declaration, 233
Baptists, 9
Baring, Sir Evelyn, Lord Cromer, 168–9,
    176, 178, 180, 181, 187–8, 195–6
Baruda Desert, 177
Bastogne, 293, 296

Bavaria, 44–7, 52
Bavaria, Elector of, 48, 49, 51
Bearns, 69
Beaumont, 99
Bedell Smith, General Walter, 294
Beersheba, 228, 229–31, 233
'Behemoth, or the Long Parliament'
    (Thomas Hobbes), 24
Beijing, 157
Beirut, 238
Beisan, 235
Beka Valley, 238
Belgians, 270
Belgium, 46, 58, 97, 141, 142, 204,
    269–70
Bennett, Private Alfred, 217
Berar, Rajah of, 123–6
Berber, 172–3, 174, 176, 179, 190
Berlin, 260, 264
Bermicourt, 244, 245
Bethlehem, 232
Bethlehem Steel Corporation, 208
Bishop, Corporal Matthew, 31, 58
Bishop of Samos, 65
Bismarck, Prince Otto von, 208
Black Watch Highlanders, 141, 173
Blenheim, Battle of, 49–53, 55, 60, 279,
    280, 299, 310
'Blockhouse and drive', 203
Bloemfontein, 199
Blücher, Field Marshal, 141, 142, 144, 306
Blues, 21, 38
Boers, 196–203, 209, 211, 218, 221, 306,
    312
Bombay, 123
Borguebus Ridge, 283, 287
Borodino, Battle of, 140
Boston, 71, 75–6
Boulogne, 111
Bourbons, 61, 97
Bowyer, Lieutenant B., 231
Boyne, Battle of the, 39, 42
Bradley, Lieutenant General Omar, 283,
    285, 286, 288–9, 291–4, 296–7
Brandywine Creek, 87, 88, 89
Breed's Hill, 71–3
British Expeditionary Force (BEF), 204,
    269
British Museum, 229
British Second Army, 283